זאת התורה

Zot ha-Torah: This is the Torah

A guided exploration of the mitzvot found in the weekly Torah portion

Jane Ellen Golub with Joel Lurie Grishaver

Torah Aura Productions

ISBN #0-933873-82-4

Hebrew and English text of this volume have been carefully copyedited by Lenore Bruckner and Marilyn Henry.
We thank them for their efforts.

© 1994 Torah Aura Productions

Published by Torah Aura Productions

All rights reserved. No part of this publication may be reproduced or transmitted in any form or by any means graphic, electronic, or mechanical, including photocopying, recording or by any information storage and retrieval systems, without permission in writing from the publisher.

Torah Aura Productions
4423 Fruitland Avenue
Los Angeles, California 90058
(800) BE-TORAH • (213) 585-7312
fax (213) 585-0327

MANUFACTURED IN THE UNITED STATES OF AMERICA

TABLE OF CONTENTS

	PARASHAH		VERSE	MITZVAH OF THE WEEK	PAGE
1.	בְּרֵאשִׁית	Bereshit	Genesis 1:27	Sh'mirat ha-Teva	1
2.	נֹחַ	Noah	Genesis 6:9	Tza'ar Ba'alei Hayyim	6
3.	לֶךְ־לְךָ	Lekh-Lekha	Genesis 17:9	Brit Milah	12
4.	וַיֵּרָא	Va-Yera	Genesis 18:2	Hakhnasat Or'him/Birkat ha-Mazon	17
5.	חַיֵּי שָׂרָה	Hayyei Sarah	Genesis 23:2	Death and Mourning	21
6.	תּוֹלְדוֹת	Toldot	Genesis 26:34–35	Jewish Continuity	25
7.	וַיֵּצֵא	Va-Yetze	Genesis 28:10-11	Daily Worship	30
8.	וַיִּשְׁלַח	Va-Yishlah	Genesis 32:25–26	Don't Eat the Thigh Vein	34
9.	וַיֵּשֶׁב	Va-Yeshev	Genesis 37:9	Honor Your Parents	39
10.	מִקֵּץ	Miketz	Genesis 41:57	Mazon	44
11.	וַיִּגַּשׁ	Va-Yigash	Genesis 45:4-5	Repentance	50
12.	וַיְחִי	Va-Yehi	Genesis 48:20	Obligations to Children	54
13.	שְׁמוֹת	Shemot	Exodus 2:1	A Hebrew Name	58
14.	וָאֵרָא	Va-Era	Exodus 6:3-4	Moving to the Land of Israel	62
15.	בֹּא	Bo	Exodus 13:8	Tell Your Children (About the Exodus)	67
16.	בְּשַׁלַּח	Beshallah	Exodus 16:29	Observing Shabbat	72
17.	יִתְרוֹ	Yitro	Exodus 20:2	Belief in God	78
18.	מִשְׁפָּטִים	Mishpatim	Exodus 22:24	Lending But Not Charging Interest	82
19.	תְּרוּמָה	T'rumah	Exodus 25:8	Making a Sanctuary	86
20.	תְּצַוֶּה	Tetzaveh	Exodus 27:20	Ner Tamid—An Everlasting Flame	90
21.	כִּי תִשָּׂא	Ki Tissa	Exodus 34:26	Not Boiling a Kid in its Mother's Milk	94
22.	וַיַּקְהֵל	Va-Yak-hel	Exodus 35:3	Not Lighting a Fire on Shabbat	97
23.	פְקוּדֵי	Pekudei	Exodus 40:31	Ritual Handwashing	101
24.	וַיִּקְרָא	Va-Yikra	Leviticus 5:1	Coming Forward to Testify	106
25.	צַו	Tzav	Leviticus 7:37	Praying the Amidah	111
26.	שְׁמִינִי	Shemini	Leviticus 10:9	Don't Abuse Alcohol	115
27.	תַּזְרִיעַ	Tazria	Leviticus 13:45	Lashon Ha-Ra—Gossip	121

	Parashah		Verse	Mitzvah of the Week	Page
28.	מְצֹרָע	M'tzora	Leviticus 14:9	Mikvah	125
29.	אַחֲרֵי מוֹת	Aharei Mot	Leviticus 18:6	Uncovering Nakedness	130
30.	קְדֹשִׁים	Kedoshim	Leviticus 19:17	Rebuke Your Friend	136
31.	אֱמֹר	Emor	Leviticus 22:32	Kiddush ha-Shem & Hillul ha-Shem	143
32.	בְּהַר	Be-Har	Leviticus 25:14	Misrepresentation	149
33.	בְּחֻקֹּתַי	Be-Hukotai	Leviticus 27:2	Taking an Oath	154
34.	בְּמִדְבַּר	Be-Midbar	Numbers 3:1-2	Teach Them Diligently	159
35.	נָשֹׂא	Naso	Numbers 7:9	Carrying the Ark	163
36.	בְּהַעֲלֹתְךָ	Be-Ha'alotekha	Numbers 9:11	Hametz and Matzah	167
37.	שְׁלַח-לְךָ	Shelah-Lekha	Numbers 15:38	Tzitzit	175
38.	קֹרַח	Korah	Numbers 18:24	Ma'aser	181
39.	חֻקַּת	Hukkat	Numbers 20:11	Do Not Embarrass	186
40.	בָּלָק	Balak	Numbers 22:6	Not Listening to a False Prophet	190
41.	פִּינְחָס	Pinhas	Numbers 29:1	Shofar	197
42.	מַטּוֹת	Mattot	Numbers 31:17	Milhemet Mitzvah	201
43.	מַסְעֵי	Mas'ei	Numbers 35:12	Two Witnesses	207
44.	דְּבָרִים	Devarim	Deuteronomy 1:1	Studying Torah Over & Over Again	213
45.	וָאֶתְחַנַּן	Va-Ethannan	Deuteronomy 6:8	Tefillin	218
46.	עֵקֶב	Ekev	Deuteronomy 8:10	Birkat ha-Mazon	222
47.	רְאֵה	Re'eh	Deuteronomy 15:8	Tzedakah	228
48.	שֹׁפְטִים	Shoftim	Deuteronomy 20:19	Bal Tash-hit	232
49.	כִּי תֵצֵא	Ki Teitzei	Deuteronomy 22:1	Returning Lost Objects	238
50.	כִּי תָבוֹא	Ki Tavo	Deuteronomy 28:9	Walking After God	243
51.	נִצָּבִים	Nitzavim	Deuteronomy 30:19	Pikuah Nefesh	247
52.	וַיֵּלֶךְ	Va-Yelekh	Deuteronomy 31:19	Writing a Torah	252
53.	הַאֲזִינוּ	Ha-Azinu	Deuteronomy 32:52	Obeying a Last Will & Testament	257
54.	וְזֹאת הַבְּרָכָה	V'Zot ha-Brakhah	Deuteronomy 34:5		262

PARASHAT HA-SHAVUA GLASSES

Our friends Vicky Kelman and Gail Dorph are both fond of quoting their teacher, Dr. Joseph Lukinsky, who regularly teaches that Jews are supposed to look at the world through the lenses of the Torah portion every week.

Here is the basis of that idea:

1. The Torah is divided into 54 portions. Because of the uniqueness of the Jewish year, which adds a whole month every couple of years, the divisions are carefully arranged so that we have a fixed part of the Torah to read each week, and can finish all of it in one year (or, at least read a part of each portion each year).

2. Each portion has many, many truths to teach, but usually we only digest them one at a time. If we only learn one great thing each year from each parashah, *Dayeinu!*

3. If we can take that one good idea with us all week, and test it, and use it as part of our life, then we will have really learned and incorporated its lesson into who we are.

4. By wearing Parashat ha-Shavua glasses we are learning the whole Torah, one piece at a time.

Consider this book a collection of 54 sets of Parashat ha-Shavua eye-glasses. We hope you see a lot of interesting and wonderful things.

Jane Golub and Joel Lurie Grishaver

BERESHIT   בְּרֵאשִׁית

GENESIS 1:1–6:8

- God **creates** the world in seven days.
- **Adam** and **Eve** are placed in the **Garden of Eden**, eat the forbidden fruit, and are driven out.
- **Cain** kills his **brother Abel**.
- List of **ten generations** from **Adam** to **Noah**.

OUR TEXT—GENESIS 1:27

On the sixth day of creation, as the last of the things created, God creates people. This verse tells that story.

וַיִּבְרָא אֱלֹהִים אֶת-הָאָדָם בְּצַלְמוֹ בְּצֶלֶם אֱלֹהִים בָּרָא אֹתוֹ זָכָר וּנְקֵבָה בָּרָא אֹתָם:

ב	[ברא] = _____	אָדָם = _____	א
ז	זָכָר = _____ male	אֱלֹהִים = _____	
נ	נְקֵבָה = _____ female	אֶת__ = _____	
צ	[צלם] = _____ image	אֹתוֹ = _____	
	בְּצַלְמוֹ = _____	אֹתָם = _____	

27. וַיִּבְרָא אֱלֹהִים _____

אֶת-הָאָדָם בְּצַלְמוֹ _____

בְּצֶלֶם אֱלֹהִים בָּרָא אֹתוֹ _____

זָכָר וּנְקֵבָה בָּרָא אֹתָם: _____

Now try reading this verse without vowels:

ויברא אלהים את האדם בצלמו בצלם אלהים
ברא אתו זכר ונקבה ברא אתם

2

EXPLORING OUR TEXT

In the Midrash on Genesis, thinking about the verse we have studied, the rabbis tell this story of an argument between two camps of angels, one of which favors the creation of people while the other objects.

> Rabbi Shimon said: When The Holy-One-Who-is-to-Be-Blessed came to create people, the angels divided themselves into two political parties.
>
> One group said, "Let people be created," while the other group argued, "Don't create people."
>
> The first group held up a sign that read "LOVE" and argued, "Create people because they will love." The other group held up a sign that read "TRUTH" and argued, "Do not create them because they will lie and cheat and steal."
>
> The first group held up a sign that read "TZEDAKAH" and argued, "Create people because they will perform *mitzvot*." The other group held up a sign that read "SHALOM" and argued, "Do not create them because they will always be fighting."
>
> The debate continued on and on. Neither side would give in.
>
> Genesis Rabbah 8.5

Somehow, despite the disagreement, people were created. Write your own ending to this midrash and tell that story.

_____
_____
_____
_____
_____
_____
_____
_____
_____
_____
_____
_____
_____

Here is the way the rabbis of the Midrash ended this story:

> Rabbi Huna, the elder of Sepphoris, said, "While the ministering angels were busy arguing and disagreeing with each other, God went off and created people. Then The Holy-One-Who-is-to-Be-Blessed said, 'It's going to do you no good to argue, people have already been made.'"

What lesson do we learn from Rabbi Huna's ending to the story? _____

_____

_____

Here is another wonderful midrash.

> Rabbi Yosi the Galilean says,
> > Whatever The Holy-One-Who-is-to-Be-Blessed created on earth,
> > > God also created in people…
> > On earth God created *forests*; in people God created *hair*.
> > On earth God created *wild animals*; in people God created *lice*.
> > On earth God created *canyons*; in people God created *ears*.
> > On earth God created *wind*; in people God created *breath*.
> > On earth God created *sun*; in people God created *a forehead*.
> > On earth God created *lakes*; in people God created *sinuses*.
> > On earth God created *salt water*; in people God created *tears*.
> > On earth God created *heavens (an open space)*; in people God created *mouths*.
> > On earth God created *fresh water*; in people God created *spit*.
> > On earth God created *stars*; in people God created *eyes*.
> > On earth God created *mountains and valleys*;
> > > when *standing* people are like *mountains*
> > > and when *lying down*, people are like *valleys*.

Avot de-Rabbi Natan 31:3

Rabbi Yosi the Galilean had a good time making this list. You should have a good time, too. Add two of your own.

On earth God created _____; in people God created _____.

On earth God created _____; in people God created _____.

MITZVAH OF THE WEEK
שְׁמִירַת הַטֶּבַע SH'MIRAT HA-TEVA

The first official mitzvah in the Torah is "Be like fruit, and multiply." It is the blessing that God gives to the first people. It teaches that families are a good thing. In the Midrash we learn that "being like fruit" is protecting the world.

> When God created the first people,
> God led them around the Garden of Eden and said:
> "Look at my works! See how beautiful they are—how excellent!
> I created them all for your sake.
>
> See to it that you do not spoil or destroy My world.
> If you do, there will be no one else to repair it."
>
> Ecclesiastes Rabbah 7:3

Here are 20 things you can do to help protect the world. Check the ones you and your family are already doing. Add five more things to the list. Share your five with the whole class.

1. ❏ Recycle paper, glass, aluminum, batteries and plastic
2. ❏ Do an energy audit at home
3. ❏ Put a water saver in your toilet
4. ❏ Turn off the water while brushing your teeth
5. ❏ Do not buy products with a lot of packaging
6. ❏ Sweep the backyard rather than hose down
7. ❏ Do not buy fur, coral or ivory
8. ❏ Check spray can for CFC's (chlorofluorocarbons)
9. ❏ Use recycled paper
10. ❏ Know what products at the store are "green"
11. ❏ Use only dolphin-safe tuna
12. ❏ Do not use tropical hardwoods
13. ❏ Carpool, bicycle or walk
14. ❏ Plant trees
15. ❏ Composte
16. ❏ Know when to turn off lights
17. ❏ Cut six-pack rings; never let helium balloons go
18. ❏ Personally clean a field or stream
19. ❏ Find a non-polluting way to light a barbecue
20. ❏ Educate yourself, educate others
21. ❏ _____
22. ❏ _____
23. ❏ _____
24. ❏ _____
25. ❏ _____

NOAH

אלה
תולדות
נח איש
צדיק
תמים היה בדרתיו
את האלהים התהלך
נח

GENESIS 6:9–11:32

- All of creation turns evil so God destroys it with a **flood**.
- No**a**h, his family, and a limited number of animals are saved. God uses a rainbow to make a **covenant** with them.
- People start to build the **Tower of Babel**, and God babbles their language.
- List of **ten generations** from **Noah** to **Abram**.

OUR TEXT—GENESIS 6:9

In the Noa<u>h</u> story, everyone but one person and his family is destroyed in the flood. God chooses to save only Noa<u>h</u> and those closest to him. This verse, which introduces Noa<u>h</u>, gives us some clues about why God picked him.

אֵלֶּה תוֹלְדֹת נֹחַ נֹחַ אִישׁ צַדִּיק תָּמִים הָיָה בְּדֹרֹתָיו אֶת־הָאֱלֹהִים הִתְהַלֶּךְ־נֹחַ:

ה	walk/go .... = [הלך]		man .... = אִישׁ	א
	_____ = הִתְהַלֶּךְ		_____ = אֱלֹהִים	
נ	_____ = נֹחַ		these .... = אֵלֶּה	
צ	justice/righteousness ...... = [צדק]		_____ = אֶת	
	_____ = צַדִּיק		generation .... = דּוֹר	ד
ת	story/offspring .... = תּוֹלְדֹת		_____ = בְּדֹרֹתָיו	
	innocent .... = תָּם		_____ = הָ	ה
	_____ = תָּמִים		_____ = [היה]	

9. אֵלֶּה תוֹלְדֹת נֹחַ _____

נֹחַ אִישׁ צַדִּיק _____

תָּמִים הָיָה בְּדֹרֹתָיו _____

אֶת־הָאֱלֹהִים הִתְהַלֶּךְ־נֹחַ: _____

Now try reading this verse without vowels:

אלה תולדת נח נח איש צדיק תמים היה בדרתיו
את האלהים התהלך נח.

EXPLORING OUR TEXT

The Torah tells us:

> *Adonai* saw that people did a lot of evil on the earth.
> All the thoughts of their hearts were evil all day long.
> *Adonai* was uncomfortable about having made people...
> But Noah found favor in *ADONAI'S* eyes.

If you were God, watching Noah, what were some of the things you would see him do in an average day that showed he was different from other people? What would be some of the things that made you comfortable with him?

_____
_____
_____
_____
_____
_____
_____
_____
_____

TZADDIKIM

The Torah tells us that Noah, who was not a Jew, was a righteous person. This teaches us that you do not have to be Jewish to be a righteous person—a *tzaddik*. List your own top seven things a person, any person, should do (or not do) to be a *tzaddik*.

1. _____
2. _____
3. _____
4. _____
5. _____
6. _____
7. _____

BASIC RIGHTEOUSNESS

In the Midrash and in the Talmud (Sanhedrin 56a), we learn that God taught Noah seven *mitzvot*, *mitzvot* that all people (not only Jews) should follow. Any person who follows these rules, which are called *Sheva Mitzvot B'nei Noah*, is considered a *tzaddik*.

Can you translate: *Sheva Mitzvot B'nei Noah*? _____

Here they are. Compare them to your list.

1. Having a system of just courts.

2. Not swearing falsely with God's name, nor teaching any untruths about God.

3. Not worshipping idols.

4. No form of sexual assault or misconduct (rape, incest, adultery, etc.)

5. Not murdering.

6. Not stealing.

7. Not cutting a limb of a living animal and eating it, while letting the animal live and suffer.

Explain why anyone would want to do number 7.

_____

_____

BASIC RIGHTEOUSNESS

MITZVAH OF THE WEEK
צַעַר בַּעֲלֵי־חַיִּים Tza'ar Ba'alei Hayyim

There is a Jewish value called *Tza'ar Ba'alei Hayyim*, preventing the pain of living creatures. The rabbis learned it from several passages they found in the Torah: "IF YOU SEE YOUR ENEMY'S DONKEY STRUGGLING UNDER A LOAD WHICH IS TOO HEAVY, YOU MUST LIFT THE BURDEN FROM THE ASS" (Exodus 23:5) and "IF YOU SEE YOUR FRIEND'S DONKEY OR OX FALLEN ON THE ROAD, DO NOT IGNORE IT; YOU MUST HELP HIM RAISE IT" (Deuteronomy 22:4). One of these laws talks about the animal of an enemy. The other talks about the animal of a friend. When we put the two laws together we learn an important lesson: it is the animal that must be helped, regardless of who owns it. This is the *mitzvah* of *Tza'ar Ba'alei Hayyim*, preventing the pain of animals.

Why is Parashat Noah a good time to learn about *Tza'ar Ba'alei Hayyim*?

_____

_____

_____

In the Talmud (Bava Metzia 85a), this story is told about Rabbi Judah the Prince, the editor of the Mishnah:

> Once Rabbi Judah the Prince sat and taught Torah before the Academy in Sepphoris, Babylonia. While he was teaching, a calf that was supposed to be slaughtered came in and hid under his robes. It began to moo, seeming to say, "Please save me." Rabbi Judah said to the calf, "What can I do for you? You were created to be eaten."
>
> For the next thirteen years, Rabbi Judah suffered from the same toothache constantly.
>
> One day a lizard ran past his daughter. She wanted to kill it. Rabbi Judah said to her, "Let it be, because it says in the Bible, 'God has mercy over all of God's creations.'"
>
> At that moment it was said in heaven, "Because he had pity, pity shall be shown to him." The toothache finally stopped.

What is the moral of this story? _____

_____

_____

_____

In the *parashah*, we learn two things:

1. That people are allowed to eat meat.
2. That people are not allowed to let animals suffer.

Today, animal rights activists are making many demands. Some of them are supported by Jewish law, others are not. Which of the following demands do you believe are reasonable and just?

1. ❏ Using make-up that does not involve animal testing.
2. ❏ Protesting hospitals that use animals for medical research.
3. ❏ Protesting hospitals that use animals for organ transplants.
4. ❏ Confronting people who wear furs.
5. ❏ Having dogs and cats spayed and neutered.
6. ❏ Demanding that everyone become a vegetarian.
7. ❏ Protesting the serving of veal.
8. ❏ Always using plastic, not leather.
9. ❏ Trying to stop all hunting and fishing.
10. ❏ Saving the spotted owls.
11. ❏ Boycotting countries that still kill whales.
12. ❏ Refusing to dissect animals in biologyclass.
13. ❏ Protesting zoos, rodeos, circuses and animal exhibitions.

The Torah forbids people to do things that will cause the extinction of a species. Even though we are permitted to use animals for our own benefit, we can do nothing that will cause them to vanish. This is the meaning of "Do not take a mother bird and her child together" (Deuteronomy 22:6).

Nahmanides, Commentary

LEKH-LEKHA

GENESIS 12:1–13:18

- **Abram, Sarai** and **Lot** move to **Canaan**.
- There is a famine, so the family moves to Egypt. While there, Pharaoh mistakes Sarai, Abram's **wife**, for Abram's sister.
- The family returns to Canaan where **Abram and Lot split up** and go their separate ways.
- Abram is the hero of a **war** fought among 9 **kings**.
- God and Abram make **The Covenant of the Pieces**.
- **Ishmael** is born.
- God changes **Abram's** name to **Abraham**, and **Sarai's** name to **Sarah**.
- God and Abraham make the **Covenant of Circumcision**.

OUR TEXT—GENESIS 17:9, 12

In this *sidrah*, Abraham receives the mitzvah of circumcision as part of the Covenant with God. This is that mitzvah:

וַיֹּאמֶר אֱלֹהִים אֶל־אַבְרָהָם וְאַתָּה אֶת־בְּרִיתִי תִשְׁמֹר אַתָּה וְזַרְעֲךָ אַחֲרֶיךָ לְדֹרֹתָם:

ב	covenant .... = בְּרִית		_____ = אַבְרָהָם	א
	.... = בְּרִיתִי	after you _____ = אַחֲרֶיךָ		
ד	generation .... = דּוֹר	to _____ = אֶל		
	.... = לְדֹרֹתָם	_____ = אֱלֹהִים		
ז	your descendants/offspring .... = זַרְעֲךָ	_____ = [אמר]		
שׁ	guard/observe .... = [שמר]	_____ = וַיֹּאמֶר		
	.... = תִשְׁמֹר	_____ = אַתָּה		

וַיֹּאמֶר אֱלֹהִים אֶל־אַבְרָהָם _____

וְאַתָּה אֶת־בְּרִיתִי תִשְׁמֹר _____

אַתָּה וְזַרְעֲךָ אַחֲרֶיךָ לְדֹרֹתָם: _____

Verse 12 says: *In every generation, when a newborn boy is eight days old, you will circumcise him.*

Now try reading this verse without vowels:

ויאמר אלהים אל אברהם ואתה את בריתי
תשמר אתה וזרעך אחריך לדרתם

EXPLORING OUR TEXT

QUESTIONS

1. What is a covenant? _____
_____

2. If you could write the covenant between God and people, what would be the conditions?

Things God Should Promise People	**Things People Should Promise God**
_____	_____
_____	_____
_____	_____
_____	_____
_____	_____
_____	_____

IF GOD WANTED MEN CIRCUMCISED, WHY WERE THEY BORN WITH A FORESKIN?

> A wicked Roman, Turnas Rufus, once asked Rabbi Akiva: "Whose creations are more beautiful, God's or people's?"
>
> Tanhumah, Tazria

If you were Rabbi Akiva, how would you answer Turnas Rufus? Explain your reasoning.

_____
_____
_____
_____
_____
_____

Rabbi Akiva answered him, "People do the prettier work." When Turnas Rufus questioned the answer, Akiva had grain and flax brought. Then he had bread and linen brought. He said, "Is not the bread more beautiful than the grain, the linen nicer than the raw flax?"

Turnas Rufus then asked: "If God wants circumcision, why aren't boys born already circumcised?" Rabbi Akiva answered him, "God gave the mitzvot to Israel as an opportunity for Israel to purify themselves."

How is *Brit Milah* like baking bread or weaving linen?

_____
_____
_____
_____
_____
_____

How is circumcision performed? Brit Milah takes place in three steps: 1. Milah, the entire foreskin that covers the glans, is cut so that the whole of the glans is exposed. 2. P'riah, a thin layer of mucous membrane beneath the foreskin is torn and turned back with the flesh of the glans completely exposed. 3. M'tzitzah, suction is applied to the wound until the blood is drawn from the more remote places so that no danger to the child's health may ensue...After this has been done, a plaster bandage or similar dressing is applied.

Maimonides, *Mishneh Torah*, Laws of Circumcision 2:2

MITZVAH OF THE WEEK
בְּרִית מִילָה Brit Milah

A *brit milah* is the sign of the covenant between God and Israel. It is a mitzvah that every male child be circumcised on the eighth day of life (health permitting). If there is a possible danger to the child, the *brit milah* must be postponed until the child is in good health. A *brit milah* is considered so important that it takes place on Shabbat, a holiday, or even Yom Kippur, if that is the eighth day.

Until May 6, 1922, there was no such thing as a *Bat Mitzvah*. Only boys became *B'nei Mitzvah*. Until 1972, all the rabbis of the world were men. The Jewish world is changing. Women are assuming equal roles in both ritual and leadership. All over the world Jews are now struggling to figure out what ceremony for girls should parallel *brit milah* for boys. Design your own version of a *brit banot*, a covenant ceremony for girls. Share it with your class.

In a number of ways, berit mila provides a perfect "teachable moment." Parents and grandparents have just shared the exhilarating experience of birth. The emotional "high" of witnessing the creation of new life, the hopes and dreams that are pinned on the new child, and the heightened awareness of relatives no longer alive to share in the experience, all make the family ready for a "teachable moment."

Michael Zeldin, *Berit Mila As Education Experience*

VA-YERA וַיֵּרָא

GENESIS 18:1-22:24
- Abraham welcomes **3 visitors**. They announce the birth of **Isaac**.
- God and Abraham **debate** the destruction of **Sodom and Gemorrah**. Lot's family is saved. The cities are **destroyed**.
- Abimelekh mistakes Abraham's **wife** for his **sister**.
- **Isaac** is born. **Hagar** and her son **Ishmael** are **sent away**. An angel saves their lives.
- Abraham is **tested** when God asks him to **sacrifice Isaac**.

OUR TEXT—GENESIS 18:2

One of Abraham's most important adventures happened one hot day when he was sitting in the opening of his tent. The adventure begins this way...

וַיִּשָּׂא עֵינָיו וַיַּרְא וְהִנֵּה שְׁלֹשָׁה אֲנָשִׁים נִצָּבִים עָלָיו וַיַּרְא וַיָּרָץ לִקְרָאתָם...

ע	eyes .... = עֵינַיִם		person .... = אִישׁ	א
	_____ = עֵינָיו		people .... = אֲנָשִׁים	
ק	call .... = [קרא]		here is/there was .... = הִנֵּה	ה
	_____ = לִקְרָאתָם		standing .... = [נצב]	נ
ר	see .... = [ראה]		_____ = נִצָּבִים	
	_____ = וַיַּרְא		pick up/lift .... = [נשא]	
	run .... = [רוץ]		_____ = וַיִּשָּׂא	
	_____ = וַיָּרָץ		on him .... = עָלָיו	ע
שׁ	three .... = שְׁלֹשָׁה			

2. וַיִּשָּׂא עֵינָיו וַיַּרְא _____

וְהִנֵּה שְׁלֹשָׁה אֲנָשִׁים _____

נִצָּבִים עָלָיו _____

וַיַּרְא וַיָּרָץ לִקְרָאתָם... _____

Now try reading this verse without vowels:

וישא עיניו וירא והנה שלשה אנשים נצבים
עליו וירא וירץ לקראתם

EXPLORING OUR TEXT

Here is what the Midrash does with our verse.

ABRAHAM AND SARAH'S HOSPITALITY

Abraham made it his goal in life to draw others to knowing and worshipping the one true God. MAIMONIDES, *GUIDE TO THE PERPLEXED* PART 3, 51

For this purpose, Abraham planted a beautiful orchard in Be'er Sheva. His tent was constructed with four entrances constantly open to attract guests from all directions, and every weary traveler was welcomed there with shelter and refreshments. Soon the word spread that a wonderful man had opened a free-for-all hotel in the desert. The guests streamed in from far and near, enjoyed their meal, thanked their host, and arose to leave.

"You must say a blessing after your meal!" Abraham urged. "Say, 'Blessed be the Ruler of the Universe of Whose bounty we have eaten.'"

"We do not want to recite this blessing," the guests complained. "Who is this Ruler of the Universe?"

"Do as you please, but in that case you owe me payment for the meal!" said Abraham.

"How much does it cost?" inquired the guests.

"A bottle of wine—ten gold pieces. A steak—ten gold pieces. A loaf of bread—ten gold pieces!" was the answer.

"This is far too expensive!" exclaimed the guests.

"Please tell me," argued Abraham, "what is the price of bread offered in the midst of a wilderness? Where else are you able to obtain wine or meat in this desert?"

"You are right!" the guests admitted. "Who was that Ruler whom you asked us to thank? Let us bless God!"

Thus Abraham, by means of his hospitality and teachings, drew tens of thousands of people to worship God.

Sarah was equally devoted to spreading the truth in the world by teaching the women. As long as Sarah was alive, the doors of the tent were always open. In her merit, the cloud of the *Shekhinah* rested above the tent, and the candle Sarah lit on *Erev Shabbat* was never extinguished, and the food in the household was blessed with abundance. GENESIS RABBAH 48:9, 49:7, 39:21, 60:15.

What point do these midrashim make? _____

_____

_____

MITZVAH OF THE WEEK
בִּרְכַּת הַמָּזוֹן Birkat ha-Mazon
הַכְנָסַת אוֹרְחִים Hakhnasat Or'him

In Deuteronomy 8:10, we are taught the mitzvah of *Birkat ha-Mazon*, the responsibility to say *brakhot* and thank God every time we eat. In the *midrashim* to this *parashah*, we learn that the mitzvah of *hakhnasat or'him,* of providing hospitality to strangers, was very important to Abraham. Interestingly, in the midrash, every time Abraham provides hospitality to a stranger, he invites him to join in *Birkat ha-Mazon*. There seems to be a connection between these two mitzvot.

How do you explain the connection between *Birkat ha-Mazon* and *Hakhnasat Or'him*? _____
_____
_____

In the *Mishneh Torah* Laws of Blessings, Maimonides' book of Jewish law, we learn that *Birkat ha-Mazon* (the Brakhot After Eating) and the mitzvah of *Hakhnasat Or'him*, (the Mitzvah of Providing Hospitality) are related.

7.2 The host should recite *ha-Motzi* to begin the meal. When the brakhah is finished, bread should be broken and distributed to all. When the meal is over, a guest should lead *Birkat ha-Mazon* in which the host and the host's family are acknowledged and God is asked to bless them.

2.7 In the fourth blessing of *Birkat ha-Mazon*, God's role as Ruler of the Cosmos is mentioned three times. In this blessing, a guest should ask God's blessing over the host by saying: "May it be Your will that my host not be disgraced in this world or shamed in the world-to-come."

(c.f. Brakhot 42a)

The most important discipline of Judaism involves the blessing. When a blessing is recited before eating, then the act itself becomes a spiritual undertaking. Through the blessing, the act of eating becomes a contemplative exercise. Just as one can contemplate a flower or a melody, one can contemplate the act of eating. One opens one's mind completely to the experience of chewing the food and fills the awareness with the taste and texture of the food. One then eats very slowly, aware of every nuance of taste.

Aryeh Kaplan, *Jewish Meditations: A Practical Guide* (1985)

HAYYEI SARAH   חַיֵּי שָׂרָה

GENESIS 23:1–25:18

- **Sarah dies**. Abraham buys the **Cave of Makhpelah** for a burial place.
- Abraham **sends a servant** to find a bride for Isaac. He plans a test. **Rebekkah** passes the test and is chosen. Isaac and Rebekkah are married.
- **Abraham dies**. Isaac and Ishmael bury him in the Cave of Makhpelah.

OUR TEXT—GENESIS 23:2

At the beginning of this *parashah*, Sarah dies. The Torah breaks that bad news this way:

וַתָּמָת שָׂרָה...וַיָּבֹא אַבְרָהָם לִסְפֹּד לְשָׂרָה וְלִבְכֹּתָהּ.

ה	_____ = הוּא = הִיא		_____ = אַבְרָהָם	א
מ	dead .... = [מות]	come .... = [בוא]	ב
	_____ = וַתָּמָת	_____ = וַיָּבֹא	
ס	mourn .... = [ספד]	cry .... = [בכה]	
	_____ = לִסְפֹּד	_____ = הָ	
שׂ	_____ = שָׂרָה	_____ = לִבְכֹּתָהּ	

2. וַתָּמָת שָׂרָה... _____

וַיָּבֹא אַבְרָהָם לִסְפֹּד לְשָׂרָה _____

וְלִבְכֹּתָהּ. _____

Now try reading this verse without vowels:

ותמת שרה...ויבא אברהם לספד לשרה ולבכתה

EXPLORING OUR TEXT

GRAPHICS

Why is the word וְלִבְכֹּתָהּ written with a small כ?

It is to teach us that Abraham did not excessively weep for Sarah because she was old and had lived a full life. (Rabbi Meir Zlotowitz)

Why is there an asterisk over the word וְלִבְכֹּתָהּ*?

It is there to tell us that this word is to be read differently than it is written. It is called a *kri u'khtiv* and if we look at the bottom of the text, we will find a footnote that reads: ב כ' זעירא, which means the kaf is supposed to be small. It is not a misprint (but read it as a normal letter). This a footnote from the Masoretes, the Jewish scholars who set the authorized text and wrote in all the vowels—around the year 200 C.E.

MITZVAH OF THE WEEK
מִצְוַת מֵת DEATH AND MOURNING

Rabbi Simlai:

The Torah begins with an act of *g'milut ḥasadim*. It also ends with an act of *g'milut ḥasadim*. It begins "AND GOD, ADONAI, CLOTHED THEM, MAKING COATS OF SKIN FOR ADAM AND HIS WIFE," and it ends "AND GOD BURIED HIM IN THE VALLEY."

The rabbis called the mitzvah of burying someone *Mitzvat ha-Met*, the mitzvah for the dead. We might imagine that a funeral is done for the sake of the survivors, but the rabbis say, "No. A funeral is a kindness, a mitzvah, done for the deceased."

Why does the dead person need a funeral?

_____

_____

Have you ever been involved in a funeral? or a shiva house? What did you do to help someone? What did someone do to help you?

_____

_____

SOME LAWS AND CUSTOMS ABOUT DEATH, BURIAL AND SHIV'AH

1. Rabbi Ben Zion Bokser wrote: "People are mortal. They only live in the world for a while. But people are not less because they die. In some ways, it is the fact that one dies which leads one to immortality. Death is the price of life."

2. It is a mitzvah to visit all sick people without regard to race, color or creed (Maimonides, *Mishneh Torah, Laws of Mourning*; Shulhan Arukh, Yoreh Deah 335.1, 335.9).

3. A dying person should not be left alone so that he or she should not feel abandoned. Also, because a person learns something important from witnessing a death (Shulhan Arukh, Yoreh Deah 339.4).

4. Because the body is the place where a holy spirit lived, it should be treated with respect, even after the spirit has left. Therefore, a body is cleaned, guarded, treated with honor, and prepared for burial with respect. This is called *Kevod ha-Met*, the honor of the dead. The mitzvah of washing and preparing a body for burial is called *Mitzvat Met* (Brakhot 18a, Shulhan Arukh, Yoreh Deah 373:5).

5. Because the act of preparing a dead body was an important, if emotionally difficult, mitzvah, Jews often organized groups called *Hevra Kadisha* (Holy Societies) (E.J., 8.439).

6. There is no standard or fixed service for funerals. The general form, however, is to recite a psalm, read a passage from the Bible, hear a eulogy, and chant the memorial prayer *El Malei Rahamim* (Harlow, *Rabbi's Manual*).

7. The rabbis of the Talmud taught: "Do not comfort people when their dead are still before them" (Pirkei Avot 4:18). At the time of death, the bereaved is in a state of shock and cannot be reached with comforting words.

8. The *Shivah* period begins after the funeral and lasts for seven days. It is then that the mourner becomes aware of the loss and can be comforted (Shulhan Arukh, Yoreh De'ah 375:1).

9. The mourners should stay at home during the seven days of *Shiv'ah*. Morning and Evening services should be conducted in their home (Shulhan Arukh, Yoreh De'ah 376:3 in Rama). Mourners should not go to work or attend to business during the *Shivah* period. However, if money is an issue, the mourner may return to work on the third day (Shulhan Arukh, Yoreh De'ah 376:3 in Rama, 380,1, 3, 393.1 in Rama).

10. It is a mitzvah to comfort mourners and to see to their needs. One goes to a funeral not only to honor the dead but to comfort the mourners (Sotah 14a).

Isaac Klein, *A Guide to Jewish Religious Practice*

TOLDOT תּוֹלְדֹת

וְאֵלֶּה תּוֹלְדֹת יִצְחָק בֶּן אַבְרָהָם אַבְרָהָם הוֹלִיד אֶת יִצְחָק

GENESIS 25:19−28:9

- Rebekkah gets **pregnant**. **Twins** are in her womb. They **fight** in her belly. **Esau** is born first. **Jacob** is pulling at his heel.
- Esau **sells** Jacob his **birthright**.
- Abimelekh thinks that Isaac's **wife** is really his **sister**.
- Isaac plans to bless Esau. Rebekkah and Jacob **trick** him.
- **Isaac blesses Jacob**. Jacob leaves to go to Paddan Aram.

OUR TEXT—GENESIS 26:34-5

Towards the end of this *parashah*, Esau, one of Isaac and Rebekkah's two sons, marries two non-Jewish women. These verses reveal his parents' reaction:

וַיְהִי עֵשָׂו בֶּן־אַרְבָּעִים שָׁנָה וַיִּקַּח אִשָּׁה אֶת־יְהוּדִית בַּת־בְּאֵרִי הַחִתִּי וְאֶת־בָּשְׂמַת בַּת־אֵילֹן הַחִתִּי וַתִּהְיֶיןָ מֹרַת רוּחַ לְיִצְחָק וּלְרִבְקָה.

ה	to be = [היה]	Elon the Hittite = אֵילֹן הַחִתִּי	א
	_____ = וַיְהִי	four = אַרְבַּע	
	_____ = וַתִּהְיֶיןָ	forty = אַרְבָּעִים	
י	Judith = יְהוּדִית	son = בֶּן	
	_____ = יִצְחָק	year = שָׁנָה	
ל	take = [לקח]	_____ = בֶּן־אַרְבָּעִים שָׁנָה	
	_____ = וַיִּקַּח	woman/wife = אִשָּׁה	
מ	bitter spirit = מֹרַת רוּחַ	Beeri the Hittite = בְּאֵרִי הַחִתִּי	ב
ע	_____ = עֵשָׂו	Bosmat = בָּשְׂמַת	
ר	_____ = רִבְקָה	daughter of = בַּת	

34. וַיְהִי עֵשָׂו בֶּן־אַרְבָּעִים שָׁנָה _____

וַיִּקַּח אִשָּׁה _____

אֶת־יְהוּדִית בַּת־בְּאֵרִי הַחִתִּי _____

וְאֶת־בָּשְׂמַת בַּת־אֵילֹן הַחִתִּי _____

35. וַתִּהְיֶיןָ מֹרַת רוּחַ _____

35. לְיִצְחָק וּלְרִבְקָה. _____

Now try reading this verse without vowels:

ויהי עשו בן ארבעים שנה ויקח אשה את יהודית בת בארי החתי ואת בשמת בת אילן החתי ותהיין מרת רוח ליצחק ולרבקה

EXPLORING OUR TEXT

Rashi explains our verse and the next one together, connecting two pieces of the story.

> **And they were a source of bitterness to Isaac and Rebekkah** because they worshiped idols. **And it came to pass, that when Isaac was old, his eyes became dim** because of the smoke of the incense that these pagan women burned to their idols.
>
> Rashi

1. According to Rashi, why were Isaac and Rebekkah unhappy?

   _____

   _____

2. According to Rashi, why did Isaac go blind?

   _____

   _____

3. What "lesson" do you think that Rashi is trying to draw from this incident?

   _____

   _____

While they profess that intermarriage is a Jewish problem and not their problem, when we look at their family life we very quickly discover, and they very quickly discover, that they are mistaken. Not that they are intentionally blind, but they are simply mistaken about the importance of culturally-bred differences within the family's evolution of lifestyle. When a couple is first married, in the so-called "honeymoon" stage of marriage, one tends to focus solely on the positive attributes of one's mate. Particularly because of the highly personalistic approach to mate selection in the first place, one tends to focus on that which is most attractive: the sexual aspects, the shared interests, shared dreams, etc. Irksome differences and incompatibilities are ignored. But they are generally not ignored for a lifetime.

Egon Mayer, Jewish Identity, Family and Intermarriage

MITZVAH OF THE WEEK
JEWISH CONTINUITY וְלֹא הִתְחַתֵּן בָּם

In Deuteronomy 22:13 we learn that it is a mitzvah to get married. Getting married is a positive mitzvah. In Deuteronomy 7:3-4 we learn that the Torah forbids marriages between Jews and non-Jews—but still recognizes such marriages as realities. Rabbi Maurice Lamm, an Orthodox rabbi, in his book *The Jewish Way in Love and Marriage* explains it this way (page 53):

> *Interfaith marriage is no marriage; it is prohibited and it is also void...Interfaith marriage is void not because it is prohibited, but because one party to the contract is incapable of contracting a marriage with a Jew within Jewish law. The contract was never a contract because both parties were not Jews.*

Traditionally, Jews marry by committing themselves to each other with this vow. Read it and then see if you can explain Rabbi Lamm's comment:

הֲרֵי אַתְּ מְקֻדֶּשֶׁת/אַתָּה מְקֻדָּשׁ לִי — Behold you are made sacred to me

בְּטַבַּעַת זוֹ — with this ring

כְּדַת מֹשֶׁה וְיִשְׂרָאֵל. — According to the law of Moses and Israel.

_____

_____

_____

Rabbi Lamm is explaining Orthodox Jewish law. Ask your own Rabbi about her or his view of the Jewish rules of interdating and intermarriage.

Our friend Cherie Kohler-Fox teaches her students a "new" mitzvah:

> "Make sure that by the time you get married, the person you are marrying is a Jew."

What Jewish rules would you create about dating and marrying non-Jews?

_____

_____

_____

EPILOGUE

Recently a report called *A Time to Act* was released. It begins with this paragraph:

> There is a deep and widespread concern in the Jewish community today that the commitment to basic Jewish values, ideas, and behavior may be diminishing at an alarming rate. A substantial number of Jews no longer seem to believe that Judaism has a role to play in their search for personal fulfillment and communality. This has great implications not only for the richness of Jewish life but for the very continuity of a large segment of the Jewish people.

This report was based on statistics like these:

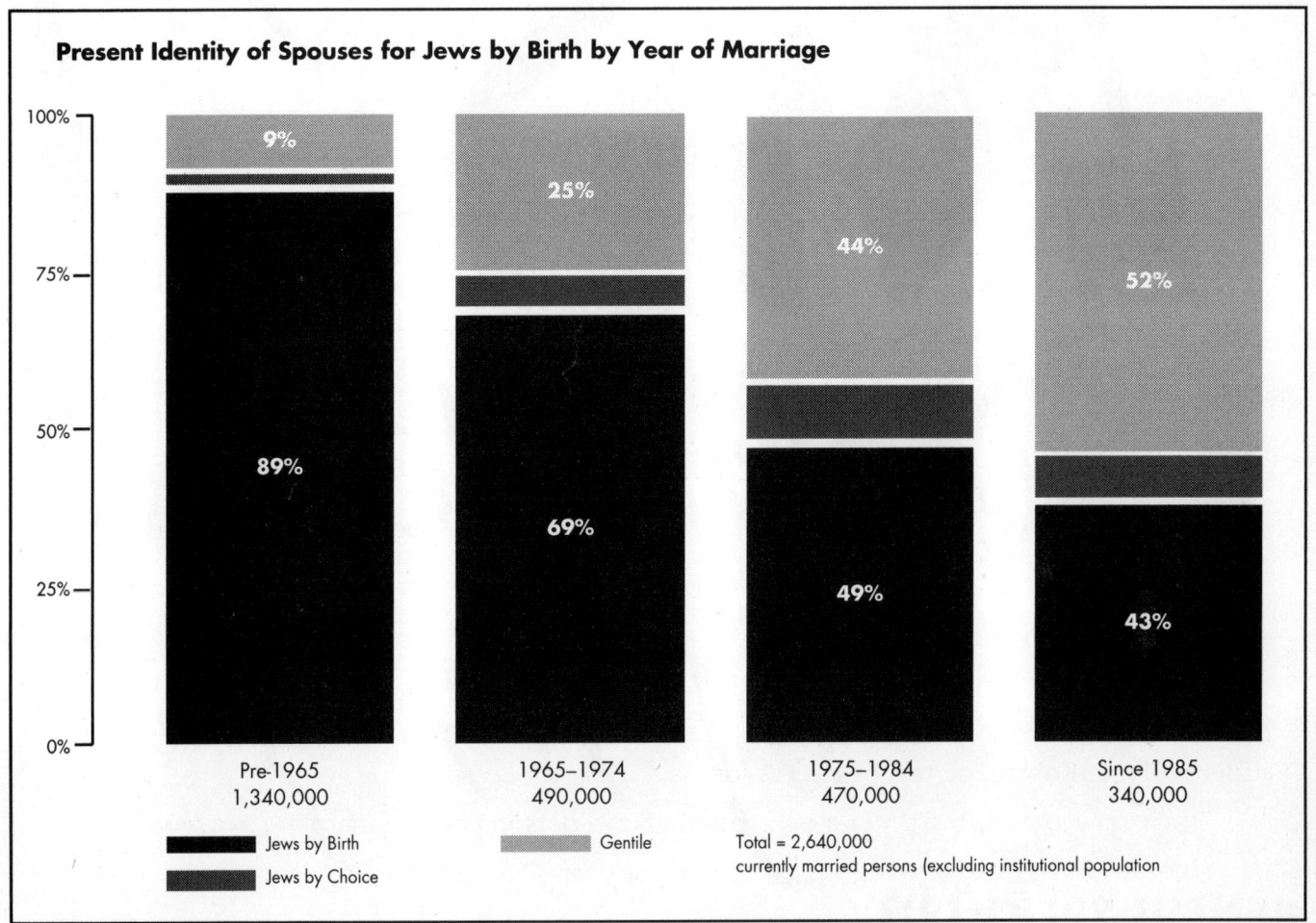

It is projected that the intermarriage rate may be as high as 70% by the year 2000.

1. What does this chart show?
2. Should we be concerned about it?
3. What are you willing to do about it?

VA-YETZE

GENESIS 28:10–32:3

- **Jacob** has a **dream** of angels going up and down. God promises to be with him. Jacob names the place Beth El.
- Jacob **meets Rachel** at the well. He works 7 years to marry her. Rachel's father Laban **tricks** Jacob into marrying **Leah**. Jacob then also marries Rachel and promises to work 7 more years.
- Rachel and Leah have children. There are 11 sons and 1 daughter. Jacob and his family **leave Laban's** household. Laban chases him. They make peace.

OUR TEXT—GENESIS 28:10-11

In this *sidrah* Jacob leaves home to seek his future. On the way he has a night adventure that changes his life and that of the Jewish people. The Torah begins that story with this verse:

וַיֵּצֵא יַעֲקֹב מִבְּאֵר שָׁבַע...וַיָּלֶן שָׁם כִּי-בָא הַשֶּׁמֶשׁ וַיִּקַּח מֵרַאֲשֹׁתָיו וַיִּשְׁכַּב בַּמָּקוֹם הַהוּא.

ל	take = [לקח]		rock = אֶבֶן	א
	_____ = וַיִּקַּח		_____ = אֲבָנִים	
מ	place = מָקוֹם		from = מִ	
ר	_____ = [ראש]		_____ = מֵאַבְנֵי	
	his = ■יו		Be'er Sheva = בְּאֵר שֶׁבַע	ב
	_____ = מְרַאֲשֹׁתָיו		_____ = יַעֲקֹב	ג
שׁ	put = [שִׂים]		go out = [יצא]	
	_____ = וַיָּשֶׂם		_____ = וַיֵּצֵא	
שׁ	lie down = [שכב]		because = כִּי	כ
	_____ = וַיִּשְׁכַּב		stay for the night = [לון]	ל
	there = שָׁם		_____ = וַיָּלֶן	
	_____ = שֶׁמֶשׁ			

10. _____ וַיֵּצֵא יַעֲקֹב מִבְּאֵר שָׁבַע...

11. _____ וַיָּלֶן שָׁם כִּי-בָא הַשֶּׁמֶשׁ...

_____ וַיִּקַּח מֵאַבְנֵי הַמָּקוֹם

_____ וַיָּשֶׂם מְרַאֲשֹׁתָיו וַיִּשְׁכַּב

_____ בַּמָּקוֹם הַהוּא.

Now try reading this verse without vowels:

ויצא יעקב מבאר שבע...וילן שם כי בא השמש ויקח מאבני המקום וישם מראשתיו וישכב במקום ההוא

EXPLORING OUR TEXT

In the Midrash, the Rabbis ask this question: How is prayer like the ladder that Jacob saw in his dream at Beth El?

Write your own version, and then read the midrashic versions below.

_____
_____
_____
_____
_____
_____
_____
_____

Our rabbis taught that the ladder that Jacob saw in his dream, the one with God's angels "going up and coming down," was also a symbol of prayer (*Zohar* I.149b).

This was a ladder that "stood on earth and reached the heavens." The rabbis taught that the ladder showed Jacob that prayer is like a ladder that connects earth and heaven, people and God. When prayer's words are meaningful, the good wishes that sincere prayer brings out become angels that go up and bring their message to God—because angels are really messengers. And God sends down other angels who bring God's blessings in return. That is why the angels in Jacob's dream were described first as "going up" and then as "coming down."

(Torah Or, 17a)

Prayer cannot mend a broken bridge, rebuild a ruined city, or bring water to parched fields. Prayer can mend a broken heart, lift up a discouraged soul, and strengthen a weakened will.

Ferdinand M. Isserman

Prayer in Judaism...is bound up with the human needs, wants, drives, and urges...Prayer is the doctrine of human needs. Prayer tells the individual as well as the community what his/her or its genuine needs are, what s/he should, or should not, petition God about...

Rabbi Joseph Soleveitchik

MITZVAH OF THE WEEK
אוֹתוֹ תַעֲבֹד DAILY WORSHIP

It is a mitzvah for Jews to praise God by saying 100 Brakhot daily, many of these during three prescribed daily services: *Shaharit*, *Minhah*, and *Ma'ariv*. Even though this mitzvah is officially connected to Deuteronomy 10:20, "**Be in awe, worship, hold fast, and swear by the name of ADONAI your God**," the Rabbis connected the creation of the daily services to our verse, "**He came to a certain place, and stopped there for the night, for the sun had set**." Explaining "stopped," Rashi comments:

> Thus we may learn that Jacob originated the custom of Evening Prayer...

Rashi was referencing this talmudic passage:

> R. Jose son of R. Hanina said: "The three daily services were instituted by the Patriarchs."
>
> R. Joshua b. Levi says: "The three daily services were instituted to replace the daily sacrifices."
>
> It has been taught in accordance with R. Jose b. Hanina: "Abraham instituted the morning service, as it says, 'And Abraham got up early in the morning... (Genesis 19:27);' Isaac instituted the afternoon Tefillah, as it says, 'And Isaac went out to meditate in the field at eventide... (Genesis 24:63);' Jacob instituted the evening prayer, as it says, 'And he came to the place...' (Genesis 28:11)."

> Brakhot 26b

Maimonides teaches these rules for communal prayer in the *Mishneh Torah*.

> Congregational prayer is always heard by God. Even if sinners are present, God does not reject public worship. One should therefore associate with congregations, and one should not pray in private when there is an opportunity to pray with the congregation.
>
> How is public worship conducted? One person recites the prayers aloud and all the rest listen. This is not done if there are fewer than ten adult men present, including the reader....
>
> The reader acts on behalf of the assembled congregation. The leader recites the prayers while people listen and respond *Amen* after each blessing; and it is as if they are praying. This only applies to one who does not know how to worship; but one who knows does not fulfill the obligation except by a personal recitation of the prayers.

> *Mishneh Torah*, Laws of Prayer, Chapter 8

VA-YISHLA**H**

וישלח

וישלח יעקב מלאכים לפניו אל עשו אחיו ארצה שעיר שדה אדום

GENESIS 32:4–36:43

- Jacob prepares to meet Esau. He **wrestles** with a stranger who **changes his name to Israel**.
- Jacob and Esau meet.
- **Dinah** gets involved with a man from Shekhem.
- God blesses Jacob and changes his name to Israel.
- Rachel dies giving birth and is buried. Jacob names his twelfth son **Benjamin**.

OUR TEXT—GENESIS 32:25-26

In this *parashah* we experience a very famous biblical wrestling match. It begins this way.

וַיִּוָּתֵר יַעֲקֹב לְבַדּוֹ וַיֵּאָבֵק אִישׁ עִמּוֹ עַד עֲלוֹת הַשָּׁחַר. וַיַּרְא כִּי לֹא יָכֹל לוֹ וַיִּגַּע בְּכַף־יְרֵכוֹ וַתֵּקַע כַּף־יֶרֶךְ יַעֲקֹב בְּהֵאָבְקוֹ עִמּוֹ.

א	[אבק] = wrestle		לוֹ = _____
	וַיֵּאָבֵק = _____	נ	[נגע] = touch/strike
	בְּהֵאָבְקוֹ = _____		וַיִּגַּע = _____
	אִישׁ = _____		[נקע] = dislocate/strain
י	יָכֹל = able to overcome		וַתֵּקַע = _____
	יַעֲקֹב = _____	ע	עַד = until
	[יתר] = remain		עֲלוֹת = rise
	וַיִּוָּתֵר = _____		עִם = with
כ	כַּף־יֶרֶךְ = socket of hipbone		עִמּוֹ = _____
	כִּי = _____	ר	[ראה] = see
ל	לֹא = _____		וַיַּרְא = _____
	לְבַדּוֹ = alone by himself	ש	שַׁחַר = dawn

.25 _____ וַיִּוָּתֵר יַעֲקֹב לְבַדּוֹ

_____ וַיֵּאָבֵק אִישׁ עִם

_____ עַד עֲלוֹת הַשָּׁחַר.

.26 _____ וַיַּרְא כִּי לֹא יָכֹל לוֹ

_____ וַיִּגַּע בְּכַף־יְרֵכוֹ

_____ וַתֵּקַע כַּף־יֶרֶךְ יַעֲקֹב

_____ בְּהֵאָבְקוֹ עִמּוֹ.

Now try reading this verse without vowels:

ויותר יעקב לבדו ויאבק איש עמו עד עלות השחר וירא כי לא יכל לו ויגע בכף ירכו ותקע כף ירך יעקב בהאבקו עמו

EXPLORING OUR TEXT

At the end of the story in the Torah we find this verse (32:33):

עַל־כֵּן	Because of this,
לֹא יֹאכְלוּ בְנֵי־יִשְׂרָאֵל	the Families-of-Israel don't eat
אֶת־גִּיד הַנָּשֶׁה עַל־כַּף הַיָּרֵךְ	the *Gid ha-Nasheh* which is on the leg
עַד הַיּוֹם הַזֶּה	until this day—
כִּי נָגַע בְּכַף־יֶרֶךְ יַעֲקֹב	because he tugged on Jacob's leg
בְּגִיד הַנָּשֶׁה.	the *Gid ha-Nasheh*

Three talmudic commentators, *Ba'alei ha-Tosafot*, the *Tur*, and <u>H</u>izkuni, have a disagreement over this verse. They all ask: "Why was Israel forbidden from eating the *Gid ha-Nasheh?*" Each of them has a different answer.

Ba'alei ha-Tosafot: It is a "remembrance" of the great event in Jacob's life. We do it to honor him, and to learn from his example.

The *Tur*: It is "to separate one's self from danger." Jacob's children separate themselves from the thing that injured their father. It is explained by this example. It is just like a person who gets a headache each time he eats a given kind of food. He learns to give up that food.

<u>H</u>izkuni: It is a "punishment"—to remind us of the sons of Jacob who left him alone that night when he was facing danger.

Do you like one of these explanations, or do you have a better one of your own? Explain or expound!

_____

_____

_____

_____

MITZVAH OF THE WEEK
לֹא יֹאכְלוּ בְנֵי יִשְׂרָאֵל אֶת־גִּיד הַנָּשֶׁה DON'T EAT THE THIGH VEIN

Don't eat the thigh vein.

Based on this verse it is forbidden to eat any part of the sinew (thigh muscle), both of the right and left hind legs, of the animal. There are two different tissues that are forbidden: the sciatic nerve (by Torah law) and the peroneal nerve (by rabbinic law).

The act of removing these veins is called "**porging**." It is just one of many technical terms used in the Kashrut process. Here is a Kashrut dictionary.

Kashrut Dictionary

1. EI-VER MIN HA-HAI—"limb from a living thing," referring to a barbaric custom of slicing off a piece of flesh from a living animal and eating it. This custom was prohibited by the Torah.

2. BODEK—"a searcher," referring to someone trained to examine the insides of a beast following *shehitah* to determine if the animal was healthy and thus kosher.

3. HAMETZ—"leaven," referring to the prohibition of eating leavened food during Passover.

4. DAM—"blood," referring to the biblical injunction against eating blood. This law of the Torah is the basis of the kashering laws that require washing, salting or broiling of meats in order to remove the forbidden blood.

5. FLEIYSHIG—"meat," referring to meat foods, dishes, utensils and silverware.

6. HADAHAH—"washing," referring to the custom of washing meats. According to the Kashrut laws, meats are washed or soaked under the following conditions:

    a. Prior to salting or boiling in order to remove any surface blood or foreign substance.

    b. After salting or broiling to remove any surface blood that has been drawn out.

    c. Following *shehitah*, if the meat has not been kashered, then after every three-day period, it must be washed with water (or at least dampened) to keep it fresh so that the blood will not coagulate and resist salting. Should a period longer than three days pass without washing the meat, it can be kashered only through broiling.

7. KOSHER—"Fit" or "proper."' While the term is commonly applied to foods, its use is not restricted in the sacred writings to food alone. For example, the word "kosher" is also used in reference to a completed Torah, Tefillin, or Marriage Contract, to indicate that the object is fit and proper for use at a Jewish religious occasion.

8. KOSHER L'PESAH—"Kosher for Passover," referring to food prepared in accordance with the special Passover dietary laws.

9. MASHGIAH—"supervisor," referring to the person who is sufficiently familiar with the laws of Kashrut to be qualified to supervise the production of the foods in accordance with the dietary laws. A *mashgiah* need not be a rabbi.

10. MILKHIG—"dairy," referring to dairy foods, dishes, utensils and silverware.

11. M'LEEHAH—"salting," referring to the Halakhic requirement to salt raw meat as a means of kashering it.

12. PAREVE—"neutral," referring to foods that are neither meat nor dairy, i.e. vegetables, fish, eggs, etc. Pareve also refers to dishes, utensils and silverware used only for these foods.

13. PLUMBA—A tag affixed to something, such as food or a package of food, testifying to the fact that it is kosher.

14. SHEHITAH—The process of Jewish ritual slaughter of animals and fowl for food. Fish do not require *shehitah*, according to the Torah.

15. SHOHET—Someone trained in the laws of Jewish ritual slaughter.

16. TREIFE—"torn," referring to an animal that was attacked by another beast and torn apart in battle. The term has taken on a general meaning that is applied to all foods that are not kosher.

17. TSA'AR BA'ALEI HAYYIM—"the suffering of living things," referring to the biblical commandment to be compassionate and not to inflict needless suffering, physical or emotional, upon God's creatures. As it relates to Kashrut, it refers to the prohibition of causing needless pain to an animal prior to or during *shehitah*.

18. TRAYBERING—A Czechoslovakian word that entered the Yiddish language, meaning "to *porg*," to clean out the veins. This refers to the process of cutting away the forbidden veins or fat from a kosher-slaughtered animal. In many countries *traybering* is still practiced as a profession, but not in America. Large slaughterhouses in America find it economically impractical to employ a *trayberer*. It is much simpler to cut away that portion of the animal that contains the forbidden part and sell it to the non-kosher trade.

19. VA'AD HA-KASHRUT—"a committee for Kashrut," referring to the synagogue or communal committee whose task it is to safeguard the dignity and observance of Kashrut.

20. YAYIN NESEKH—"wine for pouring," referring to the pagan custom of pouring wine upon the altar as part of the idolatrous worship. Observant Jews refrain from drinking wine that has been handled by a non-Jew, fearing that perhaps the non-Jew, while handling the wine, might have thought of consecrating it to his own form of worship.

VA-YESHEV

וַיֵּשֶׁב יַעֲקֹב בְּאֶרֶץ מְגוּרֵי אָבִיו בְּאֶרֶץ כְּנָעַן

GENESIS 37:1-40:23

- Joseph is Israel's **favorite son**. Israel makes him a **coat of many colors**.
- Joseph has **two dreams** in which his family bows down to him.
- Israel sends Joseph to join his brothers in the field.
- Judah, Tamar and Onan have a sub-plot.
- Joseph is **sold into slavery** and is taken to Potiphar's house. He **succeeds** and becomes **head of the household**.
- Joseph is **thrown into jail**. Again, he succeeds and becomes the **head prisoner**. Here, he interprets two dreams.

OUR TEXT—GENESIS 37:9

In this *sidrah* Joseph has two dreams that he shares with his family. Our text is Jacob's description of the second dream.

וְהִנֵּה הַשֶּׁמֶשׁ וְהַיָּרֵחַ וְאַחַד עָשָׂר כּוֹכָבִים מִשְׁתַּחֲוִים לִי.

לְ	_____ = לִי	אַחַד עָשָׂר = eleven ... א
שׁ	bow down = [שחה]	הִנֵּה = _____ ... ה
	מִשְׁתַּחֲוִים = _____	יָרֵחַ = moon ... י
	שֶׁמֶשׁ = sun	כּוֹכָבִים = stars ... כ

9. וְהִנֵּה הַשֶּׁמֶשׁ וְהַיָּרֵחַ _____
וְאַחַד עָשָׂר כּוֹכָבִים _____
מִשְׁתַּחֲוִים לִי. _____

Now try reading this verse without vowels:

והנה השמש והירח ואחד עשר כוכבים משתחוים לי

> *Judaism is not a song that is sung; it is a continuing symphony which each Jew may either swell with harmony or mar with discord.*
>
> *It is a symphony which echoes forth to the world Judaism's faith in man's possibilities of good and his power of regeneration to a nobler future.*
>
> *The past is a foundation on which Jews have to continue building and developing in loyal keeping with what has been achieved by the master builders of the past.*
>
> *It is the past which compellingly gives us the dedicated purpose to remain a people for the present and the future.*
>
> David De Sola Pool

EXPLORING OUR TEXT

1. If you were one of Joseph's brothers or one of his parents, how would you interpret this dream? What do you think it means?

   _____
   _____

2. If you were one of Joseph's brothers or one of his parents, how would you feel about this dream? What would you say to Joseph?

   _____
   _____
   _____
   _____

In the Torah, this is the actual reaction that is described:

> His father scolded him and said to him: "What kind of dream have you dreamt? Do you really expect us to come—I and your mother and your brothers—to bow down to you?" (Genesis 37:10)

Rashi explains this verse by suggesting that Jacob had more to say.

> "Your mother Rachel is long dead. Your dreams are cruel."

> Jacob did not realize that the "moon" in the dream referred to Bilhah, the handmaiden who had raised Joseph.

MITZVOT OF THE WEEK

כַּבֵּד אֶת־אָבִיךָ וְאֶת־אִמֶּךָ HONOR YOUR FATHER AND YOUR MOTHER

אִישׁ אִמּוֹ וְאָבִיו תִּירָאוּ BE IN AWE OF YOUR MOTHER AND YOUR FATHER

Even though it will not become an official mitzvah until the Ten Commandments are given on Mt. Sinai (Exodus 20:2-17), this story raises the question of the honor and respect given to parents. We are forced to ask, "Even though this dream will come true, should Joseph have told it to his family?" At the end of this lesson, give your own answer to that question.

In the Torah there are two very similar commandments:

Honor your father and your mother (Exodus 20:12).

Each person shall be in awe of his/her mother and father (Leviticus 19:3).

In the Talmud the rabbis explore the difference between these two mitzvot.

What is **awe** and what is **honor**?

Awe means that a son must neither stand nor sit in his father's place, nor contradict his words, nor side with his opponent in an argument.

Honor means that a son must give his father food and drink, and clothe and cover him.

Kiddushin 32a

Here is a test case, a real letter from the *Jewish Forward* in 1906. Based on our Torah text and this piece of Talmud, what would you advise the writer of this question?

Esteemed Editor:

I am "greenhorn," Only five weeks in the country and a jeweler by trade. I come from Russia, Where I left a blind father and a stepmother. Before I left, My father asked me not to forget him. I promised that I would send him the first money I earned in america. When I arrived in New York, I walked around for two weeks looking for a job....In the third week I was lucky, and found a job at which I earn eight dollars a week. I worked I paid my landlady board, I bought a few things to wear, and I have a few dollars in my pocket. Now I want you to advise me....Shall I send my father a few dollars for Passover, or should I keep the little money for myself? In this place the work will end soon and I may be left without a job.

_____

_____

Having studied the mitzvot of *being in awe* and *honoring* parents, should Joseph have told his second dream to his family?

_____

_____

_____

_____

Here is the answer the *Jewish Forward* columnist gave. How does it compare to your own?

> The answer to this young man is that he should send his father the few dollars for Passover because, since he is young, he will find it easier to earn a living than would his blind father in Russia.

We need Judaic stability so that the values of Jewish family life are not swept away in the maelstrom of an overly competitive, depersonalizing middle-class culture. To preserve the ideals of the Jewish family requires a reappraisal of the roles superimposed upon its members. It needs an appreciation of the values of Judaism which have been twisted out of shape. It requires collective courage and intelligence to live against the grain of middle-classism. As difficult as all this may be, history is on our side. In eras of violence, Jews did not shed blood. In environments of illiteracy, Jews read and wrote. Amidst drunkenness, Jews remained sober without vows of abstinence. Surrounded by murder and suicide, Jews cherished the sanctity of life. In a society riddled with mindless materialism, purposeless pressure, joyless hedonism, and devastating loneliness, Jews can restructure the family to oppose the shallow ethos of mass culture.

But it cannot be done alone. No family is an island. If anything, familism, the retreat of individuals into the insularity of their individual families, may prove counterproductive. Narrow familism is another form of incestuous narcissism. The traditional Jewish family did not live against the grain of mass society by isolating itself from the community. It will not save itself today without the cooperation and planning of the community.

Harold M. Schulweis, *In God's Mirror* (1990)

MIKETZ

מקץ

ויהי מקץ שנתים ימים ופרעה חלם והנה עמד על היאר

GENESIS 41:1-44:17

- Joseph interprets Pharaoh's **two dreams**, and predicts a famine.
- Pharaoh puts Joseph in charge of famine control.
- Joseph has a family. **Seven years of plenty** are followed by **famine**.
- Jacob sends **ten sons** to buy food in Egypt. Joseph's brothers **do not recognize** him. He tricks them and returns their gold. He demands that they **bring Benjamin** next time.
- Later, they return and Joseph throws Benjamin in jail.

OUR TEXT—GENESIS 41:57

This *parashah* is the one where Joseph exits jail, passes go, and winds up as Pharoah's right-hand man. He sets up both a tax and a welfare system. This verse tells us what happens.

וְכָל־הָאָרֶץ בָּאוּ מִצְרַיְמָה לִשְׁבֹּר אֶל־יוֹסֵף כִּי־חָזַק הָרָעָב בְּכָל־הָאָרֶץ.

כ	כִּי = _____	to	אֶל = א
מ	מִצְרַיִם = Egypt	....	אֶרֶץ =
	מִצְרַיְמָה = to Egypt	come	[בוֹא] = ב
ר	[רָעָב] = hunger/famine	they come	בָּאוּ =
ש	[שבר] = buy grain	strong	[חזק] = ח
	לִשְׁבֹּר = to buy grain	....	יוֹסֵף = י
		....	כָּל = כ

וְכָל־הָאָרֶץ בָּאוּ מִצְרַיְמָה _____ .57

לִשְׁבֹּר אֶל־יוֹסֵף _____

כִּי־חָזַק הָרָעָב _____

בְּכָל־הָאָרֶץ. _____

Now try reading this verse without vowels:

וכל הארץ באו מצרימה לשבר אל יוסף כי חזק
הרעב בכל הארץ

45

EXPLORING OUR TEXT

QUESTIONS

Why did Joseph set up a system to feed non-Jews and non-Egyptians? _____
_____

When the rabbis looked at this passage, they asked two questions: (1) If the Egyptians were going to hurt the Jews and make them slaves, why did Joseph help them and feed them? (2) Even if Joseph wanted to help the Egyptians, why does he set up a system that feeds the whole world?

What is your theory? _____
_____
_____
_____

What is the meaning of the verse, "He donned victory like a coat of mail" (Isaiah 59:17)?
It tells us that just as in a coat of mail every small scale joins with others to form a piece of armor, so every little sum of money given to charity combines with the rest to form a large sum.

Babylonian Talmud, tractate Bava Batra, page 9b

Here is a Jewish folk story. See if it can expand our understanding.

A BANQUET IN HEAVEN

A righteous man was permitted by God to get a preview of the world to come. In a celestial palace, he was ushered into a large room where he saw people seated at a banquet table laden with delicious food, but not a morsel had been touched. The righteous man gazed in wonder at the people seated at the table. They were hungry and wanted to eat—but did not!

"If they are hungry, why is it they don't eat and enjoy the food before them?" asked the righteous man.

"They cannot feed themselves," said his heavenly guide. "If you will notice, each has his arms strapped so that no matter how he tries, he cannot get the food into his mouth."

"Truly, this is hell," said the righteous one as they left the hall.

The heavenly attendant escorted him across the hall into another room, where the righteous man observed another beautiful table, equally laden with delicacies. Here, however, he noticed those seated around the table were well fed, happy, and joyous. To his amazement, he saw these people also had their arms strapped.

He turned to his guide and asked: "How is it that they are so well fed even though they are unable to transport the food to their mouths?"

"Behold," said the heavenly guide. The righteous man looked on with wonder as he watched each one feeding his neighbor. The straps, he noticed, were tied to allow enough freedom for each individual to feed his neighbor, even though he was unable to feed himself.

"This is really heaven," said the righteous man.

"In truth it is," the guide answered. "As you can see, the difference between hell and heaven is a matter of cooperation—of serving one's fellow man."

What is the message of this story? _____

_____

_____

How does it help us answer our questions about Joseph's actions? _____

_____

_____

MITZVAH OF THE WEEK
מָזוֹן Mazon

While it is not on the official list of 613 and an individual *mitzvah*, this week we will focus on one aspect of *Gemilut Hasadim* called *mazon*—feeding the hungry. (It is part of some other *mitzvot* dealing with all kinds of caring.)

There is an American Jewish organization called *Mazon: A Jewish Response to Hunger* that feeds both the Jewish and the non-Jewish poor. On its brochure Mazon has a quote from the prophet Isaiah. What does it mean?

> If you offer your compassion to the hungry and you feed the famished creatures—then your light will shine in the darkness and your gloom will be like noonday (Isaiah 58:10).

What MAZON Does

MAZON asks that you contribute a suggested amount of 3% of the cost of your *simha*—a *bar* or *bat mitzvah*, a wedding, a birthday, or anniversary, any joyous occasion. Three percent: to a cost of $1,000, add $30, to $5,000 add $150, to $ 10,000 add $300...

MAZON funds a variety of organizations: Kosher meals-on-wheels programs for homebound elderly people; food banks and food pantries in the inner cities and rural areas; multi-service centers that provide homeless families with food, shelter and counseling; state and national organizations that work for long-term solutions to hunger.

MAZON is, of course, responsive to hunger that exists in the Jewish community, but in keeping with the best of our tradition, we respond to all who are in need.

What YOU Can Do

Our ancestors left the corners of their fields for the needy. You can follow in their footsteps by sending MAZON 3% of the cost of your celebrations...For a hungry person, it is a gift of life.

On Yom Kippur you can respond to Isaiah's challenge to "share your bread with the hungry" by providing MAZON with the dollars you would ordinarily spend to feed your family. Deepen the meaning of voluntary fasting by helping to alleviate endless days of involuntary fasting—the fast of the poor.

During Passover, you can remember that we were strangers in the land of Egypt, and respond to the needs of the hungry stranger today by sending MAZON the dollars that would have been spent to feed one extra guest at your *seder*. Add meaning to the words of the Haggadah: "Let all who are hungry come and eat."

The rabbis taught, "Bread is the comfort of the heart." You can offer comfort to those who mourn with a contribution honoring the memory of loved ones. You can also honor friends or family with a contribution to their joyous occasions.

How is *Mazon* a lot like Joseph?

_____

_____

_____

Consider being like Joseph on the day of your *bat* or *bar mitzvah*.

_____

_____

_____

For more information:
MAZON, 2940 Westwood Blvd., Suite 7, Los Angeles, CA 90064-4102. (310) 470-7769.

VA-YIGASH

ויגש אליו יהודה ויאמר בי אדני ידבר נא עבדך דבר באזני אדני ואל יחר אפך בעבדך כי כמוך כפרעה

GENESIS 44:18–47:27

- **Judah pleads** for Benjamin.
- **Joseph reveals himself** to his brothers.
- Pharaoh welcomes Joseph's family.
- Jacob moves the family to Egypt. They settle in the land of Goshen.

OUR TEXT—GENESIS 45:4-5

We are almost at the end of the book of Genesis. In this *sidrah* comes the climax of the Joseph story. In these two verses, Joseph finally reveals himself to his brothers. When he does, the outcome is a surprise.

וַיֹּאמֶר אֲנִי יוֹסֵף אֲחִיכֶם אֲשֶׁר־מְכַרְתֶּם אֹתִי מִצְרָיְמָה. וְעַתָּה אַל־תֵּעָצְבוּ וְאַל־יִחַר בְּעֵינֵיכֶם כִּי־מְכַרְתֶּם אֹתִי הֵנָּה כִּי לְמִחְיָה שְׁלָחַנִי אֱלֹהִים לִפְנֵיכֶם.

כ	_____ = כִּי	brothers............... = אֲחִים	א
	_____ = ■+כֶם	do not............... = אַל	
ל	before............... = לִפְנֵי	_____ = אֱלֹהִים	
מ	sell............... = [מכר]	_____ = [אמר]	
	_____ = מְכַרְתֶּם	_____ = אֲנִי	
	_____ = מִצְרָיְמָה	_____ = אֲשֶׁר	
ע	eyes............... = עֵינַיִם	here............... = הֵנָּה	ה
	sad/grieve............... = [עצב]	_____ = [חי]	ח
	_____ = תֵּעָצְבוּ	_____ = לְמִחְיָה	
	now............... = עַתָּה	angry............... = [חרה]	
ש	sent............... = [שלח]	_____ = יִחַר	
	_____ = שְׁלָחַנִי	_____ = יוֹסֵף	י

4. וַיֹּאמֶר אֲנִי יוֹסֵף אֲחִיכֶם _____
_____ אֲשֶׁר־מְכַרְתֶּם אֹתִי מִצְרָיְמָה.

5. וְעַתָּה אַל־תֵּעָצְבוּ _____
_____ וְאַל־יִחַר בְּעֵינֵיכֶם
_____ כִּי־מְכַרְתֶּם אֹתִי הֵנָּה
_____ כִּי לְמִחְיָה
_____ שְׁלָחַנִי אֱלֹהִים לִפְנֵיכֶם.

Now try reading this verse without vowels:

ויאמר אני יוסף אחיכם אשר מכרתם אתי מצרימה
ועתה אל תעצבו ואל יחר בעיניכם כי מכרתם אתי
הנה כי למחיה שלחני אלהים לפניכם

EXPLORING OUR TEXT

Joseph has been playing games with his brothers for a long time. He has sent them back and forth to Canaan. He has hidden things in their bags. He has even put Benjamin in jail. Why does he finally give in and reveal himself?

Write your answer and then look below to find a traditional Jewish answer.

_____
_____
_____
_____
_____
_____
_____

With Judah's selfless offer of himself as a substitute for Benjamin, Joseph finally had the irrefutable proof of the change in his brothers' old attitude, as exemplified by their filial devotion to Jacob, their love for Benjamin, their sincere contrition for their crimes against Joseph himself.

(Akeidah, Abrabanel, Hirsch, Munk)
The Family Chumash, Artscroll 1989

MITZVAH OF THE WEEK
תְּשׁוּבָה REPENTANCE

In Numbers 5:7 we are specifically told: "**They shall confess their sin which they have committed**." From that verse, the mitzvah of *T'shuvah*, repentance, is rooted. However, the story of this week's Torah portion, the reconciliation of Joseph and his brothers, gives us a great opportunity to talk about forgiveness and change.

> As Joseph became reconciled to his brothers from the midst of weeping, so will the Holy One redeem Israel from the midst of weeping, as it says, *"They shall come with weeping, and with supplications will I lead them; I will cause them to walk by rivers or waters."* (Jeremiah 31:9)
>
> Genesis Rabbah XCIII.8,11-12

Here are a few of Maimonides' *T'shuvah* guidelines:

2.3 Anyone who makes a verbal confession without resolving in his heart to abandon his sin is like one who takes a ritual bath while grasping a defiling reptile—the bath is useless unless he first casts the reptile away.

2.10 One must not show himself cruel by not accepting an apology; he should be easily pacified, and provoked with difficulty. When an offender asks his forgiveness, he should forgive wholeheartedly and with a willing spirit. Even if he has caused him much trouble wrongfully, he must not avenge himself, he must not bear a grudge.

7.2 A man should always consider himself as if he is about to die. He may die when his time is up while still behaving sinfully, so he should therefore repent of his sins immediately. Let him not say: "When I grow old I shall repent," since he may die before getting old. Solomon in his wisdom said: "Let your garments be always white" (Ecclesiastes 9:8).

7.3 Do not say that repentance is limited to sinful acts, such as fornication, robbery and theft. Just as a man must repent of these, so he must scan and search his evil traits, repenting of anger, hatred, envy, scoffing, greed, vainglory, excessive desire for food, and so on. One must repent of all these failings. They are worse than sinful acts. When a person is addicted to them, he finds it hard to get rid of them.

7.4 Let not the repentant person imagine that he is far removed from the merit of the righteous on account of the iniquities and sins he committed. This not so. He is tenderly loved by the Creator as if he never sinned. Besides, his reward is great, since he had tasted sin and got rid of it by suppressing his evil impulse.

7.8 Those who repent should be exceedingly humble in their behavior. If ignorant fools insult them by mentioning their past deeds and saying to them:"Last night you were doing this and that; last night you were saying this and that," they should pay no attention to them, but upon hearing this they should rejoice, knowing that this is a merit. As long as they feel ashamed of their past deeds and are disgraced because of them, their merit and worth are enhanced. It is a flagrant sin to say to a person, "Remember your past deeds," with all kinds of insulting words.

VA-YE<u>H</u>I

ויחי

ויהי יעקב בארץ מצרים שבע עשרה שנה ויהי ימי יעקב שני חייו

GENESIS 47:28–50:26

- Joseph **promises** Jacob that he will not bury him in Egypt.
- Jacob **blesses** Joseph's sons and his own twelve sons.
- Jacob **dies** and is taken to the Cave of Makhpelah and is buried.
- Joseph **dies** and is buried in Egypt. The Children of Israel **promise** to move his remains to **Canaan**.

OUR TEXT—GENESIS 48:20

Close to his death, Jacob blesses Joseph's sons, Ephraim and Menashe. Our verse is this famous blessing.

וַיְבָרְכֵם בַּיּוֹם הַהוּא לֵאמוֹר בְּךָ יְבָרֵךְ יִשְׂרָאֵל לֵאמֹר יְשִׂמְךָ אֱלֹהִים כְּאֶפְרַיִם וְכִמְנַשֶּׁה וַיָּשֶׂם אֶת־אֶפְרַיִם לִפְנֵי מְנַשֶּׁה.

י	יִשְׂרָאֵל = _____	א	[אמר] = _____
כ	כְּ = like		לֵאמוֹר = _____
ל	לִפְנֵי = _____		אֶפְרַיִם = Ephraim
מ	מְנַשֶּׁה = Menashe	ב	בַּיּוֹם הַהוּא = on that day
ש	[שים] = put		בְּךָ = _____
	יְשִׂמְךָ = _____		[ברך] = _____
	וַיָּשֶׂם = _____		וַיְבָרְכֵם = _____
			יְבָרֵךְ = _____

20. _____ וַיְבָרְכֵם בַּיּוֹם הַהוּא לֵאמוֹר

_____ בְּךָ יְבָרֵךְ יִשְׂרָאֵל לֵאמֹר

_____ יְשִׂמְךָ אֱלֹהִים

_____ כְּאֶפְרַיִם וְכִמְנַשֶּׁה

_____ וַיָּשֶׂם אֶת־אֶפְרַיִם לִפְנֵי מְנַשֶּׁה.

Now try reading this verse without vowels:

ויברכם ביום ההוא לאמור בך יברך ישראל לאמר ישמך אלהים כאפרים וכמנשה וישם את אפרים לפני מנשה

EXPLORING OUR TEXT

It is a custom for Jewish parents to bless their children at the Erev Shabbat (Friday Night) dinner table. It grows from our verse. Here is the ceremony.

BLESSING THE CHILDREN

1. Place your hands on your child's head.
2. Say the appropriate blessings (sons or daughters).
3. Add your own wishes and thoughts.
4. Say the "Priestly Blessing" (for all children).
5. Hug, kiss, etc.

FOR SONS

יְשִׂימְךָ אֱלֹהִים כְּאֶפְרַיִם וְכִמְנַשֶּׁה.

Y'simkha Elohim k'Efrayim v'khi-Menashe
May ADONAI make you like Ephraim and Menashe.

FOR DAUGHTERS

יְשִׂימֵךְ אֱלֹהִים כְּשָׂרָה רִבְקָה רָחֵל וְלֵאָה.

Y'simekh Elohim k'Sarah, Rivka, Ra_hel, v'Leah.
May ADONAI make you like Sarah, Rebekkah, Rachel and Leah.

Here is a formula for your own blessing (fill in the blanks for your own children).

May God bless you with _____ and _____.

May you be (like) _____ and _____.

May this Shabbat of _____ fill you with _____ and _____.

FOR ALL CHILDREN

יְבָרֶכְךָ יהוה וְיִשְׁמְרֶךָ.

יָאֵר יהוה פָּנָיו אֵלֶיךָ וִיחֻנֶּךָּ.

יִשָּׂא יהוה פָּנָיו אֵלֶיךָ וְיָשֵׂם לְךָ שָׁלוֹם.

Y'varekh'kha Adonai v'Yishm'rekha.

Ya'er Adonai Panav Elekha vi-_H_uneka.

Yissa Adonai Panav Elekha v'Yasem L'kha Shalom.

May ADONAI bless and guard you. May ADONAI shine Divine light upon you and be good to you. May ADONAI face you and give you peace.

> *As far as I know no such explicit formulation is to be found in our Midrashic literature. The oldest literary work containing reference to, and dealing with, the blessing of children on Friday nights is, to my mind, the Ma'avar Yabbok by R. Aaron Berechiah b. Moses of Modena (d. 1639 C.E.). In the section entitled Sifre Renanot, Chap. 43 p. 245, he writes: 'It was stated in the section dealing with raising children: When someone lays his hand on the head of a young child receiving the blessing, as is said (Gen. 48:14): 'And Israel stretched out his hands', and (v. 20) 'And he blessed them that day...'"*
>
> B.S. Jacobson, *The Shabbat Siddur*

MITZVAH OF THE WEEK
OBLIGATIONS TO CHILDREN

While blessing one's children is not a mitzvah (only a *minhag*) the Torah does list a series of obligations parents have towards children. The Talmud puts it way:

> A father is obligated to circumcise his son, redeem him, teach him Torah, take a wife for him, and teach him a trade. Some authorities say to teach him to swim, also.
>
> *Kiddushin 29a-30b*

> A father must provide for his daughter clothing and covering and must also give her a dowry so that people may be anxious to woo her and so proceed to marry her. And to what extent?...Up to a tenth of his wealth.
>
> *Ketubot 52b*

> When a father who refused to support his child was brought before Rabbi Hisda, he would say: "Make a public announcement and proclaim: 'The raven cares for its young, but this man does not care for his young.'"
>
> *Ketubot 48b*

SHEMOT שְׁמוֹת

שְׁמוֹת וְאֵלֶּה בְּנֵי יִשְׂרָאֵל הַבָּאִים מִצְרָיְמָה אֵת יַעֲקֹב אִישׁ וּבֵיתוֹ בָּאוּ

EXODUS 1:1–6:1

- A new generation of the Children of Israel grows into a **nation**.
- A **new Pharaoh** comes to rule.
- The Jewish people are turned into **slaves**.
- Moses is born, hidden, found floating in a basket, raised in Pharaoh's house, turned into an outlaw when he kills to defend a Hebrew slave, and married to the daughter of the High Priest of Midian.
- God talks to him from inside a **Burning Bush**.

OUR TEXT—EXODUS 2:1

In the first *sidrah* in Exodus we meet Moses. His story begins with this seemingly unremarkable sentence.

וַיֵּלֶךְ אִישׁ מִבֵּית לֵוִי וַיִּקַּח אֶת־בַּת־לֵוִי.

ה	go/walk = [הלך]		_____ = אִישׁ	א
	_____ = וַיֵּלֶךְ		_____ = אֶת	
ל	Levi = לֵוִי		_____ = בַּיִת	ב
	take = [לקח]		_____ = מִבֵּית	
	_____ = וַיִּקַּח		_____ = בַּת	

1. וַיֵּלֶךְ אִישׁ מִבֵּית לֵוִי _____
   וַיִּקַּח אֶת־בַּת־לֵוִי. _____

Now try reading this verse without vowels:

וילך איש מבית לוי ויקח את בת לוי

> ...the reason for the Egyptian exile, the persecution and suffering of bondage accompanying the birth of the Jewish people prior to giving of the Torah and their entry into the Promised Land, was that they themselves should experience the taste of slavery and humiliation. They were to be made to realize just what it felt like to be subjected to the violence and domination of people.
>
> Just as the Egyptian exile prefigures every exile to which Israel was subjected, and just as Egyptian bondage provided the motivation and impulse for many moral imperatives, so did the redemption from Egypt serve as a spur for a religious duty; that imposed on every Jew to redeem fellow-beings from slavery. This duty too is motivated in the Torah by the Almighty's rescuing God's people from Egypt.
>
> Nehama Leibowitz, *Studies in Shemot* (1976)

EXPLORING OUR TEXT

1. In Exodus 6:20, the Torah tells us that Moses' father's name was Amram and that his mother's name was Yokheved. In our text, they are only referred to as a "man" and a "woman." Why do you think the Torah chose to delay the introduction of their names?

   _____

   _____

2. The first *parashah* of Shemot seems to go out of its way to say that women were crucial to Jewish survival. We meet the "midwives," Moses mother and sister, Pharaoh's daughter, and Jethro's daughter—all of whom have an important role in saving the Jewish people. In fact, no men seem to help. What lesson can you learn from this?

   _____

   _____

3. In the Midrash on Numbers we are given a clue. It says:

   In that generation the women rebuilt many of the Torah laws that men had broken.

   When Aaron asked everyone to give their gold jewelry to make the golden calf, the men agreed and the women refused.

   When the spies urged everyone to abandon the Promised Land of Israel as a destination, the men were unwilling to enter the land, but the women retained their faith in God's command.

   In other midrashim we learn that (a) after Pharaoh condemned all Jewish baby boys to death, the men wanted to abandon having children but the women insisted on continuing; (b) women insisted on teaching their children Hebrew and giving them Hebrew names rather than adopting Egyptian culture; and (c) when most Jews abandoned infant circumcision, the women of the tribe of Levi maintained it.

   How do you explain these insights? What do they teach us about the man and the woman from the tribe of Levi?

   _____

   _____

MITZVAH OF THE WEEK
שֵׁם עִבְרִי A Hebrew Name

In the Midrash on Song of Songs (IV. 12.1) we learn:

> Rabbi Huna said in the name of Bar Kappara: As a reward for four practices the Jews were redeemed from Egypt: (a) they did not change their Hebrew names, (b) they continued speaking Hebrew as their language, (c) they did not inform one on the other, and (d) they did not intermarry with the Egyptians.

Even though it is not an official mitzvah, based on this midrash we know that it is good for Jews to learn Hebrew and to have Hebrew names.

Tell everything you know about your Hebrew name. Explain: How it works? What it means? Where it came from?

_____

_____

_____

_____

_____

_____

The Book of Exodus gives an expanded picture of what Jewish biblical women were like. Jacob's extended family went into Egypt, beginning an exile that was to last for 210 years.

The men settled a little too comfortably in an Egyptian district called Goshen, where they led a prosperous material existence. The women did not want to trade the spirituality of the land of Israel, even in a time of famine, for the lack of holiness in a land of plenty.

Through the women's demonstrations of their love of God in these matters, they showed themselves to be in tune with God's will. Their behavior was so exemplary that had the men acted as the women did, the Messiah would have surely come during the time of the desert generation.

Women's loving actions will be one of the most fundamental contributions that will help bring about the coming of the Messiah.

Dr. Lisa Aiken, *To Be A Jewish Woman* (1993)

VA-ERA וָאֵרָא

וידבר אלהים אל משה
ויאמר אליו אני יהוה
וארא אל אברהם
אל יצחק ואל יעקב באל שדי
ושמי יהוה לא נודעתי להם

EXODUS 6:2-9:35

- **Moses and Aaron** visit **Pharaoh** and do the staff-into-snake trick. They tell him: "**Let My People Go**."
- The first seven plagues: **Blood, frogs, lice, insect swarms, cattle blight, boils** and **hail**.

OUR TEXT: EXODUS 6:3-4

At the end of the last *sidrah*, Moses and Aaron confront Pharaoh for the first time. It gets them nowhere. This *sidrah* begins with God giving Moses a pep-talk to keep on struggling. Our verses are the first time God speaks in this conversation.

וָאֵרָא אֶל־אַבְרָהָם אֶל־יִצְחָק אֶל־יַעֲקֹב בְּאֵל שַׁדָּי וּשְׁמִי יהוה לֹא נוֹדַעְתִּי לָהֶם.

וְגַם הֲקִמֹתִי אֶת־בְּרִיתִי אִתָּם לָתֵת לָהֶם אֶת־אֶרֶץ כְּנַעַן אֵת אֶרֶץ מְגֻרֵיהֶם אֲשֶׁר־גָּרוּ בָהּ.

י	_____ = יַעֲקֹב		_____ = אַבְרָהָם	א
	_____ = יִצְחָק		_____ = אֶל	
כ	_____ = כְּנַעַן		_____ = אֶל	
ל	_____ = לֹא		_____ = אֶרֶץ	
	_____ = לְ + הֶם = לָהֶם		_____ = אֲשֶׁר	
נ	give = [נתן]		_____ = אֶת + הֶם = אֹתָם	
	_____ = לָתֵת		_____ = בְּ + הּ = בָהּ	ב
ק	establish/rise up = [קום]	covenant _____ = בְּרִית	
	_____ = הֲקִמֹתִי	dwell/sojourn/settle _____ = [גור]	ג
ר	see = [ראה]	_____ = גָּרוּ	
	_____ = וָאֵרָא	_____ = מְגֻרֵיהֶם	
ש	Shaddai = שַׁדָּי	also _____ = גַם	
	name = שֵׁם	know _____ = [ידע]	י
	_____ = וּשְׁמִי	_____ = נוֹדַעְתִּי	

3. וָאֵרָא אֶל־אַבְרָהָם _____

אֶל־יִצְחָק אֶל־יַעֲקֹב _____

בְּאֵל שַׁדָּי _____

וּשְׁמִי יהוה לֹא נוֹדַעְתִּי לָהֶם. _____

4. וְגַם הֲקִמֹתִי אֶת־בְּרִיתִי אִתָּם _____

לָתֵת לָהֶם אֶת־אֶרֶץ כְּנַעַן _____

אֵת אֶרֶץ מְגֻרֵיהֶם אֲשֶׁר־גָּרוּ בָהּ. _____

Now try reading this verse without vowels:

וארא אל אברהם אל יצחק ואל יעקב באל שדי ושמי יהוה
לא נודעתי להם וגם הקמתי את בריתי אתם לתת להם את
ארץ כנען את ארץ מגריהם אשר גרו בה

EXPLORING OUR TEXT

In our text we learn that God makes a formal gift to the Jewish People of the Land of Canaan. Here is the question: Just because God gave it to us, is it a mitzvah to live there? Here are two *t'shuvot*, legal "Dear Abby"-style questions, sent to famous Jewish legal scholars. Both ask about the obligation to live in Israel. Write your own answers to each. You'll find the scholars' actual answers at the end of this chapter.

THE QUESTIONS

T'shuvot Rabbeinu Nissim Gerondi, no. 38

Question: Reuven, Shimon, and Levi joined together in a plan to cross the Mediterranean Sea together to be closer to Eretz Yisrael. They made the following agreement which they signed under solemn oath: Before us, the undersigned witnesses, and before Rabbi Yosef of Marseilles and Rabbi Chaim Tzarfati, they agreed to sail in October or November on a vessel from the port of Barcelona, Spain, bound for that destination, for the purpose of settling in Eretz Yisrael or near it, in Cyprus or Alexandria, Egypt. Now Shimon wants to recant his vow because his wife refuses to go along with him. Her relatives convinced her not to follow her husband and to refuse to accept a *Get* from him. Besides, he surmises that she is pregnant. He says that if he had known that she would not join him, he would not have sworn to emigrate. He is asking whether his vows can be annulled and, if so, whether he needs Reuven's and Levi's consent, since they swore to go together.

_____

_____

_____

_____

_____

_____

Tashbatz, no. 3:288

Question: Is it correct to say that upon entering Eretz Yisrael all of a person's sins of which he repents are forgiven? And can it be said that a person who died while on his way to Eretz Yisrael is considered as having lived in Eretz Yisrael if his intentions were upright?

_____

_____

_____

_____

MITZVAH OF THE WEEK
עֲלִיָּה לְאֶרֶץ יִשְׂרָאֵל Moving to the Land of Israel

When you read the Ramban (Rabbi Moshe ben Nahman, who is not the Rambam) he points you directly to Numbers 33:53:

> You shall take possession of the Land (of Israel)
> and settle it—
> For I have given the Land to you
> to possess it.

The Ramban reads this verse and says: "Living in the Land of Israel is a Mitzvah"—and he seems to be right.

Here is the problem: When you look into Maimonides' list of mitzvot, *Aliyah* is not there. When you read *Sefer ha-Hinukh*, another famous list of mitzvot, *Aliyah* is also missing. When you dig deep into the Talmud, you can find a lot of statements that say living in Eretz Yisrael is good, desirable, meritorious, and probably better for Jews—but it is hard (except for Nachmanides—the Ramban) to find a legal source that says Jews have an obligation to move to Israel (before the Messiah comes).

In both Maimonides and the *Sefer ha-Hinukh* we find this mitzvah (Deuteronomy 17:16): "It is forbidden to dwell in the land of Egypt. Jews may return there for business purposes but may not permanently live there."

Based on your opinion, which of these should be Jewish obligations regarding Eretz Yisrael?

____ Every Jew should include Israel in their prayers.
____ Every Jew should study about the Land of Israel.
____ Every Jew should financially support the State of Israel.
____ Every Jew should politically support the State of Israel.
____ Every Jew should visit the Land of Israel at least once in their life.
____ Every Jew should spend at least one year studying in and/or volunteering in the Land of Israel.
____ Every Jew should seriously consider moving to the Land of Israel.
____ Every Jew should move to the Land of Israel.

THE ANSWERS

T'shuvot Rabbeinu Nissim Gerondi, no. 38

Answer: This is indeed a severe oath, one that you should avoid like a snake...But a man is not permitted to leave his wife, and he cannot demand that she follow him to the ends of the world....I agree that this vow should be annulled. As for the question whether the consent of Reuven and Levi is needed....In this case, if Shimon received no consideration of favor from Reuven and Levi to induce him to make the vow, it may be annulled in their presence, even without their consent. But if he did receive a consideration or favor from them and because of it he made the vow, then he must do his utmost to obtain Reuven's and Levi's agreement to the annulment. However, if they are unwilling to give their consent, the vow may be annulled in any event, for the reason set forth.

Tashbatz, no. 3:288

Answer: To live in Eretz Yisrael is a great mitzvah. The Ramban counts it as one of the 613 mitzvot of the Torah, and he writes that living in Eretz Yisrael is equal to all the mitzvot in the Torah....Whoever lives in Eretz Yisrael lives without sin...Whoever is buried in Eretz Yisrael is as though he is buried underneath the altar. The sages of Israel would risk their lives fording raging rivers in their attempts to reach Eretz Yisrael. They would say, "The land that Moshe and Aharon did not merit to enter, will we deserve to enter it?" They would kiss the stones and roll in the dust, in fulfillment of the verse, "For your servants take pleasure in her stones, and love her dust." You are permitted to leave Eretz Yisrael only for the purpose of learning Torah, if you cannot find anyone there to teach you, or in order to honor your father and mother. From all this it is evident that if a person is a *Ba'al T'shuvah* (a returnee to Torah observance) and wishes to move to Eretz Yisrael (although *T'shuvah* [repentance] itself brings about forgiveness), by moving to Eretz Yisrael he gains additional merit, and it will save him from sin all his life. As for your question regarding a person who was unable to complete the mitzvah, our sages state that virtuous thoughts count as deeds. As Rav Asi said, "Even if you planned to do a mitzvah but you did not perform it, you are deemed as though you had actually done the mitzvah." May God help you to carry out your good intentions.

BO

בֹּא

ויאמר יהוה אל משה

אֶל פַּרְעֹה כִּי אֲנִי הִכְבַּדְתִּי אֶת לִבּוֹ וְאֶת לֵב עֲבָדָיו לְמַעַן שִׁתִי אֹתֹתַי אֵלֶּה בְּקִרְבּוֹ

EXODUS 10:1-13:16

- God sends the last three plagues: **Locusts, darkness** and the **death of the firstborn.**
- God teaches the *mitzvah* of the **new month**.
- The Jews **celebrate Passover** while still slaves in Egypt.

OUR TEXT—EXODUS 13:8

The first Passover took place in Egypt before the Exodus ever happened. It took place on the last night in Egypt, the night of the death of firstborn sons. Our verse comes from the directions for that Seder.

וְהִגַּדְתָּ לְבִנְךָ בַּיּוֹם הַהוּא לֵאמֹר בַּעֲבוּר זֶה עָשָׂה יהוה לִי בְּצֵאתִי מִמִּצְרָיִם.

ל	to .... = לְ		_____ = [אמר]	א
מ	Egypt .... = מִצְרַיִם		son .... = בֵּן	ב
	_____ = מִמִּצְרָיִם		this .... = זֶה	ז
נ	tell/explain .... = [נגד]		_____ = יוֹם	י
	_____ = וְהִגַּדְתָּ		on this day .... = בַּיּוֹם הַהוּא	
ע	because .... = עֲבוּר		went out/took out .... = [יצא]	
	because of .... = בַּעֲבוּר		I/me .... = י ■
	_____ = [עשה]		_____ = בְּצֵאתִי	

8. _____ וְהִגַּדְתָּ לְבִנְךָ

_____ בַּיּוֹם הַהוּא לֵאמֹר

_____ בַּעֲבוּר זֶה עָשָׂה יהוה לִי

_____ בְּצֵאתִי מִמִּצְרָיִם.

Now try reading this verse without vowels:

והגדת לבנך ביום ההוא לאמר
בעבור זה עשה יהוה לי בצאתי ממצרים

EXPLORING OUR TEXT

The verse we have just studied is the reason we have a Seder each year. A Seder is a family lesson plan, a way for parents to tell the story of the Exodus from Egypt to their children. The ones who transformed this verse into a Seder were the rabbis of the Mishnah. In that book we find the first rules for a Seder. When you open up the Mishnah to chapter 10 of Pesahim you find the first Seder blueprint. Here is an edited version of that passage. Read it and see if you can figure out the steps that are involved. See if you can figure out which of the steps in our Seder are missing.

MISHNAH PESAHIM 10

1. On *Erev Pesah*, from after *Minhah* one may not eat until after dark. Even a poor Jew may not eat until s/he reclines at The Seder. Even a poor Jew—a person who lives off Tzedakah—must not drink less than four cups.

2. When the first cup is filled, one says the Kiddush. Beit Shammai and Beit Hillel differ over the order of the two Kiddush brakhot.

3. One then brings vegetables. The green is dipped before the breaking of the loaf. Then they bring *matzah,* greens, *haroset*, and two cooked dishes. In the days when the Temple existed the bones of the *Pesah* offering were also brought.

4. Then the second cup is poured. Next the child asks the four questions. If the child doesn't have enough understanding, the parents just provide instruction. According to the child's knowledge so is the teaching done. The parent begins with the story of our shame and ends with the story of God's glory. The parent starts the explanation with the words: *"My ancestor was a wandering Aramean"* (Deuteronomy 26:5) and then works through the entire portion.

5. Rabban Gamaliel taught that every Seder must include a discussion of *Pesah*, *Matzah*, and *Maror*. Then one says the beginning of the *Hallel*.

6. Beit Shammai and Beit Hillel disagree on how much of the *Hallel* is said before the meal. Then comes a concluding brakhah about redemption. Rabbi Tarphon and Rabbi Akiva disagree about the text of this brakhah.

7. Then the third cup is poured and *Birkat ha-Mazon* (the Grace After Meals) is said, followed by the rest of the *Hallel*.

When you open a modern Haggadah you find a list of 15 steps in our Seder. Match each of these steps with the things that are done or said. Clue: Some steps have more than one thing.

1. קַדֵּשׁ   Kadesh (Sanctification)   _____ Four Questions

2. וּרְחַץ   Urhatz (Washing)   _____ Four Children

3. כַּרְפַּס   Karpas (Greens)   _____ First Cup

4. יַחַץ   Yahatz (Breaking)   _____ Second Cup

5. מַגִּיד   Maggid (The Telling)   _____ Third Cup

6. רָחְצָה   Rohtzah (Washing)   _____ Fourth Cup

7. מוֹצִיא   Motzi (Bread Brakhah)   _____ Salt Water and Parsley

8. מַצָּה   Matzah (Unleaven Bread)   _____ Break Middle Matzah

9. מָרוֹר   Maror (Bitter Herb)   _____ Eat Matzah

10. כּוֹרֵךְ   Koreikh (Hillel Sandwich)   _____ Matzah + Maror + Haroset

11. שֻׁלְחָן עוֹרֵךְ Shulhan Orekh (Meal)   _____ Eat Horseradish

12. צָפוּן   Tzafun (Afikoman)   _____ Chicken Soup with *Matzah* Ball

13. בָּרֵךְ   Bareikh (Birkat ha-Mazon)   _____ Hunt for Afikoman

14. הַלֵּל   Hallel   _____ First Part of Hallel

15. נִרְצָה   Nirtzah   _____ Rest of Hallel

                                              _____ Door for Elijah

                                              _____ L'shanah ha-Ba'ah vi'Yerushalayim

                                              _____ Dayeinu

                                              _____ Who Knows One?

                                              _____ Had Gadya

                                              _____ Light Candles

MITZVAH OF THE WEEK
וְהִגַּדְתָּ לְבִנְךָ Tell Your Children

It is a mitzvah on the eve of the fifteenth of *Nissan* to tell your child the story of the Exodus from Egypt. We hold a Passover Seder as a formal way of doing this telling. Rather than a Seder being a Temple service, it is intentionally held in the home so that each family will have their own way of telling each of their own children. The Talmud makes it very clear that each child must be told this story in the way that will make it most real and most significant for her or him. A Seder is a family affair.

List three special things your family does at your Seder. How does each enhance the holiday?

1. _____

2. _____

3. _____

Seder nights are magic. They both transcend and unite history. Torah teaches us that the first Seder took place on the evening of the Exodus. It was a watch night filled with fear and anticipation. While the angel of death stalked the Egyptian firstborn, slave families gathered to eat the paschal lamb. Since then, our families have relived that evening more that three thousand times. For generations we have sat together to remember, retell, recreate, and relive that Exodus experience. Over time, the Seder has become more than an historic remembrance; it has evolved its own memories and significance. We cannot return to the lessons of that first Seder night in Egypt without its being enriched by the memories of our own Seder celebrations. As I sit to write of Seder traditions and customs, I return in my mind to Omaha. Such is the Jewish way. Family history and national history are interwoven. I cannot prepare to experience the spiritual liberation from Egypt without first returning in memory to Nebraska.

Dr. Ron Wolfson, *The Art of Jewish Living: The Passover Seder* (1988)

BESHALLAḤ

בְּשַׁלַּח

בשלח

ויהי בשלח פרעה את העם ולא נחם אלהים דרך ארץ פלשתים כי קרוב הוא כי אמר אלהים פן ינחם העם בראתם מלחמה ושבו מצרימה

EXODUS 13:17–17:16

- The Children of Israel flee from Egypt.
- Pharaoh and his army chase them.
- The Children of Israel cross the **Reed Sea** while Pharaoh and Company drown.
- The **Song of the Sea** is sung.
- The people complain about the water. Moses **hits a rock** and brings water.
- Israel fights a **battle with Amalek**.

72

OUR TEXT—EXODUS 16:29

In this *sidrah* we meet manna, the miracle food that falls like dew every night to feed the Families-of-Israel in the wilderness. The daily manna collection conflicts with the rules of Shabbat and causes some disagreement. Our verse comes from the middle of this situation, but you'll understand it better if you open a *Tanakh* and read all of Exodus 16 first.

רְאוּ כִּי־יהוה נָתַן לָכֶם הַשַּׁבָּת עַל־כֵּן יהוה נֹתֵן לָכֶם בַּיּוֹם הַשִּׁשִּׁי לֶחֶם יוֹמָיִם שְׁבוּ אִישׁ תַּחְתָּיו אַל־יֵצֵא אִישׁ מִמְּקֹמוֹ בַּיּוֹם הַשְּׁבִיעִי.

מ	place .... = מָקוֹם	_____ = אִישׁ	א
	_____ = מִמְּקֹמוֹ	do not .... = אַל	
נ	_____ = [נתן]	_____ = יהוה	י
ע	therefore .... = עַל־כֵּן	_____ = יוֹם	
ר	see .... = [ראה]	_____ = יוֹמָיִם	
	_____ = רְאוּ	go out/leave .... = [יצא]	
שׁ	seven .... = שְׁבִיעִי	sit .... = [ישב]	
	six .... = שִׁשִּׁי	_____ = שְׁבוּ	
ת	under/bottom .... = תַּחַת	_____ = כִּי	כ
	_____ = תַּחְתָּיו	_____ = לֶחֶם	ל

29. רְאוּ כִּי־יהוה נָתַן לָכֶם הַשַּׁבָּת _____

עַל־כֵּן יהוה נֹתֵן לָכֶם _____

בַּיּוֹם הַשִּׁשִּׁי לֶחֶם יוֹמָיִם _____

שְׁבוּ אִישׁ תַּחְתָּיו _____

אַל־יֵצֵא אִישׁ מִמְּקֹמוֹ _____

בַּיּוֹם הַשְּׁבִיעִי. _____

Now try reading this verse without vowels:

ראו כי יהוה נתן לכם השבת על כן יהוה נתן לכם ביום הששי לחם יומים שבו איש תחתיו אל יצא איש ממקמו ביום השביעי

73

EXPLORING OUR TEXT

THE MEANING OF SHABBAT

MORDECHAI M. KAPLAN

An artist cannot be continually wielding his brush. He must stop at times in his painting to freshen his vision of the object, the meaning of which he wishes to express on his canvas. Living is also art. We dare not become absorbed in its technical processes and lose our consciousness of its general plan...

The Shabbat represents those moments when we pause in our brushwork to renew our vision of this object. Having done so, we take ourselves to our painting with clarified vision and renewed energy. This applies to the individual and to the community alike.

ABRAHAM JOSHUA HESCHEL

Judaism is a religion of time, aiming at the sanctification of time. Unlike the space minded man to whom time is unvaried, iterative, homogeneous, to whom all hours are alike, qualitiless, empty shells, the Bible sense the diversified character of time. There are no two hours alike. Every hour is unique and the only one given at the moment, exclusive and endlessly precious.

Judaism teaches us to be attached to holiness in time, to be attached to sacred events, to learn how to consecrate sanctuaries that emerge from the magnificent stream of a year. The Sabbaths are our great cathedrals; and our Holy of Holies is a shrine that neither the Romans nor the Greeks were able to burn....

The meaning of the Sabbath is to celebrate time rather than space. Six days a week we live under the tyranny of things of space; on the Sabbath, we try to become attuned to the holiness of time. It is a day on which we are called to share in that which is eternal in time, to turn from the world of creation to the creation of the world.

Excerpted from The Sabbath

ERIC FROMM

The Sabbath seems to have been an old Babylonian holy day, celebrated every seventh day (Shapatu). But its meaning was quite different from that of the biblical Sabbath. The Babylonian Shapatu was a day of mourning and self-castigation. It was a somber day, dedicated to the planet Saturn (our "Saturday" is still, in its name, devoted to Saturn—Saturn's Day), whose wrath one wanted to placate by self-castigation and self-punishment.

Saturn (in the old astrological and metaphysical tradition) symbolizes time. he is the god of time and hence the god of death. Inasmuch as man is like God, gifted with a soul, with reason, love and freedom, he is not subject to time or death. But inasmuch as man is an animal, with a body subject to the laws of nature, he is a slave to time and death. The Babylonians sought to appease the lord of time by self-castigation.

The Bible in its Sabbath concept makes an entirely new attempt to solve the problem: by stopping interference with nature for one day you eliminate time; where there is no change, no work, no human interference, there is no time. Instead of a Sabbath on which man bows down to the lord of time, the biblical Sabbath symbolizes man's victory over time; time is suspended, Saturn is dethroned on his very day, Saturn's Day.

The Forgotten Language, pp. 242 ff.

Why is Shabbat such an important mitzvah?

___

MITZVAH OF THE WEEK
שְׁמִירַת שַׁבָּת Observing Sabbath

In a home that follows traditional Jewish practices, these things are never done on Shabbat: driving a car, switching an electric light on or off, watching television, playing a stereo—and many, many other things. For Jews who believe that the Torah (as interpreted by the Talmud and other books of Jewish Law) forms a code of law that Jews must follow without question, each of these actions would be working on Shabbat—so they aren't done.

If you are studying from this book, chances are you are a student at a non-Orthodox Jewish school in North America and those probably aren't ways Shabbat is celebrated in your home. However, to understand the Jewish tradition, you'll need to understand how those rules work.

In the Torah, in the Ten Commandments, we find:

> FOR SIX DAYS YOU MAY LABOR AND DO ALL YOUR WORK
> BUT THE SEVENTH DAY SHOULD BE A SABBATH
> FOR ADONAI, YOUR GOD.
> YOU SHALL NOT DO ANY KIND OF WORK.
>
> Exodus 20:9-10

While this text tells us that we cannot work on Shabbat, it doesn't tell us what is work and what is not work. When we look through the rest of the Torah, we find only one specific example of a forbidden kind of work:

> YOU SHALL LIGHT NO FIRE IN YOUR HOUSES ON SHABBAT.
>
> Exodus 20:9-10

Because the rabbis had very legal minds and wanted to know exactly what was to be considered work, they carefully studied the problem and formulated a specific list. It is found in the Mishnah.

THE FOLLOWING 39 CATEGORIES OF WORK ARE FORBIDDEN ON SHABBAT:

THESE STEPS IN TURNING GRAIN INTO BREAD: SOWING, PLOUGHING, REAPING, BINDING SHEAVES, THRESHING, WINNOWING, SORTING, GRINDING, SIFTING, KNEADING, BAKING.

THESE STEPS TURNING WOOL INTO CLOTH: SHEARING, BLEACHING, BEATING, DYEING, SPINNING, STRETCHING IT ON THE LOOM, MAKING TWO LOOPS, WEAVING TWO THREADS, SEPARATING TWO THREADS, TYING A KNOT, UNTYING A KNOT, SEWING TWO STITCHES, TEARING IN ORDER TO SEW.

THESE STEPS IN MAKING LEATHER: TRAPPING, SLAUGHTERING, FLAYING, SALTING, CURING, SCRAPING, CUTTING.

THESE STEPS IN WRITING: WRITING TWO LETTERS, ERASING IN ORDER TO WRITE TWO LETTERS. AND THESE STEPS IN CONSTRUCTION: BUILDING, PULLING DOWN, PUTTING OUT A FIRE, LIGHTING A FIRE, HAMMERING, CARRYING FROM INSIDE TO OUTSIDE OR OUTSIDE TO INSIDE.

Shabbat 7:2

In the Talmud, the rabbis got even more specific, explaining that each of these is really a general category that has many other specific subheadings. Hundreds of actions became forbidden as work.

By traditional standards each of the following actions is forbidden on Shabbat. Here are two examples with explanations. After reviewing the examples, state which category defines the remaining actions as "work" and then explain your answers.

ploughing 1. Playing soccer. *It was feared that in kicking the ball one's foot might also cut a hole in the soil—an action that would be "ploughing" the ground, even though it wasn't intended for agricultural purposes.*

dyeing 2. Putting a tea bag in hot water. *Tea stains things brown. When you are putting tea in water (adding dry powder to a liquid) you are making a dye.*

_____ 3. Watching television. _____

_____ 4. Playing a trumpet. _____

_____ 5. Doing needlepoint. _____

_____ 6. Cooking. _____

_____ 7. Riding a bicycle. _____

_____ 8. Driving a car. _____

_____ 9. Tearing toilet paper. _____

_____ 10. Going swimming. _____

_____ 11. Carrying a Swiss army knife. _____

For someone who doesn't follow these rules, Shabbat may sound a lot like being in prison (there are so many rules to follow and things you can't do). But, for Jews who give their lives over to the celebration of Shabbat, these rules make Shabbat a day of total freedom and peace. (You'd have to try it to fully understand.)

The basic idea, however, is simple. God created and made things for six days and then rested on the seventh day. Shabbat is when we are like God. Six days we are like God. Six day we make things, manipulate, and try to change the world. We use nature for our own purposes. On Shabbat, we leave the world alone, and change nothing—rather we let creation change us. Simply put, these 39 kinds of work are all involved in using and changing nature—resting is leaving creation alone and just experiencing it.

What set of "Shabbat rules" does your synagogue/Jewish school teach?

_____
_____
_____
_____

If your family were to adopt a set of Shabbat rules in order to create a "time" that is different from the rest of the week what would they be? How do you interpret "don't work on Shabbat." What authority do you follow?

_____
_____
_____
_____
_____
_____

YITRO

יִתְר֖וֹ

ידתרו

וישמע כהן מדין חתן משה
את כל אשר
עשה אלהים למשה
ולישראל עמו
כי הוציא יהוה
את ישראל ממצרים

EXODUS 18:1–20:26
- Yitro bring Tzipporah, Gershom and Eliezer to Moses.
- Moses follows Yitro's advice and **appoints judges**.
- The Children of Israel prepare and God gives them the **Ten Commandments**.
- The Children of Israel ask Moses to serve as a go-between for God and the people.

OUR TEXT—EXODUS 20:2

This is the *parashah* where the Ten Commandments are given. Our verse is the first commandment.

אָנֹכִי יהוה אֱלֹהֶיךָ אֲשֶׁר הוֹצֵאתִיךָ מֵאֶרֶץ מִצְרַיִם מִבֵּית עֲבָדִים.

י	_____ = יהוה	_____ = אֱלֹהִים	א
	_____ = [יצא]	_____ = אֱלֹהֶיךָ	
	_____ = הוֹצֵאתִיךָ	I .... = אָנֹכִי	
מ	Egypt .... = מִצְרַיִם	_____ = אֶרֶץ	
ע	slave/work _____ = [עבד]	_____ = אֲשֶׁר	
	_____ = עֲבָדִים	_____ = בֵּית	ב

2. _____אָנֹכִי יהוה אֱלֹהֶיךָ

_____אֲשֶׁר הוֹצֵאתִיךָ

_____מֵאֶרֶץ מִצְרַיִם

_____מִבֵּית עֲבָדִים.

Now try reading this verse without vowels:

אנכי יהוה אלהיך אשר הוצאתיך מארץ מצרים מבית עבדים

EXPLORING OUR TEXT

In Hebrew, the word *mitzvot* means "commandments." This is not the word the Jewish tradition uses to describe the ten things God taught the Jewish People at Mount Sinai. In Hebrew they are called *Aseret ha-Dibrot,* the Ten Speakings or Ten Things. In English we call them the Ten Commandments.

> I am *Adonai* your God
> who brought you out of Egypt
> out of the house of bondage.

What do you think this "teaching" commands?

_____
_____
_____

In the Jewish tradition there is an argument over this "commandment." Read the two opinions that follow the debate.

ABRAVANEL
The phrase "I am *Adonai* your God..." is not a commandment either of belief or action. It is just an introduction to the commandments that follow. It is a statement addressed to the Families-of-Israel to let them know Who is commanding them.

RAMBAM
The first commandment is that God commands us to believe in God. The mitzvah is to believe that there is a cause and an organizing force behind all existing things. This idea is expressed in the statement, "I am *Adonai* your God."

1. Restate the two opinions in your own words:

   Abravanel: _____
   _____

   Rambam: _____
   _____

2. Do you believe that it is a mitzvah (a commandment) to believe in God? _____
   _____
   _____

MITZVAH OF THE WEEK
BELIEF IN GOD

Basing ourselves on Maimonides, we've chosen "Belief in God" as our Mitzvah of the Week.

He describes this mitzvah this way:
> The foundations of all foundations and the pillar of wisdom is to know that there is a Primary Being Who brought into being all existence. All the beings of the heavens, the earth, and what is between them came into existence only from the truth of God's being.

Maimonides teaches that there are ten mitzvot that are connected to the belief in God. Discuss them as a class. See if you can figure out what was intended by each mitzvah.

1. To know that there is a God.
2. Not to consider the thought that there is another divinity aside from God.
3. To unify God.
4. To love God.
5. To fear God.
6. To sanctify God's name.
7. Not to profane God's name.
8. Not to destroy those things associated with God's name.
9. To listen to a prophet who speaks in God's name.
10. Not to test God.

Hilkhot Yesodei Hatorah

Vision looks inward and becomes duty.
Vision looks outward and becomes aspiration.
Vision looks upward and becomes faith.

Stephen S. Wise

MISHPATIM מִשְׁפָּטִים

וְאֵלֶּה הַמִּשְׁפָּטִים אֲשֶׁר תָּשִׂים לִפְנֵיהֶם

EXODUS 21:1-24:18
- God has Moses teach the Jewish People a basic law code. It includes:
  - Rules of owning slaves.
  - A list of capital crimes.
  - Rules of damages.
  - Assorted rules including social codes and fair courts.
- Then the Children of Israel accept the law.

OUR TEXT—EXODUS 22:24

Parashat Mishpatim is a law code. According to *Sefer ha-Hinukh* it contains 53 different mitzvot. We've chosen a verse that generates three of these mitzvot, all of which have to do with lending money and interest.

אִם-כֶּסֶף תַּלְוֶה אֶת-עַמִּי אֶת-הֶעָנִי עִמָּךְ לֹא-תִהְיֶה לוֹ כְּנֹשֶׁה לֹא-תְשִׂימוּן עָלָיו נֶשֶׁךְ.

נ	creditor = נֹשֶׁה	if = אִם	א
	interest = נֶשֶׁךְ	be = [היה]	ה
ע	on him = עָלָיו	_____ = תִהְיֶה	
	with = עִם	like/as = כְּ	כ
	_____ = עִמָּךְ	money = כֶּסֶף	
	nation/people = עַם	_____ = לֹא	ל
	_____ = עַמִּי	_____ = לוֹ	
	poor = עָנִי	lend = [לוה]	
ש	assess = [שׂוּם]	_____ = תַּלְוֶה	
	_____ = תְשִׂימוּן		

24. אִם-כֶּסֶף תַּלְוֶה אֶת-עַמִּי _____

אֶת-הֶעָנִי עִמָּךְ _____

לֹא-תִהְיֶה לוֹ כְּנֹשֶׁה _____

לֹא-תְשִׂימוּן עָלָיו נֶשֶׁךְ. _____

Now try reading this verse without vowels:

אם כסף תלוה את עמי את העני עמך לא תהיה לו כנשה
לא תשימון עליו נשך

EXPLORING OUR TEXT

Here are four excerpts from *Sefer ha-Hinukh*. All of them teach laws regarding loans.

Exodus 22:24: If you lend money to My people, the poor among you...
It is a mitzvah to lend money to a poor man in order to lighten his burden and relieve his anguish. This mitzvah is even greater than the mitzvah of giving charity. For by accepting a loan, the unfortunate person can be helped in a dignified manner, whereas those who receive charity experience some degree of shame.

Exodus 22:24: You shall not be to him as a creditor...
We are forbidden to demand payment of a loan from a borrower at a time when we know that she lacks the means with which to pay her debt. The purpose of this mitzvah is that we firmly implant in our hearts the qualities of kindness and compassion for another person.

Exodus 22:24: You shall not set upon him interest...
We are forbidden to assist or support in any way a borrower or a lender in transacting a loan with interest. Besides the lender and borrower, the scribe, guarantor, and witnesses are also forbidden to take part in a transaction involving a loan with interest.

Deuteronomy 23:20: You shall not pay your brother interest...
It is forbidden to borrow money at interest from a Jew. This mitzvah prohibits the borrower from paying interest, while other mitzvot prohibit the lender from accepting interest.

Based on these four laws, what should a Jew do when s/he is asked to lend money to another Jew?

_____
_____
_____
_____

Why is this a set of laws?

_____
_____

What is the problem with this set of laws?

_____
_____

Read this short piece of Talmud.

> In the Yeshiva at Nehardea, they developed a new kind of business arrangement called an *iska*. An *iska* is a half loan/half trust agreement made between an investor and a trader.
>
> It works like this: If A gives B an amount of merchandise to sell so that the two of them can split the profits, half of that amount is considered a loan to B that will have to be repaid (without interest), and half of that amount is still considered to belong to A and was merely entrusted to B to bring to sale. That way it is a full partnership.
>
> *Bava Metzia 104b-105a*

How does the *iska* solve the problem with the no-loan laws?

_____

_____

_____

P.S. Today, Israeli banks use the concept of an *iska* when they lend money to Jewish people and Jewish businesses.

MITZVAH OF THE WEEK
לֹא-תְשִׂימוּן עָלָיו נֶשֶׁךְ Lending but Not Charging Interest

Our mitzvah of the week is the collection of laws about Jews lending money for interest. Based on all of these passages we've looked at, write your own summary of the Jewish laws about loans.

_____

_____

_____

_____

_____

_____

_____

TERUMAH תְּרוּמָה

וידבר יהוה אל משה לאמר
דבר אל בני ישראל
ויקחו לי **תרומה**
מאת כל איש
אשר ידבנו לבו תקחו את תרומתי

EXODUS 25:1–27:19

- Moses asks the Children of Israel to donate gifts and materials for the Tabernacle.
- Thirteen specific kinds of material gifts are described.
- The **aron**, the **shulhan** and the **menorah** are each described in detail.

OUR TEXT—EXODUS 25:8

In this *sidrah,* the Families-of-Israel begin to build the *Mishkan,* the portable sanctuary used in the wilderness. This verse is the culmination of God's directions.

וְעָשׂוּ לִי מִקְדָּשׁ וְשָׁכַנְתִּי בְּתוֹכָם.

שׁ	dwell .... = [שכן]		_____ = לִי	ל
	_____ = וְשָׁכַנְתִּי	sanctuary .... = מִקְדָּשׁ	מ
ת	among .... = תּוֹךְ	_____ = [עשׂה]	ע
	_____ = בְּתוֹכָם	_____ = וְעָשׂוּ	

8. _____ וְעָשׂוּ לִי מִקְדָּשׁ

_____ וְשָׁכַנְתִּי בְּתוֹכָם.

Now try reading this verse without vowels:

ועשו לי מקדש ושכנתי בתוכם

EXPLORING OUR TEXT

Our text deals with creating holy space, making a sanctuary. Here is a real case that happened in our Hebrew School. It is a case of the "rules" for holy space and what it takes to make a sanctuary.

> We had services every time that classes met, and we expected heads to be covered while we were in the sanctuary. (Actually, we required the boys to wear *kippot* and allowed the girls to do so.) Many of the boys wore baseball caps (usually backwards) to school and thought that was good enough to fulfill the obligation to cover one's head. The principal argued that the purpose of a *kippah* was to set the sanctuary apart and make it a special place for prayer.
>
> We got into a big argument. The boys argued that if hasidic rabbis could wear their big hats when they prayed, then Reform boys certainly ought to be able to wear baseball caps. One of the teachers remembered a case where Samson Raphael Hirsch forbade English Jews from wearing their *kippot* under their white powdered wigs (and hiding them). The debate went on and on.

If you had to decide this case, would you allow the boys to wear baseball caps instead of *kippot*?

_____
_____
_____
_____
_____

To help you out, here are a couple of sources on the laws of *kippot*.

> Of one thing we can be sure, however; in the generations preceeding ours, the general practice among traditional Jews was to have their heads covered at all times.
>
> The reasons given were twofold. First, it was the Jewish way of showing reverence and respect. Secondly, uncovering the head was the custom of the Gentiles; hence, it must be avoided by Jews. Covering the head thus served as a means of identification and a barrier against assimilation.
>
> While the practice was uniform in the generations preceding ours, it now runs the gamut from those Orthodox who retain the old practice of having the head covered at all times to those Reform who discard the custom entirely. Our practice should be:
>   a. To cover the head when in the sanctuary of a synagogue.
>   b. To cover the head when praying and when studying or reading from our sacred literature.
>   c. To cover the head when performing a ritual.
>   d. To cover the head when eating, since is preceded and followed by a benediction. (Some follow the custom of certain Jewish communities in Germany and cover their heads during the benedictions before and after the meal but not during the meal itself.)
>
> Klein, *A Guide to Jewish Religious Practice*

Even the Vilna Gaon writes that to cover the head for prayer and study of the Torah is not a sacred obligation but a saintly practice. Nevertheless, particularly since Christians leave their heads bare in church, it became the established practice for Jews to pray with heads covered.

Rabbi Louis Jacobs, *The Book of Jewish Practice*

MITZVAH OF THE WEEK
וְעָשׂוּ לִי מִקְדָּשׁ MAKING A SANCTUARY

It is a mitzvah to build a house for God's sake. This house (Beit ha-Mikdash) is where we offer our sacrifices to Him, and it is this holy site where we are commanded to ascend for the pilgrimage festivals every year.

In this day and age, when there is no longer a single Temple in Jerusalem, this sense of holiness is transferred to the Synagogue sanctuary. In the Mishnah (*Megillah* chapter 3) we find the rules for keeping holy the space where Jews study and worship.

1. If the people of a town have sold an open space they may purchase a synagogue with its proceeds. If they have sold a synagogue, they may purchase an Ark. If they have sold an Ark, they may buy Torah mantles. If they have sold Torah mantles, they may buy books. If they have sold books, they may purchase a scroll of the Law. But if they sold a Scroll of the Law they may not buy books. If they have sold books, they must not buy mantles. If they have sold mantles, they may not purchase an Ark. If they have sold an Ark, they may not buy a synagogue. If they have sold a synagogue, they may not purchase an open space.
2. They may sell a synagogue except for four purposes: For a bath-house, for a tannery, for a ritual bath, or for a urinal.
3. R. Judah said, "If a synagogue be derelict, they may not deliver a funeral oration therein, nor may they twist ropes therein, nor may they spread nets therein, nor spread out produce upon its roof, nor make of it a short-cut."

Do any of these laws help you with the case of the baseball cap? If so, how?

_____

_____

_____

TETZAVEH

תְּצַוֶּה

ואתה תצוה את בני ישראל ויקחו אליך שמן זית זך כתית למאור להעלת נר תמיד

EXODUS 27:20–30:10

- The Children of Israel are instructed to bring pure olive oil for the menorah.
- Aaron and his sons, Nadav, Avihu, Eleazar and Itamar, are chosen to serve as priests.
- God instructs Moses to make special clothes for the priests including **tunic**, **breeches**, **belt**, **hat**, **mantle**, **apron**, **breastplate** and **headplate**.
- We are given a description of the sacrifices to consecrate the priests.

OUR TEXT—EXODUS 27:20

In this *parashah* we continue with the description of the holy items that will be needed to worship in the *Mishkan*. Our verse focuses on a very small detail, the olive oil burned in the menorah.

וְאַתָּה תְּצַוֶּה אֶת־בְּנֵי יִשְׂרָאֵל וְיִקְחוּ אֵלֶיךָ שֶׁמֶן זַיִת זָךְ כָּתִית לַמָּאוֹר לְהַעֲלֹת נֵר תָּמִיד.

מ	light = מָאוֹר		to = אֶל	א
נ	_____ = נֵר		_____ = אֵלֶיךָ	
ע	raise up = [עלה]		_____ = אַתָּה	
	_____ = לְהַעֲלֹת		בְּנֵי יִשְׂרָאֵל = _____	ב
צ	command = [צוה]		olive = זַיִת	ז
	_____ = תְּצַוֶּה		pure = זָךְ	
שׁ	oil = שֶׁמֶן		beaten = כָּתִית	כ
ת	eternal = תָּמִיד		take/bring = [לקח]	ל
			_____ = וְיִקְחוּ	

20. וְאַתָּה תְּצַוֶּה אֶת־בְּנֵי יִשְׂרָאֵל _____

וַיִקְחוּ אֵלֶיךָ _____

שֶׁמֶן זַיִת זָךְ כָּתִית לַמָּאוֹר _____

לְהַעֲלֹת נֵר תָּמִיד. _____

Now try reading this verse without vowels:

אתה תצוה את בני ישראל ויקחו אליך שמן זית זך כתית למאור כהעלת נר תמיד

EXPLORING OUR TEXT

In the midrash on this passage, they quote another verse from Proverbs:

The commandment is a lamp, and the teaching is light (Prov. 6:23).

In the midrash, the rabbis use this verse to give a symbolic meaning to the mitzvah of the Ner Tamid.

> A parable of one who stands in a dark place. No sooner does s/he start walking than s/he stumbles over a stone or comes to a gutter and falls into it, striking the ground with her/his face. Why does this happen? Because they have no light in their hand. So, too, is the unlearned person who possesses no Torah. When s/he comes upon a transgression, s/he stumbles and dies. But they who study Torah give light wherever they are.
>
> A parable of one who stands in the dark with a lamp in his hand. When s/he comes upon a stone, s/he does not stumble over it; when s/he comes upon a gutter, s/he does not fall into it. Why not? Because s/he has a lamp in his/her hand, as Scripture says, "Thy word is a lamp unto my feet, and a light unto my path".
>
> Exodus Rabbah 36.3

What is the symbolic meaning the rabbis give to the *Ner Tamid*?

_____

_____

Here is a song called "Light One Candle" sung by Peter Yarrow of Peter, Paul, and Mary.

Light One Candle

Light one candle for the Maccabee children with thanks that their light didn't die.
Light one candle for the pain they endured when their right to exist was denied.
Light one candle for the terrible sacrifice justice and freedom demand.
But light one candle for the wisdom to know when the peacemaker's time is at hand.

CHORUS   **Don't let the light go out; it's lasted for so many years.**
                 Don't let the light go out; let it shine through our love and our tears.

Light one candle for the strength that we need to never become our own foe.
Light one candle for those who are suffering the pain we learned so long ago.
Light one candle for all we believe in, let anger not tear us apart.
And light one candle to bind us together with peace as the song in our heart.

CHORUS   **Don't let the light go out; it's lasted for so many years.**
                 Don't let the light go out; let it shine through our love and our tears.

What is the memory that's valued so highly that we keep it alive in that flame?
What's the commitment to those who have died when we cry out they've not died in vain.
We have come this far always believing that justice will somehow prevail.
This is the burden and this is the promise and this is why we will not fail.

CHORUS   **Don't let the light go out; it's lasted for so many years.**
                 Don't let the light go out; let it shine through our love and our tears.

What symbolic meaning for the *Ner Tamid* can you draw from it?

___

MITZVAH OF THE WEEK
נֵר תָּמִיד An Everlasting Flame

It is a mitzvah for the Kohanim to kindle the menorah in the Beit ha-Mikdash every evening. This mitzvah also included discarding old wicks, removing the ashes, cleaning the oil cups, and refilling them with sufficient oil to burn through the night.

This mitzvah can't be done today because there is no longer a Temple in Jerusalem. In its place is a *zekher mitzvah,* a practice we do to remember the original mitzvah. Describe what we do to remember this mitzvah.

___

This is a mitzvah we can also do symbolically. List seven things we can do to keep the *Ner Tamid* burning.

1. _____
2. _____
3. _____
4. _____
5. _____
6. _____
7. _____

KI TISSA
כִּי תִשָּׂא

וידבר יהוה אל משה לאמר
את ראש בני ישראל לפקדיהם
ונתנו איש כפר נפשו
ליהוה בפקד אותם
ולא יהיה בהם נגף
בפקד אותם

EXODUS 30:11–34:35

- God instructs Moses in the taking of a census.
- Description of the **kiyyor**—a basin for washing.
- The formulas for **incense** and **anointing oil**.
- God restates rules of **Shabbat**
- God gives Moses the first tablets of the **Ten Commandments**.
- Moses breaks the tablets when he sees the **Golden Calf**.
- Moses goes up to get a second set of tablets after punishing the Children of Israel.

OUR TEXT: EXODUS 34:26

In the middle of the Tabernacle rules, the Torah does a "flashback" to Moses getting laws and bringing down the Two Tablets of the Law. In the middle of a short law code we find this rule:

רֵאשִׁית בִּכּוּרֵי אַדְמָתְךָ תָּבִיא בֵּית יהוה אֱלֹהֶיךָ לֹא תְבַשֵּׁל גְּדִי בַּחֲלֵב אִמּוֹ.

ב

בֵּית = _____		אֲדָמָה = land/earth/soil	א
[בשל] = boil		אַדְמָתְךָ = _____	
תְבַשֵּׁל = _____		אֵם = mother	
גְּדִי = goat		אִמּוֹ = _____	ג
חָלָב = milk		[בוא] = _____	ח
לֹא = _____		תָּבִיא = _____	ל
[ראש] = _____		[בכר] = first born/first choice	ר
רֵאשִׁית = _____		בִּכּוּרֵי = _____	

26. רֵאשִׁית בִּכּוּרֵי אַדְמָתְךָ _____

תָּבִיא בֵּית יהוה אֱלֹהֶיךָ _____

לֹא תְבַשֵּׁל גְּדִי _____

בַּחֲלֵב אִמּוֹ. _____

Now try reading this verse without vowels:

ראשית בכורי אדמתך תביא בית יהוה אלהיך לא תבשל גדי בחלב אמו

EXPLORING OUR TEXT

The verse teaches us that we should not boil a kid in its mother's milk. As a "fence around the Torah" the rabbis expand this to forbid all mixing of milk and meat products. However, there is no clear reason why the two should not be mixed. Why do you think the Torah teaches this mitzvah?

_____

_____

_____

Neither the Bible nor the Talmud explain why milk and meat cannot be mixed. Maimonides explains their origin as a Jewish disgust at the fertility rites practiced by the pagan cults of Canaan (Guide 3:48). One of these rites was the cooking of a kid in its mother's milk. Dr. Nelson Glueck reports that this practice is still found among the Bedouin of today, not as a pagan rite but as an act of hospitality to a distinguished guest.

To us this regulation reflects reverence for life and the teaching of compassion. To seethe a kid in its mother's milk is callous. Professor Abraham Joshua Heschel expresses it thus: The goat—in our case, more commonly the cow—generously and steadfastly provides man with the single most perfect food that she possesses, milk. It is the only food which, by reason of its proper composition of fat, carbohydrates, and protein, can by itself sustain the human body. How ungrateful and callous we would be to take the child of an animal to whom we are thus indebted and cook it in the very milk which nourishes us and is given us so freely by its mother (Dresner and Siegel, *Jewish Dietary Laws*, p. 70).

Klein, Jewish Religious Practice

MITZVAH OF THE WEEK
לֹא תְבַשֵּׁל גְּדִי בַּחֲלֵב אִמּוֹ You Shall Not Cook a Kid in its Mother's Milk

You shall not cook a kid in its mother's milk. It is forbidden to eat meat and milk that were cooked together. This prohibition is different from other forbidden foods, for even if one does not benefit from it while eating it, he is liable.

It is customary to place special marks on dairy and meat utensils and flatware, to differentiate between them and make them easily recognizable. A pot in which meat and milk were cooked becomes forbidden until it is purified to make it kosher. Bread that comes in contact with meat, may not be eaten with dairy. Similarly, if bread comes in contact with cheese, it may not be eaten with meat.

After eating meat, one must wait at least one, three, or six hours before eating dairy. However, one may eat meat a short while after eating dairy, provided he thoroughly rinses his mouth and/or brushes his teeth, so as not to leave any particles of the dairy food lodged between his teeth.

VA-YAK-HEL

וַיַּקְהֵל

ויקהל משה את כל עדת בני ישראל ויאמר אלהם אלה הדברים אשר צוה יהוה לעשת אתם

EXODUS 35:1–38:20

- Moses again teaches the rules of **Shabbat** and the **building of the Mishkan**.
- The actual work of building the Mishkan is described.
- Moses refuses more donations since there have been too many.
- Description of the kiyyor, which was made from copper mirrors.

OUR TEXT—EXODUS 35:3

We've already learned the "don't work on Shabbat" rule earlier in the Torah. Now the Torah teaches another Shabbat rule:

לֹא־תְבַעֲרוּ אֵשׁ בְּכֹל מֹשְׁבֹתֵיכֶם בְּיוֹם הַשַּׁבָּת.

sit = [ישב]		fire = אֵשׁ	א
dwelling = מוֹשָׁב		___ = בְּ ■	ב
___ = מֹשְׁבֹתֵיכֶם		burn = [בער]	
___ = כֹּל		___ = תְבַעֲרוּ	
___ = לֹא		___ = הַ ■	ה
___ = שַׁבָּת		___ = יוֹם	י

3. לֹא־תְבַעֲרוּ אֵשׁ ___

בְּכֹל מֹשְׁבֹתֵיכֶם ___

בְּיוֹם הַשַּׁבָּת. ___

Now try reading this verse without vowels:

לא תבערו אש בכל משבתיכם ביום השבת

EXPLORING OUR TEXT

Our text forbids lighting fires on Shabbat. In contemporary Jewish law the firing of a spark plug in a car and the use of electricity are considered to be a violation of Jewish law.

Here are some test cases for this law. Put a "T" next to those items that are permitted under Traditional Jewish law. Put a "C" next to those activities that Conservative Judaism allows. Because Reform Judaism believes that individuals should make their own decisions about Shabbat observance, put an "I" next to any of these activities that you will allow.

_____ Driving to synagogue for services.

_____ Driving to the woods to enjoy nature.

_____ Driving a friend to the emergency room.

_____ Leaving the kitchen light on all Shabbat.

_____ Turning the lightbulb in the refrigerator on and off each time the door is opened.

_____ Turning the lights on and off with a Shabbat clock.

_____ Turning the television on and off with a Shabbat clock.

_____ Turning on the television to watch a "cultural" program.

Here are a few legal texts to help you work out the "official" positions on these cases.

> Most modern travel is by car. It is often claimed that driving requires less effort than walking, but, in fact, it is easy to find halakhic reasons to avoid driving on Shabbat. First there is the prohibition against creating fire. Even according to the opinion that electricity is not fire, actual fire is created in the engine of the car.
>
> Klein, *A Guide to Jewish Ritual Practice*

> If someone is trapped in a building that has collapsed, you are allowed to violate the Sabbath to dig for them. If at first you find only dead bodies you must continue digging for as long as there is a little bit of hope that one person is alive.
>
> Yoma 8.6

> Under the conditions of our day, many congregants live far from the synagogue and cannot attend services unless they ride. For many of these people, attendance at services is their only contact with religious life...therefore it is our considered opinion that the positive value involved in the participation in public worship on the Sabbath outweighs the negative value of refraining from riding in an automobile. Yet this must not be seen as a general *heter*..every other alternative must be exhausted first.
>
> The Law Committee of the Rabbinical Assembly

> It is permissible to start filling a garden with water just before Shabbat, even if it keeps filling all day. A perfume brazier may be placed under clothes before Shabbat, even though the clothes keep absorbing the odor. Similarly, silver vessels may rest in sulfer all of Shabbat. The same is true of traps for fish and animals that are set before Shabbat. Why are these permitted? Because they require no human action on Shabbat.
>
> Shabbat 18a

MITZVAH OF THE WEEK
לֹא־תְבַעֲרוּ אֵשׁ   **NOT LIGHTING A FIRE ON SHABBAT**

If you open up Maimonides' Book of Mitzvot you get a surprise when you look up this mitzvah. Based on some talmudic readings, he tells you that this verse "really means" that a *Bet Din* (a rabbinical court) may not execute someone on Shabbat.

The explanation is more simple than it first appears. It has to do with the way the rabbis of the Talmud read the Torah. They believed that God wrote it—every word. That it was perfect, and that a perfect God never repeated anything. Therefore, because we have already learned "no work on Shabbat," the "no fire" rule was already obvious. Thus, the "no fire" rule was included here to teach us something different—no executions.

Be like the rabbis. Think of five other things we might learn from the "no fire" on Shabbat rule:

1. _____
2. _____
3. _____
4. _____
5. _____

When a person labors not for a livelihood but to accumulate wealth, then that person is a slave. Therefore it is that God granted us the Sabbath. For it is by the Sabbath that we know we are not work animals, born to eat and to labor; we are people. It is the Sabbath which is a person's goal—not labor, but the rest which a person earns from the labor. It is because the Jews made the Sabbath holy to God that they were redeemed from slavery in Egypt. It was by the Sabbath that they proclaimed that they were not slaves but free people.

Sholem Asch

PEKUDEI פְּקוּדֵי

אֵלֶּה פְקוּדֵי הַמִּשְׁכָּן מִשְׁכַּן הָעֵדֻת אֲשֶׁר פֻּקַּד עַל פִּי מֹשֶׁה עֲבֹדַת הַלְוִיִּם בְּיַד אִיתָמָר בֶּן אַהֲרֹן הַכֹּהֵן

EXODUS 38:21–40:38

- Moses reports how the donations were given and how they were used.
- Moses sets up the Mishkan and the priests are established therein.
- A description is given of a **cloud** that covers the Mishkan **by day** and a **fire that burns by night** indicating God's presence therein.

OUR TEXT—EXODUS 40:31

In Pekudei, the *Mishkan* is finally set up and put into use. As part of that larger event, our verse is one little part!

וְרָחֲצוּ מִמֶּנּוּ מֹשֶׁה וְאַהֲרֹן וּבָנָיו אֶת-יְדֵיהֶם וְאֶת-רַגְלֵיהֶם.

מ	from it .... = מִמֶּנּוּ		_____ = אַהֲרֹן	א
	_____ = מֹשֶׁה	sons .... = בָּנִים	ב
	foot .... = רַגְלַיִם	_____ = בָּנָיו	
כ	_____ = רַגְלֵיהֶם	hands .... = יָדַיִם	י
ר	wash .... = [רחץ]	_____ = יְדֵיהֶם	
	_____ = וְרָחֲצוּ		

וְרָחֲצוּ מִמֶּנּוּ _____ .31

מֹשֶׁה וְאַהֲרֹן וּבָנָיו _____

אֶת-יְדֵיהֶם _____

וְאֶת-רַגְלֵיהֶם. _____

Now try reading this verse without vowels:

ורחצו ממנו משה ואהרן ובניו את ידיהם ואת רגליהם

EXPLORING OUR TEXT

Looking at our verse, this is what Rashi says:

> And Moses and Aaron and his sons washed their hands and feet.
>
> On the eighth day of the dedication of the Tabernacle, all of the people mentioned above, Moses, Aaron and Aaron's sons, were equal in the priesthood. That day, all of them washed their hands together and (as we learn in the *Targum*)—they made themselves holy.
>
> *Note: The Targum is an Aramaic translation of the Torah that sometimes gives additional insights.*

Rashi suggests that this verse teaches two lessons.

1. That all those from the family of Kohein from the tribe of Levi were "equally" priests. How does this verse show that?

   _____

   _____

2. That ritual washing is a way of making yourself holy. How does this work?

   _____

   _____

Here is a poem from our friend and teacher Danny Siegel:

> If the Torah were forgotten
> (If? If? If?)
> If no one knew a single line
> I would start again this way—
> Son,
>   when you finish urinating
>   wash your hands
>   and say the brakhah
> For as our faith fades
> in the presence of our own-made desolation
> there remains a hope
>   that a towel
>   will liven your hands
> and you will say
>   that feels fine
>   I feel good
> Now let's get down to work.
> With a hand towel
>   and a blessing
> We will start again
>   somehow
> as in the days of our Father Abraham
> who left home
> because
>   they would not
>   wash and sing

1. What do you think this poem means?

   _____

   _____

2. How does it connect to our verse from this *parashah*?

   _____

   _____

   _____

MITZVAH OF THE WEEK
עַל נְטִילַת יָדַיִם RITUAL HANDWASHING

The official mitzvah here is for the *Kohanim* to wash before performing their rituals. However, there is a direct echo of this mitzvah in daily Jewish practice. The Torah says (Exodus 19:6) that the Jews should be "a nation of *Kohanim* and a holy people." Simultaneously, we know that the table where we dine is like an altar. Therefore, like priests, it is a Jewish custom to ritually wash before eating.

In the *Kitzur Shulḥan Arukh,* there are pages of rules about how to wash before meals. Read these excerpts, then answer these questions:

What is the difference between "ritual washing" and practical washing? How does "ritual washing" help you to reach a level of holiness?

_____
_____
_____
_____
_____
_____
_____

40.1 Before eating bread over which the brakhah *ha-Motzi* is to be said, one must first wash hands. If the bread is larger than the size of an egg, both the handwashing and the brakhah are required.

40.2 The water used for ritual handwashing must be poured out of a vessel that is perfect, one that has neither a crack nor a hole. If it has a spout, we must not pour the water out of the spout.

40.4 There is no precise amount of water that must be poured, but the entire hand up to the wrist must be covered with one outpouring of the water. It is best to pour water twice on each hand—to make sure they have been completely covered.

40.5 After the hands have been covered, rub them together and lift them up. Before drying we say the brakhah:

בָּרוּךְ אַתָּה, יהוה Praised are You, *Adonai*
אֱלֹהֵינוּ, מֶלֶךְ הָעוֹלָם Our God, Ruler of the Cosmos
אֲשֶׁר קִדְּשָׁנוּ בְּמִצְוֹתָיו וְצִוָּנוּ who made us holy with the mitzvot and made it a mitzvah
עַל נְטִילַת יָדַיִם. for us to wash our hands.

41.2 One must be careful not to linger between the washing and the brakhah *ha-Motzi*, but one may say "*Amen*" to any brakhot that are heard. One doesn't talk or do any other act in between the washing and the saying of *ha-Motzi*.

VA-YIKRA

וַיִּקְרָא

ויקרא

וידבר יהוה אליו אהל מועד לאמר משה

LEVITICUS 1:1–5:26

- The introduction of sacrifices:
- The *Olah*—regular **daily offering**.
- The *Min̲hah*—**meal offering** of flour and water.
- The *Shelamim*—**peace offering**.
- The *H̲atat*—**sin offering**.
- The *Asham*—**guilt offering**.

OUR TEXT—LEVITICUS 5:1

In the middle of a lot of laws about "guilt" offerings and other sacrifices comes our verse, which teaches an important lesson about civic responsibility.

וְנֶפֶשׁ כִּי־תֶחֱטָא וְשָׁמְעָה קוֹל אָלָה וְהוּא עֵד אוֹ רָאָה אוֹ יָדָע אִם־לוֹא יַגִּיד וְנָשָׂא עֲוֺנוֹ.

ל	_____ = לוֹא	or .... = אוֹ	א
נ	carry .... = [נשא]	call for witness/oath .... = אָלָה	
ע	witness .... = עֵד	if .... = אִם	
	sin/punishment/guilt .... = [עוֹן]	speak/tell .... = [הגד]	ה
	_____ = עֲוֺנוֹ	_____ = יַגִּיד	
ק	voice .... = קוֹל	_____ = הוּא	
ר	_____ = [ראה]	sin .... = [חטא]	ח
שׁ	_____ = [שמע]	_____ = תֶחֱטָא	
		_____ = [ידע]	י

1. וְנֶפֶשׁ כִּי־תֶחֱטָא _____

וְשָׁמְעָה קוֹל אָלָה _____

וְהוּא עֵד _____

אוֹ רָאָה אוֹ יָדָע _____

אִם־לוֹא יַגִּיד וְנָשָׂא עֲוֺנוֹ. _____

Now try reading this verse without vowels:

ונפש כי תחטא ושמעה קול אלה והוא עד או ראה או ידע
אם לוא יגיד ונשא עונו

EXPLORING OUR TEXT

THE CASE OF CREBBS VS. GALUF
JUDGE THIS CASE:

A man, Robert Galuf, rented a car from Mr. Crebbs' "Rent-A-Beaut." He had the car for three days. The day after it was returned, Mr. Crebbs' mechanic, Charles X. Kahn, found a large dent in the rear left fender. Mr. Crebbs asked Robert to pay $750 for the damage, but he claims that the dent was there when he picked up the "beaut." The written contract signed by Mr. Galuf showed that he was responsible for any damage to the car, but both he and Mr. Kahn had failed to initial the boxes that showed the car had been inspected prior to leaving the garage. The matter was taken to court. Here is the collected testimony.

Mr. Crebbs: I own a car rental service called "Rent-A-Beaut." Our cars are all older used models, but they are all in perfect condition. I personally checked out the 1972 Lincoln that Mr. Galuf rented. It had just been repainted. There wasn't a scratch on it. When it was returned, we found this $750 dent.

Mr. Galuf: When the major rental companies were out of cars, I had to get a car from this "Rent-A-Beaut." When I came in to pick up the car, I noticed the dent, but the mechanic told me not to worry about it. He said, and I quote, "All our beauts have dents."

Mrs. Galuf: My husband, Bob, is telling the truth. While I didn't go with him to pick up the car, he complained about the dent and showed it to me as soon as he got back to the hotel.

W. INO: I lost my job about six months ago. I've been living next to a dumpster in an alley across the street from the "Rent-A-Beaut" lot. On the day that this Mr. Galuf returned the car, I saw a big dent in the left-hand side. I know, 'cause he sped down my alley and almost hit me. I yelled at him, "No wonder your car looks that way!" Then I saw him pull into "Rent-A-Beaut."

D. Lemon: I am a blues guitarist known as "Blind Lemon Blue." I've been blind since I was twelve, but I make great music. Mr. Galuf and I had a meeting. He drove me back to the club. When he dropped me off, I heard him back into another car. I'm sure he must have dented his car.

Mrs. Aydut: My son, Darren-Paul, and I were walking past the Nexus Club when we heard this crash. We saw this old Lincoln back into a big trash container. I didn't see the dent, but the right fender must have been badly banged up.

D.P. Aydut: I'm only eleven, but I know what I see. It happened just like my mother said. We saw this guy with a white can and a guitar standing on the sidewalk. We ran up to Mr. Blind Lemon Blue and made sure that he was O.K. When the Lincoln pulled away, I saw the dent in the trunk.

C.X. Kahn: It's true that I was arrested a couple of years ago, but I've gone straight since then. This is the truth. When Mr. Galuf brought the car back, he slipped me $20 not to tell anyone about the dent.

J. Crebbs: I don't like to air family dirty laundry in public, but my brother Milton runs a dishonest business. He always tries to cheat the public. He and I went our separate ways because he was always pulling scams like this.

E. Sheib: I painted a blue Lincoln for Mr. Crebbs' "Rent-A-Beaut" and did a real nice job on it. We dropped it off at his lot on the morning of September 23rd. *(Judge's note: The 23rd was the day that Mr. Galuf rented the car.)*

BE FAIR! WHAT IS YOUR VERDICT?

_____

_____

_____

In Jewish law we are given these rules for acceptable witness. Read them and see how they would change the case.

> A person cannot be found guilty or blamed because of the testimony of *just* one witness. For every offense, two (or even three) witnesses are needed to establish a verdict.
>
> *Deuteronomy 19:15*

> Ten categories of people are not qualified to serve *as witnesses (or judges)*: women, slaves, minors (under 13), the insane, the deaf, the blind, the wicked, the contemptible, relatives, and interested (involved) parties.
>
> *Yad, Laws of Evidence 9.1*

> The following are ineligible to be *witnesses (or judges)*: gamblers, loan-sharks, grifters.
>
> *Sanhedrein 3.3*

> *Also ineligible (to be a witness or a judge)* is a friend or an enemy.
>
> *Sandhedrin 3.5*

1. Based on these "Jewish" rules of evidence, what should be the verdict in this case? _____

   _____

   _____

2. What important insights into the process of justice are manifest by these "Jewish" rules? _____

   _____

   _____

3. What (if any) "value" problems do you find with these "Jewish" rules of evidence? _____

   _____

   _____

MITZVAH OF THE WEEK
עֵדוּת Coming Forward to Testify

It is a mitzvah to give testimony before the *Bet Din* about all we know whether a person will be sentenced through our testimony to death, or to payment of goods and possessions or whether someone will thus be spared goods, possessions, or life. This is the meaning of Leviticus 5:1. In any matter of guilt or obligation, we have a mitzvah to give testimony.

In civil cases, cases involving goods, money, and possessions, we need not come forward to testify. But, if called, we must tell the truth. In criminal cases, in cases of the violation of Torah laws, we have an obligation to come forward and tell all we know—whether or not we are called.

TZAV

וידבר יהוה אל משה לאמר

צו את אהרן ואת בניו לאמר זאת תורת העלה הוא העלה על מוקדה על המזבח כל הלילה עד הבקר ואש המזבח תוקד בו

LEVITICUS 6:1-8:36

- There is a description of what the Kohanim have to do in the Mishkan.
- Then the Kohanim are taught how to offer the sacrifices.
- Finally, we are given the rules for eating meat.

OUR TEXT—LEVITICUS 7:37

Leviticus is the book of the priests. We are now far enough into the book to establish that the *Kohanim* have their own mitzvot that effect all of Israel.

זֹאת הַתּוֹרָה לָעֹלָה לַמִּנְחָה וְלַחַטָּאת וְלָאָשָׁם וְלַמִּלּוּאִים וּלְזֶבַח הַשְּׁלָמִים.

מ	ordination offering = מִלּוּאִים	guilt = אָשָׁם	א
	meal offering = מִנְחָה	_____ = זֹאת	ז
ע	burnt offering = עֹלָה	sacrifice = זֶבַח	
שׁ	well-being = שְׁלָמִים	sin offering = חַטָּאת	ח

37. זֹאת הַתּוֹרָה _____
לָעֹלָה לַמִּנְחָה _____
וְלַחַטָּאת וְלָאָשָׁם _____
וְלַמִּלּוּאִים וּלְזֶבַח הַשְּׁלָמִים. _____

Now try reading this verse without vowels:

זאת התורה לעלה למנחה ולחטאת לאשם ולמלואים

EXPLORING OUR TEXT

Maimonides asked the following really good question. "Why would God, the most rational of all Beings, ask people to sacrifice? God doesn't need sacrifice! And, sacrifice doesn't seem to be the highest spiritual form for people, either."

In his big philosophical work, the *Guide for the Perplexed*, he gives a long and complicated answer. Here are a few excerpts.

> It is impossible to suddenly go from one extreme to the other. People's natures will not allow them to suddenly discontinue everything to which they have become accustomed. Now, God sent Moses to make the Families-of-Israel into a "Nation of Priests and a Holy People" (Exodus 19:6). The key tool in the transformation was to be knowledge of God.
>
> The general mode of worship in which the Israelites were brought up consisted of sacrificing animals in temples containing images, to bow down to those images, to burn incense before them. The wisdom in God's plan, as revealed by all the wisdom of all the acts of creation, was that God didn't ask people to give up all these "acts" of worship, only to abandon the idolatry to which these "acts" were originally connected.
>
> The primary object of the mitzvot is not the actual sacrifice, but to move people closer to supplications, prayers, and similar kinds of worship—nearer to the primary objective, knowing God. Whereas sacrifices can only be offered by the *Kohanim*, every Jew can involve him-or-her-self in prayer and study. This is what Jeremiah was teaching: "I did not speak to your ancestors in Egypt about sacrifices, nor did I command them to bring offerings in Egypt. The only thing I said to them there was, 'Obey My voice.'"

Restate Maimonides' theory of worship in you own words.

_____
_____
_____

Do you agree with this theory or do you have another explanation?

_____
_____
_____

MITZVAH OF THE WEEK
תְּפִלַּת עֲמִידָה Praying the Amidah

It is a positive commandment, taught in the Torah, that a Jew should pray every day. The origins of this are Exodus 23:25, "You shall serve *Adonai*, Your God…" and Deuteronomy 11:13. Originally Jews fulfilled this mitzvah with sacrifices. Later, these were replaced with the Amidah. How do you serve God with all your heart? The sages taught: Through prayer.

Ezra and his court fixed informal prayers into a formal practice, taking a practice that had been happening since the time of Moses and giving it an official structure.

1. Everyone would pray facing the Temple in Jerusalem.
2. They established 18 benedictions. (A 19th brakhah was added later.)
3. The first three brakhot are praise of God. The last three brakhot are offerings of thanksgiving. The middle brakhot contain requests.
4. The rabbis taught that the number of times the Amidah was to be said each day was to correspond to the number of sacrifices that were to be done each day. This took the Temple service and turned it into "Service of the Heart."
5. What is proper *Kavanah* (intention) for prayer?

    One should clear the mind from all other thoughts and see oneself standing before the Divine presence. Then, one should sit a while before praying in order to focus attention and then pray in a pleasant and supplicatory fashion. One should not pray as one carrying a burden who throws it off and walks away. Therefore, one must sit a short while after praying, and then withdraw. The pious ones of the previous generation would wait an hour before praying and an hour after praying. They would also extend their prayers for an hour.

    Excerpts from Yad, the Laws of the Amidah

In his commentary on the Siddur, Abudarham asks: "Why are there 18 brakhot in the Amidah?" He gives many reasons, among them, because there are 18 bones in the human spine. He then asks: "How is the Amidah like the spine of the Jewish People?" How would you answer this question?

_____

_____

_____

_____

SHEMINI שְׁמִינִי

וַיְהִי בַּיּוֹם הַשְּׁמִינִי קָרָא מֹשֶׁה לְאַהֲרֹן וּלְבָנָיו וּלְזִקְנֵי יִשְׂרָאֵל

LEVITICUS 9:1–11:47

- The Mishkan is dedicated and sacrifices are offered.
- **Nadav and Avihu die** after offering a strange fire before God.
- God warns Aaron that priests should not drink before doing priestly service.
- **Rules** are given about which **animals, birds, fish** and **insects can be eaten**.

OUR TEXT—LEVITICUS 10:9

In this Torah portion, Nadav and Avihu, two of Aaron's sons, *Kohanim*, are burned to death in an accident in the Mishkan. After than accident, Torah teaches this rule:

יַיִן וְשֵׁכָר אַל־תֵּשְׁתְּ אַתָּה וּבָנֶיךָ אִתָּךְ בְּבֹאֲכֶם אֶל־אֹהֶל מוֹעֵד וְלֹא תָמֻתוּ חֻקַּת עוֹלָם לְדֹרֹתֵיכֶם.

מ	meeting = מוֹעֵד		tent = אֹהֶל	א
	die/death = [מות]		do not = אַל	
	_____ = תָּמֻתוּ		_____ = [בוא]	ב
ע	_____ = עוֹלָם		_____ = בָנֶיךָ	
ש	intoxicating liquor = שֵׁכָר		generation = דוֹר	ד
	drink = [שתה]		law = חֻקָּה	ח
	_____ = תֵּשְׁתְּ		_____ = יַיִן	י
			_____ = לֹא	ל

9. _____יַיִן וְשֵׁכָר אַל־תֵּשְׁתְּ

_____אַתָּה וּבָנֶיךָ אִתָּךְ

_____בְּבֹאֲכֶם אֶל־אֹהֶל מוֹעֵד

_____וְלֹא תָמֻתוּ

_____חֻקַּת עוֹלָם לְדֹרֹתֵיכֶם.

Now try reading this verse without vowels:

יין ושכר אל תשת אתה ובניך אתך בבאכם אל אהל מועד
חקת עולם לדרתיכם

EXPLORING OUR TEXT

Be a detective. Open up a *Tanakh* and read Leviticus 10:1-10. Write your own summary of the deaths of Nadav and Avihu. Give your own best guess as to what caused their deaths.

_____
_____
_____
_____
_____

Rashi did the same thing. In his commentary he cites two possible explanations of the deaths (based on discussions the rabbis held previously).

    Rabbi Eliezer said,

    "The sons of Aaron died only because they gave decisions on religious matters in the presence of their teacher, Moshe."

    Rabbi Ishamel said,

    "They died because they entered the *Mishkan* intoxicated by wine. You may know that this is so, because after their death God admonished those who arrived that they should not enter the *Mishkan* intoxicated by wine…"

1. What evidence is there for the first explanation?

_____
_____

2. What evidence is there for the second explanation?

_____
_____

3. What do you think "really" happened?

_____
_____

MITZVAH OF THE WEEK
יַיִן וְשֵׁכָר אַל-תֵּשְׁתְּ Don't Abuse Alcohol

If you look in *Sefer ha-Hinukh*, our verse generates this mitzvah for priests and for rabbis who are acting as judges:

> It is forbidden to enter the Temple or to give a legal verdict while drunk.

The Talmud (*Zevakhim 17*) explains:

> Intoxication produces three changes in a person, drowsiness, overconfidence, and a reduction of mental clarity. A *Kohein* must possess his full mental capacities when performing his service. A rabbi must have a perfectly clear mind before giving a verdict. Therefore, both are forbidden to drink before they do their sacred work.

In later commentaries we find:

> Nowadays, since our prayers have replaced sacrifices, and every Jew is responsible for the offerings of his or her heart, it is forbidden to pray while drunk. Drunken prayers are unacceptable and must be reoffered when sober (*Kreetot 13*).

Read this autobiographical essay by Gil Peters, thinking about additional commentaries to this mitzvah you may write.

MY OWN PERSONAL T'SHUVAH JOURNEY
Gil Peters

The myth for hundreds of years has been that Jews are not alcoholics—that "only Goyim are shikkers."

Clearly, the myth makers never meant me and my family. Although no one ever discussed it, both of my grandfathers were alcoholics, of two distinct kinds.

My father's father was a shlepper in the Boston meat market who downed a tumbler of moonshine at dawn before heading to work, then drank a bathtub of gin out of coffee cups at the local deli at day's end, until my dad was dispatched to drag him home.

My mother's father owned a hardware store that had everything, including a bottle in his office desk drawer. He'd come home from work, have two Scotches, which he called "my heart medicine," and fall asleep after dinner in his leather chair.

Probably as a result of their fathers' alcoholic behaviors, neither of my parents were drinkers. But I've heard that some diseases skip a generation.

Whatever the reasons, I displayed the addictive personality from the time I was in kindergarten. I remember, hazily, one Passover at my grandparents' when I managed to wrap my six-year-old lips around enough Manischewitz Concord Grape to pass out on the living room floor.

By my pubescent years I was crashing bar mitzvahs in search of Screwdrivers and "7&7's," or a drink left unattended. In daily life, though, liquor wasn't readily available, so I resorted to an easier drug to procure—mass quantities of food—in order to numb my self-perceived inadequacies.

Why? Well, to my adolescent mind, I had a nose that looked like a map of Mount Sinai, two broken and badly capped teeth, black-frame Nerd glasses and a pudgy body. I saw myself as an ugly, klutzy shlub—someone so average that I would never be special in the classroom, on the playground or at the drive-in.

And so the only way I knew how to get love was to do whatever I was told...or whatever I sensed would make someone else happy. I was ripe for addiction. I wanted to rebel but was afraid of losing whatever love I had built up, so I acted out in a manner that wouldn't hurt anyone but me. Food and alcohol were my solution.

As a teenager, I made sure I slept over at someone else's house whenever I'd drink, so as not to disappoint my ever-vigilant Jewish mother. But once married at age 22, the first thing I did was buy several six-packs of beer to put in my fridge. The following year, upon graduation from college, I became a sportswriter—the perfect job for a budding alcoholic.

Around this time I also cultivated an addiction to marijuana. Again, as a people pleaser, I had never touched the stuff while everyone around was going up in smoke during the Sixties. I still wanted to be a good boy in my parents' eyes. But in 1970, married and out of school, I experimented with the drug once, soon becoming an every day and every night smoker—a pothead.

Over the next decade I developed a nightly regimen: I'd finish work around 1 A.M. (feeling very insecure and sure I'd be fired the next day) and rush down to the newsmen's hangout, where I'd order two shots of Jack Daniels and three beers, which I'd drain before the 2 A.M. closing time. Then I'd light a joint in my car and negotiate the 45-minute drive home, often in rain or snow. Once in the house, I'd have another beer or two, another joint or two and raid the refrigerator and cookie box. By the time I crashed into bed around 4 A.M., I'd feel nothing. Mission accomplished yet again.

What I've just described wasn't an occasional scenario; it was a nightly routine. I moved from Boston to California in the late seventies and stopped working nights, but my eating–drinking–smoking orgies continued.

I stumbled my way through each day thinking I was in charge of and responsible for the universe. Of course, I was constantly let down because, in truth, I had no control over anything or anyone. All I knew how to do, really, was blame, resent and feel guilty. To dull that unending pain, I turned to food, alcohol and drugs, without realizing that I was killing myself on the installment plan.

In the throes of an emotional disease that manifested itself physically through a variety of substance abuses, I didn't have a clue how bad off I was—until about six years ago. That's when I learned the hard way, that finding spirituality was the only cure for my disease.

Until that time, I was pretty much an agnostic. Sure, I had some Hebrew School training and even had become a bar mitzvah. Then I quit religious training—cold turkey. Four years of college taught me that a belief in God simply was not logical, and the death of my mother from cancer at age 51 proved to me that God was dead or living in seclusion somewhere on Fiji.

My only recourse, it seemed, was to abuse myself with substances and behavior—because, to me, that was the one freedom I had in the world. This collision course with disaster lasted until I got very drunk one more time in 1986, winding up with my head in the toilet, praying at the porcelain altar, as alcoholics say. I was in such physical pain that I cried out: "Oh, God, please don't let this happen to me again!"

The incident changed my life—eventually. The immediate effect was that I stopped drinking; yet I continued to hurt myself with food, pot and self-loathing.

As fate would have it—I now know there are no coincidences, just God acting anonymously—someone very close to me had recently joined a 12-step, self-help group and had begun talking to me about that program. I was desperate enough to hear some of what was said, even though I tried mightily not to listen.

Five months later, after gorging myself yet again one night on ice cream, cake, peanut butter, nuts and anything that wasn't nailed down, I crawled into bed with a distended stomach and wicked heartburn. Lying there in distress, I took the first of the 12 steps—admitting I was powerless over food, just as I knew I was powerless over alcohol.

I began attending 12-step meetings once a week at a nearby church. In another six months I actually became willing to give up my last addiction—marijuana, which I had continued to smoke morning, noon and night.

Now clean, sober and abstinent, I finally was willing to take the second and third steps to the 12-step programs: "Come to believe that a power greater than myself could restore me to sanity," and "Make a decision to turn my will and my life over to the care of God as I understood God." The last phrase was the key. I got to fashion my own God, one that loved me all the time, regardless of my transgressions; a God who wanted only the best for me.

What I discovered was that the God I fashioned was very Jewish—only without the punishing aspects I had come to associate with the Judaism of my upbringing. I started going to temple more and more and actually enjoyed it.

I became involved with the Reform movement's task force on Jews and addiction, started visiting temples to discuss the long-hidden truth about compulsive behavior among our people, and ways to recover Jewishly.

More than five years into recovery, I now realize that my addiction and recovery from it was all part of God's plan for me. Only by following the winding path that is me today, could I be spreading the message that *t'shuvah* is just around the corner for those Jews who are willing to go to any lengths to get it.

Gil Peters is the former chairman of the Union of American Hebrew Congregations Pacific Southwest Council Task Force on Addictions.

In my commentary on this Mitzvah, I would expand the prohibition about doing things while drunk to include:

_____

_____

_____

Write your additional commentaries here.

_____

_____

_____

TAZRIA　　　　　　　　　　　　　　　　　תַּזְרִיעַ

וידבר יהוה אל משה לאמר דבר אל בני ישראל לאמר אשה כי תזריע וילדה זכר וטמאה שבעת ימים

כִּי אִשָּׁה נִדַּת דְּוֺתָהּ וְטָמְאָה

LEVITICUS 12:1–13:59

- Laws of the **impurity** of women after giving birth.
- Laws of **skin disease**.
- Laws of conditions that are considered leprosy.
- Procedures for dealing with leprosy.

OUR TEXT—LEVITICUS 13:45

In this *sidrah*, and in the next, we are given a lot of rules about leprosy. In Hebrew, *Mitzorah* is the word for leprosy. Our verse gives the basics.

וְהַצָּרוּעַ אֲשֶׁר־בּוֹ הַנֶּגַע בְּגָדָיו יִהְיוּ פְרֻמִים וְרֹאשׁוֹ יִהְיֶה פָרוּעַ וְעַל־שָׂפָם יַעְטֶה וְטָמֵא טָמֵא יִקְרָא.

פ	tear open = [פרם]	_____ = אֲשֶׁר	א
	uncover = [פרע]	clothing = בֶּגֶד	ב
צ	leper = צָרוּעַ	_____ = [היה]	ה
ק	call = [קרא]	unclean = טָמֵא	ט
ר	_____ = רֹאשׁ	infected with leprosy = נֶגַע	נ
שׁ	lip/moustache = שָׂפָם	cover = [עטה]	ע
		_____ = עַל	

45. וְהַצָּרוּעַ אֲשֶׁר־בּוֹ הַנֶּגַע בְּגָדָיו _____
יִהְיוּ פְרֻמִים _____
וְרֹאשׁוֹ יִהְיֶה פָרוּעַ _____
וְעַל־שָׂפָם יַעְטֶה _____
וְטָמֵא טָמֵא יִקְרָא. _____

Now try reading this verse without vowels:

והצרוע אשר בו הנגע בגדיו יהיו פרמים וראשם יהיה פרוע
ועל שפם יעטה וטמא טמא יקרא

EXPLORING OUR TEXT

In the Talmud and the Midrash, the rabbis ask, "Why does the Torah devote so much space to curing a skin disease?" They give several answers, including this one, which says that *Mitzorah* is also a metaphor.

> Rabbi Yoḥanan said in the name of Rabbi Yosi ben Zimra: "The spreading of *Lashon ha-Ra* (evil talk/gossip) is equal to denying God."
> He also said: "Whoever retells *Lashon ha-Ra* will be visited by plagues."
> Resh Lakish said, "What is the real meaning of the verse (Leviticus 14:2) 'This is the Torah of מְצֹרָע *M'tzora?*' It really means, 'This is the Torah of one who is a מוֹצִיא שֵׁם רָע *Motzi-Shem-Ra* (one who spreads gossip)."
>
> *Arakhim 15b*

1. In the Talmud, the rabbis connect "gossip" and "leprosy." How do they make this connection?

   _____
   _____

2. This "pun" is not just a word play. It is based on another biblical story. Read Numbers 12 and then again explain the connection between *Lashon ha-Ra* and *Mitzorah*.

   _____
   _____

MITZVOT OF THE WEEK
לָשׁוֹן רָע GOSSIP
מוֹצִיא שֵׁם רָע DEFAMATION OF CHARACTER

The *Ḥafetz Ḥayyim* explained the mitzvah of not speaking *Lashon ha-Ra* this way:

> You are forbidden to relate anything negative about others. If a negative statement is true, it is still considered to be *Lashon ha-Ra*. If it is false, even partly false, it is considered to be *Motzi-Shem-Ra* (defamation of character)—and is a much more severe offense. It cannot be repeated often enough that true negative statements are considered to be *Lashon ha-Ra*. The most common defense to a criticism for speaking *Lashon ha-Ra* is, "But it is true." That is exactly what categorizes the statement as being *Lashon ha-Ra*.

1. What is the difference between *Lashon ha-Ra* and *Motzi-Shem-Ra*?

   _____
   _____

2. Which is forbidden under Torah law?

_____

_____

Here are two sayings about *Lashon ha-Ra*:

> Why is the tongue like an arrow? If a person draws a sword to kill a neighbor, and the neighbor begs for mercy, the person's mind can change, and the sword can be returned unused. However, once an arrow is loosed, it can never be called back, even if the person who shot it has a change of mind.
>
> *Midrash Soher Tov*

> It says in Proverbs 18:21: "Death and life are in the power of the tongue. A person's tongue is more powerful than the sword. A sword can only kill someone who is nearby—a tongue can cause the death of someone who is far away."
>
> *Arakhim 15b*

Write your own saying about the power of a tongue:

_____

_____

_____

_____

_____

M'TZORA

מְצֹרָע

וידבר יהוה אל משה לאמר

זאת תהיה תורת המצרע ביום טהרתו והובא אל הכהן

LEVITICUS 14:1–15:33

- Leprosy Part II:
- The priests' duties in curing leprosy.
- Procedures for curing leprosy.
- Laws concerning house leprosy.
- Laws of discharges from the body with required acts of purification.

OUR TEXT—LEVITICUS 14:9

In this passage, we learn that once a leper is cleansed of *M'tzora*, immersion in water is the next step towards returning to society.

וְהָיָה בַיּוֹם הַשְּׁבִיעִי יְגַלַּח אֶת-כָּל-שְׂעָרוֹ אֶת-רֹאשׁוֹ וְאֶת-זְקָנוֹ וְאֵת גַּבֹּת עֵינָיו וְאֶת-כָּל-שְׂעָרוֹ יְגַלֵּחַ וְכִבֶּס אֶת-בְּגָדָיו וְרָחַץ אֶת-בְּשָׂרוֹ בַּמַּיִם וְטָהֵר.

י	יוֹם הַשְּׁבִיעִי = _____	ב	בֶּגֶד = _____
כ	[כבס] = launder		בָּשָׂר = body
	כָּל = _____	ג	גַּבֹּת עֵינָיו = eyebrows
מ	מַיִם = _____		[גלח] = shave
ר	רֹאשׁ = _____	ה	[היה] = _____
	[רחץ] = wash	ז	זָקָן = beard
שׂ	שֵׂעָר = hair	ט	טָהֵר = purify

9. _____ וְהָיָה בַיּוֹם הַשְּׁבִיעִי

_____ יְגַלַּח אֶת-כָּל-שְׂעָרוֹ

_____ אֶת-רֹאשׁוֹ וְאֶת-זְקָנוֹ

_____ וְאֵת גַּבֹּת עֵינָיו

_____ וְאֶת-כָּל-שְׂעָרוֹ יְגַלֵּחַ

_____ וְכִבֶּס אֶת-בְּגָדָיו

_____ וְרָחַץ אֶת-בְּשָׂרוֹ בַּמַּיִם וְטָהֵר.

Now try reading this verse without vowels:

היה ביום השביעי יגלח את כל שערו את ראשו ואת זקנו ואת גבת עיניו ואת כל שערו יגלח וכבס את בגדיו ורחץ את בשרו במים וטהר

EXPLORING OUR TEXT

In order to become pure after recovering from the skin disease, a leper must dip him/her self in a *mikvah* (a ritual bath of water).

In order to become pure and be ready to perform the holy work of the sacrifices, the *Kohein* must dip himself in a *mikvah*.

After our hands are clean, to become pure, a person must ritually wash them and say a brakhah before eating the meal.

In order to become pure and again be permitted to her husband at the end of her menstrual period, a woman must dip herself in the *mikvah*.

In order to enact the final transformation, and as the ritual moment of change, a convert immerses him/her self in a *mikvah* and becomes a Jew.

1. What is the difference between "pure" and "clean?"

   _____

   _____

2. What do all five of these rituals have in common?

   _____

   _____

3. What seems to be the purpose of a *mikvah*?

   _____

   _____

All streams flow into the sea,
Yet the sea is never full.
To the place from which the water flows,
There it returns.

Ecclesiastes 1:7

MITZVAH OF THE WEEK
מִקְוָה Mikvah

In brief, Jewish law requires husband and wife to refrain from any kind of physical contact during menstruation and for a period of seven days after its cessation. At the end of this period, the woman, who is referred to as a *nidah*, or menstruant, bathes herself thoroughly and then immerses herself in a mikvah (literally, "a gathering of waters"). The mikvah, designed according to specific and ancient guidelines, is a specially constructed ritual pool with a natural water source. The wife recites the following blessing: "Blessed are You, O God, King of the Universe, Who has sanctified us with His precepts and has commanded us to observe the mitzvah of *t'vilah*, ritual immersion." Thereafter, husband and wife renew their physical relationship.

Michael Kaufman, Love, Marriage and Family in Jewish Law and Tradition, Jason Aronson, 1992, page 195

Read these passages:

A married woman's immersion in the natural waters of the mikvah prior to resuming martial relations is parellel to the *kohein's* immersion in the mikvah prior to entering the Sanctuary. The climax of the Temple ritual was the entry of the *Kohein Gadol*, the High Priest, into the Holy of Holies. Five times during this day, before each major service, he would immerse himself in a mikvah. The immersions were symbolic acts of purification which had the effect of raising his spiritual status to allow him to enter the Holy of Holies, a place to which entry ordinarily was strictly forbidden.

Samson R. Hirsch, Torah Commentary, Chapter 15

The institution of family purity possesses grand symbolic significance when seen in the context of all of the Torah's legislation concerning *tum'ah* and *taharah*, terms which are loosely and misleadingly translated as "uncleanliness" and "cleanliness," or "purity" and "impurity." The reason we term these translations as inaccurate is because they imply, or at least they allow the listener to infer, that there is some hygienic element involved in them. This, of course, as explained above, is simply not so. They are spiritual states, and have no relation to physical disgust or attractiveness....

The Torah itself defines for us the purpose of all the commandments: "And one shall live by them and not die" (Lev. 18:5; Sanhedrin 74a). An analysis of the various species of *tum'ah* reveals that what they all have in common is the awareness of death. So that *tum'ah*, the intimation of death, whether it be through *nidah* (menstrual impurity) or any other form, is counteracted by immersion in the water of the mikvah, the symbol of life.

By means of this symbolism, we may understand the special requirements for a mikvah. The mikvah must be a gathering of natural water, such as a well or lake or rain-water, and not a pool of bath artificially accumulated by such means as plumbing. The question "what is the difference between (natural) water and (artificial) water?" already perplexed the ancients. According to what has been said above concerning the symbolic significance of water, we may begin to appreciate the difference between the two. By insisting upon the naturalness of the water of the mikvah, we affirm that God alone is the Author of Life and to God alone do we turn for continued life for us and our descendants after us. People are not the absolute master of their own lives and destinies; *mayim she'uvim*, water artificially accumulated, does not therefore possess the power of purification that appertains to natural water. Life is of God.

Pardes Rimonim: A Marriage Mannual for the Jewish Family, by Dr. Moses Tendler

Why then was I, a Reform rabbi and a committed feminist, splashing around in the mikvah? Was I going to make myself "kosher" for my new husband? Hardly. For me, it was an experience of reappropriation. The mikvah has been taken from me as a Jewish woman by sexist interpretations, by my experiences with Orthodox "family purity" committees who run communal mikvaot as Orthodox monopolies, by a history of male biases, fears of menstruation and superstitions. I was going to take back the water.

To take back the water means to see mikvah as a wholly female experience: as Miriam's well gave water to the Israelites, so too, will the mikvah give strength back to Jewish women. Water is the symbol of birth—now it can be a symbol of rebirth.

Elyse M. Goldstein, "Take Back the Waters: A Feminist Re-Appropriation of Mikvah, Lilith no. 15 (Summer 1986)

What meaning do you see in the mitzvah and ritual of mikvah?

(For the boys: Remember, men go to the mikvah too. Often, just before Shabbat. Also, *Sofrim*, scribes go to the mikvah before writing the name of God in a Torah scroll.)

_____

_____

_____

_____

_____

AHAREI MOT

אַחֲרֵי מוֹת

וידבר יהוה אל משה

אחרי מות

שני בני אהרן

בקרבתם לפני יהוה

וימתו

LEVITICUS 16:1–18:30

- God gives additional laws and duties for the Kohanim.
- The responsibilities of the **Head Kohein** on **Yom Kippur**.
- Laws for fasting and atonement on Yom Kippur.
- Laws about blood.
- Laws of eating meat.
- Prohibitions of nakednesses.

OUR TEXT: LEVITICUS 18:6

This *sidrah* contains a whole series of "Just Say No" rules about sexual practices. It forbids incest and other acts, starting with this verse.

אִישׁ אִישׁ אֶל־כָּל־שְׁאֵר בְּשָׂרוֹ לֹא תִקְרְבוּ לְגַלּוֹת עֶרְוָה אֲנִי יהוה.

ל	_____ = לֹא	a person .... = אִישׁ אִישׁ	א
ע	naked .... = עֶרְוָה	I _____ = אֲנִי	
ק	come near _____ = [קרב]	blood relative .... = בָּשָׂר	ב
	_____ = תִקְרְבוּ	reveal .... = [גלה]	ג
שׁ	flesh .... = שְׁאֵר	_____ = יהוה	י

6. אִישׁ אִישׁ _____
אֶל־כָּל־שְׁאֵר בְּשָׂרוֹ _____
לֹא תִקְרְבוּ לְגַלּוֹת עֶרְוָה _____
אֲנִי יהוה. _____

Now try reading this verse without vowels:

איש איש אל כל שאר בשרו לא תקרבו לגלות ערוה אני יהוה

EXPLORING OUR TEXT

Open up and read chapter 18 of Leviticus.

List all of the sexual relations that are forbidden:

18:7 _____

18:8 _____

18:9 _____

18:10 _____

18:11 _____

18:12 _____

18:13 _____

18:14 _____

18:15 _____

18:16 _____

18:17 _____

18:18 _____

18:19 _____

18:20 _____

18:21 _____

18:22 _____

18:23 _____

In your own words, summarize the basic prohibitions. What is the bottom line principle?

_____

_____

_____

Today, a major debate is raging over verse 22: "*Do not lie with a man the way one lies with a woman.*" The Orthodox community has maintained that physical homosexual relations are a sin—they see no room to compromise on God's laws. The Reform movement has stated that the biblical prohibitions against homosexuality are outmoded and reflect a primitive bias. They have said, in essence, that this law is a place where the people who wrote down the Torah reflected an understanding that fell short of the ideal God was really teaching. They have also, however, voiced a statement that heterosexual marriage and family remains a preferable Jewish practice. The Conservative movement is still debating the issue. They have as yet expressed no opinion that differs with the tradition. One Conservative Rabbi, Bradley Shavit Artson, has argued that the opening of the passage, "You shall not copy the practices of the Land of Egypt...or of the land of Canaan" is the key to a different understanding. He suggests that a committed gay relationship (akin to a marriage) is different from what the Torah is prohibiting as "the practices of Canaan." His opinion is still being discussed.

What does your synagogue teach about homosexuality?

_____

_____

How do you think that Jews today should respond to this verse?

_____

_____

Look at this case from Manis Friedman's *Doesn't Anyone Blush Anymore?* (Manis Friedman is an Orthodox rabbi who teaches, in a wonderfully creative way, a very traditional Jewish view of sexual ethics and responsibility.)

> A man confided to his rabbi, "I don't know how far I should go in trying to make friends with my stepdaughter. It's been three years now and she won't let me near her. When do I just throw in the towel and say, 'I quit'?"
>
> "How old is this girl?" the rabbi asked.
>
> "Fifteen," the man replied. "She was twelve when I married her mother. Why is she so cold to me every time I try to be friendly? What's wrong with the girl?"
>
> "Nothing's wrong with her," the rabbi explained. "A fifteen-year-old wants her privacy. You're imposing on her. She's trying to tell you, 'You're not my father. I have a father, even if I don't know where he is. I may hate his guts, but that doesn't make you my father, either. So I don't want you walking into my room, and I'm not comfortable having you put your arm around me. I don't want it, and I don't like it. It's an invasion of my privacy, of my modesty.'"
>
> His stepdaughter felt violated not necessarily out of an understanding of sexual ethics, but out of her innate sense of modesty. A door was opened that should have remained closed; a border was crossed that should have remained inviolate.

Do you disagree or agree with the analysis and counsel given in this passage? It comes from a traditional Jewish concept, both based on our verse, and on an idea called *Yihud* (being alone together).

_____

_____

Rabbi Friedman clarifies *Yihud* this way:

> A man and a woman alone together is a sexual event—even if nothing else happens. According to Jewish tradition, a man and a woman who are not married to each other, and who are not blood relatives, may not be alone together in a room in which the door is locked. This applies to every man and to every woman. Moses himself being alone with Sarah, wife of Abraham, would constitute a sexual event.
>
> *Manis Friedman, Doesn't Anyone Blush Anymore, Harper SanFrancisco 1990*

MITZVAH OF THE WEEK
לְגַלּוֹת עֶרְוָה UNCOVERING NAKEDNESS

Simply put, the mitzvot found in this passage ask you to establish and respect sexual boundaries. There are some sexual relationships that should not take place, and some times when sexual relationships are not appropriate. The set of laws in this passage asks Jews to know and respect those boundaries. Today, for non-Orthodox Jews, defining and understanding these boundaries is not easy. It requires thinking and studying.

Two famous Reform educators have said this about sex and Torah learning:

> We do not believe that sex in Judaism can be considered apart from love, from personhood, from the ideal of holiness. To turn sex education into basic biology is to debase it from a Jewish point of view. Biological data are important, but only as a means. The end is a loving human being whose sexuality is expressed with another in a way that makes them both holier—that is, closer to God—than they were before.
>
> *Rabbi Eugene and Estelle Borowitz*

To follow the Borowitz's example, look at the following passage from Michael Gold's *Does God Belong in the Bedroom?*

> To teach Jewish values, I gave high school students in a Hebrew high school setting the following eighteen situations and asked them to respond before I shared what I considered the appropriate Jewish response.
>
> 1. Luann, a high school senior, has a boyfriend who says: "If you love me, you will sleep with me."
> 2. Jack and Jill decided to live together to see if they are really compatible before marriage.
> 3. A public high school wants to establish a clinic that will provide birth control for students.
> 4. Sally is sexually abused by her stepfather, who tells her not to tell anyone.
> 5. Fred discovers that his wife, Sheila, has carried on an extramarital affair.
> 6. Howard and Kate decide to have an open marriage, with permission to seek other sexual partners.
> 7. Barry decides to remain a virgin until marriage although other boys make fun of him.
> 8. Janet, fifteen years old, is pregnant after sleeping with her boyfriend.
> 9. A Jewish high school decides to hold a special sex education class taught by a nurse and a rabbi.
> 10. Jeff want his wife, Debbie, to go to the mikvah each month.
> 11. Steve and Judy tell the rabbi before their wedding that they plan not to have children.
> 12. A new gay synagogue wants to advertise in the local Jewish newspaper.
> 13. Rhonda, married with a child, wants to leave her husband for a lesbian lover.
> 14. George's parents have told him that masturbation is a sin that leads to disease.
> 15. A pornographic theater opens in a Jewish neighborhood.
> 16. Jon likes to brag about his sexual conquests.
> 17. A youth group is having an overnight trip and want boys and girls to sleep in the same room.
> 18. Bob and Laurie, married ten years with no children, decide to have a baby using in vitro fertilization.
>
> *Michael Gold, Does God Belong in the Bedroom, JPS, 1992*

Discuss these situations in class. And, if you want to learn more, you can get either Rabbi Gold's or Rabbi Friedman's books.

KEDOSHIM

קְדֹשִׁים

וידבר יהוה אל משה לאמר דבר אל כל עדת בני ישראל
ואמרת אלהם

קדשים

תהיו

כי קדוש

אני יהוה אלהיכם

LEVITICUS 19:1-20:27

- **The Holiness code.**
- These laws include: **respecting parents, not worshipping idols, observing Shabbat, eating sacrifices right away, leaving the corners of fields, not stealing, not taking advantage of handicaps, judging cases fairly, not hating people**, and **loving your neighbor as yourself.**

OUR TEXT—LEVITICUS 19:17

In the verse right after our verse, we are told: וְאָהַבְתָּ לְרֵעֲךָ כָּמוֹךָ—you should love your neighbor as yourself. Our verse is about doing something that at first doesn't seem like love:

לֹא-תִשְׂנָא אֶת-אָחִיךָ בִּלְבָבֶךָ הוֹכֵחַ תּוֹכִיחַ אֶת-עֲמִיתֶךָ וְלֹא-תִשָּׂא עָלָיו חֵטְא.

נ	lift/carry = [נשא]	brother = אַח	א
	‗‗‗‗‗ = תִשָּׂא	sin = חֵטְא	ח
ע	‗‗‗‗‗ = עַל	correct/reprimand = [יכח]	י
	‗‗‗‗‗ = עָלָיו	‗‗‗‗‗ = הוֹכֵחַ תּוֹכִיחַ	
	friend/neighbor = עָמִית	‗‗‗‗‗ = לֹא	ל
שׂ	hate = [שנא]	heart = לֵב	
	‗‗‗‗‗ = תִשְׂנָא	‗‗‗‗‗ = בִּלְבָבֶךָ	

17. ‗‗‗‗‗לֹא-תִשְׂנָא אֶת-אָחִיךָ בִּלְבָבֶךָ

‗‗‗‗‗הוֹכֵחַ תּוֹכִיחַ אֶת-עֲמִיתֶךָ

‗‗‗‗‗וְלֹא-תִשָּׂא עָלָיו חֵטְא.

Now try reading this verse without vowels:

לא תשנא את אחיך בלבבך הוכח תוכיח את עמיתך ולא תשא עליו חטא

EXPLORING OUR TEXT

1. How is it "loving" and "not hating" your neighbors to tell them what they are doing wrong?

   _____
   _____

2. What problems can you see in the performance of this mitzvah?

   _____
   _____
   _____
   _____
   _____
   _____

MITZVAH OF THE WEEK
הוֹכֵחַ תּוֹכִיחַ REBUKE YOUR FRIEND

It is a mitzvah to rebuke a fellow Jew who does not behave properly either in matters between people and God, or between people. The proper way of reproving someone is to do it privately, in a soft tone, and with gentle, sincere words, so that the person will not be shamed.

If the alleged sinner does not accept private reproval, one may correct the person in the presence of close friends and relatives. Should this too prove unsuccessful, it is permissible to publicly admonish the person, even thought it may be humiliating.

If you see a person doing wrong and the sinner will not accept your words, then you are exempt from this mitzvah. For the rabbis of the Talmud teach us, "Just as it is a mitzvah to say something that will be heeded so is it a mitzvah **not** to say what will not be heeded" (*Yevamot* 65b).

Sefer ha-Hinukh

Our friend Mark Borovitz brought us this problem:

> Sam is 12 years old. He and Davis, a "good bud," are at the school playground, hanging. No one else is around. Davis starts talking about breaking into the school and messing up the Science Lab to get even with the teacher who is "a piece of work." Sam "hates" the teacher, too. He also knows that "breaking and entering" and "vandalizing" are against the law and he is afraid that they might get caught. He tells Davis, "I don't think that this is a good idea. We're gonna get busted." Davis calls him a wimp.

How should Sam respond?

___

To answer Mark's problem, we collected a number of Jewish sources and began to think about writing a Responsum—a Jewish legal answer. Use these sources to create your Jewish answer to Sam's problem. If Sam's case was brought to you, and you were asked to write a Responsum, how would these texts guide your answer? Cite the sources you use.

Your Responsum

0. Obviously, Sam should not break into the school and destroy someone else's property. We will not insult you with that question. These other questions are also important.

1. What should Sam say to Davis?

___

2. If Davis decides to break in on his own, should Sam go to the police?

___

3. If the police suspect Davis and question Sam, what should Sam do?

___

Sources

1.

YOU MUST TELL YOUR "PEOPLE" WHEN THEY ARE DOING SOMETHING WRONG.
THIS WILL KEEP YOU FROM BEING RESPONSIBLE FOR HIS/HER "SIN."

Leviticus 19:17

Even though you must confront your friend about wrong doings, you must not do it publicly, where your friend could be embarrassed by your words—this, too, would be a "sin."

This is why the last part of the verse says: "THIS WILL KEEP YOU FROM BEING RESPONSIBLE FOR HIS/HER "SIN,"" meaning that your friend's "sin" should not lead you to also "sin" in trying to stop it.

Rashi on Leviticus 19:17

2.

Rabbi Iliya said: "This I learned from Rabbi Elazar ben Rabbi Shimon—Just as it is a *mitzvah* to confront friends with their wrong-doings when it **will** be listened to—so, too, is it a *mitzvah* **not** to confront friends when it **will not** make a difference.
Rabbi Abba explained: In the Bible (Proverbs 9:8) it says, "DO NOT CONFRONT A HARDENED ASSOCIATE LEST THEY HATE YOU, BUT, CONFRONT A WISE PEOPLE AND THEY WILL LOVE YOU."

Yevamot 65b

Do not confront a person who is sure to ignore you.

Rashi on Yevamot 65b

3.

The Holy-One-Who-Is-To-Be-Blessed hates three kinds of people:
A person who says one thing with words while thinking another thing in his/her heart.
A person who has evidence or information to help neighbors and who holds back that evidence.
A person who is the **only** person to see a crime and comes alone to testify against his/her neighbor in court.
To explain this last point, the Talmud tells this story:
Tobias committed a crime and Zigud saw it. He brought the case before Rabbi Papa to judge. Surprisingly, Rabbi Papa had Zigud punished. Zigud complained, "Tobias committed the crime and I got punished? Why?" Rabbi Papa explained, "It says in Deuteronomy 19:15, 'One witness should not testify alone against a person.' Because you 'alone' brought this case before me, and I cannot find him guilty on the words of one witness, all you did was destroy his reputation."
Rabbi Samuel ben Rabbi Isaac said, "I have learned from Rav, that even though you cannot be the only one to testify against a criminal, you can 'disapprove' of that person."

Pesaḥim 113b

4.

If a person sees flood waters approaching someone else's field, that person must make a barrier or a dam and try to stop them in order to prevent damage to the neighbor's property. This obligation is based on the responsibility taught in the Torah: "If you see your neighbor's ox or sheep lost, you must not ignore it. You must take it back to your neighbor...You must do the same for anything that is your neighbor's—you must not remain indifferent" (Deuteronmy 22:1-3).

Bava Metzia 30b

Our Responsum

We know that this case presents a difficult choice. Sam's heart is being pulled in several directions. Everyone wants to be "loyal" to his friends. No one wants to be known as a "squealer" and get someone else in trouble. Emotionally, the easiest thing to do is nothing. It is easy in this case to simply look the other way and not say a word. That way Sam can say, "I didn't do anything. I even told him not to do it—because he would get caught. I am not responsible. I am innocent."

At the same time, we know that what Davis is going to do is wrong. It is against the law. It hurts someone else. It destroys public and, probably, private property. It causes harm. If we do nothing, we are allowing the damage to be done. That, too, seems wrong.

These two sets of feelings pull at each other. We are caught between two sets of actions, each of which feels wrong. If we can't stop Davis (and it seems like we can't), telling on him feels like a betrayal of a friendship. If we don't have someone else stop him, we are being bad citizens, bad neighbors, and bad members of our community. The two sets of values have to be balanced. Jewish law struggles with this dilemma.

0. Obviously, Sam should not break into the school and destroy someone else's property.

1. What should Sam say to Davis?
Jewish Law teaches that Sam should try to stop Davis by showing him that his actions would be wrong and harmful. That is the lesson taught by Leviticus 19:17: "YOU MUST TELL YOUR 'PEOPLE' WHEN THEY ARE DOING SOMETHING WRONG. THIS WILL KEEP YOU FROM BEING RESPONSIBLE FOR HIS/HER 'SIN'." The mistake that Sam makes is that he limits his warning to "getting caught," not that the action is "wrong." Sam fails to be a good friend and teach his "bud" an important ethical lesson.

However, Jewish Law understands that this is not always easy. It understands that sometimes trying to change someone's mind only makes things worse. Therefore, it teaches in the Talmud (*Yevamot* 65b) "JUST AS IT IS A *MITZVAH* TO CONFRONT A FRIEND WITH WRONG-DOING WHEN IT **WILL** BE LISTENED TO—SO, TOO, IT IS A *MITZVAH* **NOT** TO CONFRONT A FRIEND WHEN IT **WILL NOT** MAKE A DIFFERENCE." Sam has a choice to make. If he thinks he can change Davis' mind, he **must** try. If he thinks he cannot, or especially if it will make things worse, then he **should not** even try.

2. If Davis decides to break in on his own, should Sam go to the police?
First of all, we must be honest. In America, this is an ethical issue, not a legal one. If Sam fails to inform on Davis, he has broken no law. He may be doing "the wrong thing," but his non-action is not criminal.

In America, if we see a person's property being destroyed by flood or fire, we have no legal obligation to either get involved or to send for help. It is the right thing to do. It is what a good neighbor does, but it is not a legal obligation. It is not a crime if we don't do it. Jewish law teaches differently. It teaches that we must protect our neighbor's property. This is the meaning of the Talmudic text (*Bava Metzia* 30b): "IF A PERSON SEES FLOOD WATERS APPROACHING SOMEONE ELSE'S FIELD, THAT PERSON MUST MAKE A BARRIER OR A DAM AND TRY TO STOP THEM IN ORDER TO PREVENT DAMAGE TO THE NEIGHBOR'S PROPERTY." Based on this text, it would seem that Sam has an obligation to get an authority to stop Davis from doing harm. It is not that simple, however.

Jewish Law is very concerned with criminal rights, too. It never wants anyone who is innocent to ever be convicted falsely. For that reason, Jewish Law always demands two witnesses to every crime. Jewish Law would rather let a guilty person go free, if there are not enough witnesses, than have an innocent person convicted by one person's mistake. For that reason, the Talmud teaches that a good Jew should never be the only witness against a criminal. This is why the Talmud tells the story of Tobias and Zigud (*Peas͟him 113b*).

One could think that this would mean that Sam should not tell. It does not. Being a witness is something that takes place during the crime. Here, Sam is reacting to a danger to property. He is building a dam. Therefore he must try to stop Davis by warning someone of the impending crime. (Jewish Law might encourage an anonymous tip—not incriminating Davis in advance of the crime.) If Davis is caught, there will be two or more witnesses. If he is not caught, but under suspicion, Jewish Law would then prohibit Sam's sole testimony.

3. If the police suspect Davis and question Sam, what should Sam do?

Believe it or not, Jewish Law encourages Sam to ask the police a question: "Do you have other witnesses?" If the answer is "yes" and Sam establishes that the other witness has incriminating evidence, then he must testify. This is taught in this same passage in the Talmud when it says: "THE HOLY-ONE-WHO-IS-TO-BE-BLESSED HATES THREE KINDS OF PEOPLE...A PERSON WHO HAS EVIDENCE OR INFORMATION TO HELP NEIGHBORS AND WHO HOLDS BACK THAT EVIDENCE." However the passage continues: "A PERSON WHO IS THE **ONLY** PERSON TO SEE A CRIME AND COMES ALONE TO TESTIFY AGAINST HIS/HER NEIGHBOR IN COURT." So, if Sam will be the only witness, he is correct in refusing to "rat" on his friend.

EMOR אֱמֹר

ויאמר יהוה אל משה אמר אל הכהנים בני אהרן ואמרת אלהם לנפש לא יטמא בעמיו

LEVITICUS 21:1–24:23

- More rules about Kohanim:
- Rules about a Kohein coming in contact with the dead.
- Rules about serving as a Kohein.
- Rules about how to celebrate holidays:
- **Shabbat, Passover**, the **Omer, Shavuot, Rosh ha-Shanah, Yom Kippur** and **Sukkot** are described.
- The story of a man who cursed God.

OUR TEXT—LEVITICUS 22:32

From our verse we learn two important mitzvot about God's public image—the state of God's name.

וְלֹא תְחַלְּלוּ אֶת־שֵׁם קָדְשִׁי וְנִקְדַּשְׁתִּי בְּתוֹךְ בְּנֵי יִשְׂרָאֵל אֲנִי יהוה מְקַדִּשְׁכֶם.

ק	[קדש] = _____	אֲנִי = _____	א
	קָדְשִׁי = _____	בְּנֵי יִשְׂרָאֵל = _____	ב
	וְנִקְדַּשְׁתִּי = _____	[חלל] = curse/profane	ח
	מְקַדִּשְׁכֶם = _____	תְחַלְּלוּ = _____	
שׁ	שֵׁם = _____	יהוה = _____	י
ת	תּוֹךְ = middle/midst	לֹא = _____	ל

וְלֹא תְחַלְּלוּ אֶת־שֵׁם קָדְשִׁי _____ .32

וְנִקְדַּשְׁתִּי _____

בְּתוֹךְ בְּנֵי יִשְׂרָאֵל _____

אֲנִי יהוה מְקַדִּשְׁכֶם. _____

Now try reading this verse without vowels:

ולא תחללו את שם קדשי ונקדשתי בתוך בני ישראל אני יהוה מקדשכם

EXPLORING OUR TEXT

From this verse, and a couple of others, the rabbis suggest that we can make God's name holy, and we can dishonor God's name, too.

What can we do to make God's name holy?

_____

_____

_____

What can we do to dishonor God's name?

_____

_____

_____

MITZVAH OF THE WEEK
Hillul ha-Shem and Kiddush ha-Shem — חִלּוּל הַשֵׁם and קִדּוּשׁ הַשֵׁם

The assertion that people, with all their limitations and faults, can hallow God, and that God requires people to hallow the Divine Name, is known in rabbinic literature as *Kiddush ha-Shem*. People are sanctified by God if they choose to follow the *mitzvot*, thus imitating God's ways. It is likewise the duty of people to hallow God. "I will be hallowed among the children of Israel; I am *Adonai* who hallows you," proclaims the Torah.

The verse quoted from Leviticus was originally directed to the priesthood, who, as guardians of the Sanctuary, were warned in this manner to fulfill their duties to God. Later, however, the obligation to sanctify God's name was extended to the "Kingdom of Priests"—the whole Jewish People.

Kiddush Ha-Shem and its opposite, *Hillul ha-Shem* (profanation of God's name), became two of the basic polarities of Judaism. The Jew was required to look upon himself as a guardian of her or his people's reputation. Any extraordinary act that would bring honor to the Jewish People was regarded as *Kiddush Ha-Shem*.

One of the best-known examples of *Kiddush ha-Shem* that the Talmud relates, concerns an incident in the life of Simeon ben Shetah, who found a valuable gem hanging around the neck of a camel he had bought from an Arab. His disciples urged him to keep the treasure that God had bestowed upon him. However, Simeon quickly returned the stone saying, "I purchased an animal, not a precious stone."

When the Arab was given back the stone he exclaimed: "Blessed be the God of Simeon ben Sheta<u>h</u>; blessed be the God of Israel." Here God's name became hallowed because Simeon demonstrated that his belief in God was real, so real that he did not succumb to the temptation of taking advantage of an innocent person. He caused a non-Jew (prior to Islam) to praise the God of Israel.

The most extreme form of *Kiddush ha-Shem* is martyrdom—the instance of a Jew's faith in God biding so strong that one is willing to forego the privilege of living, if necessary, to prevent the desecration of God's name. It was during the war against the Romans who imperiled the existence of the Jewish People and the Torah that *Kiddush ha-Shem* became associated with martyrdom. Did this mean that a Jew could destroy her/himself if she/he believed that the cause for which she/he stood was important enough?

Life was too precious for the individual to make such a crucial decision. The rabbis then decreed that only with regard to three cardinal sins—idolatry, incest, murder—should a person prefer to make the supreme sacrifice rather than be forced to commit any of these transgressions. If one were coerced into violating any other commandment, one should spare one's self from death and violate the law.

The opposite of *Kiddush ha-Shem* is <u>Hillul ha-Shem</u>. Just as *Kiddush ha-Shem* is an act which helps to encourage belief in God, <u>Hillul ha-Shem</u> is an act which causes others to withdraw from God. For this reason both *Kiddush ha-Shem* and <u>Hillul ha-Shem</u> are usually associated with acts committed in public. This is not to say that a person may feel free to violate the commandments in private. Nevertheless, public violation is regarded to be a more serious offense, for it shows a complete disregard for the religious sensitivities of others and contributes to a general break-down of religious loyalty.

The more prominent the individual, the more vulnerable one is to committing a <u>Hillul ha-Shem</u>, Rav, the founder of the Babylonian academy, said: "In my case, if I should buy meat from a butcher and not pay for it immediately." Here it is the responsibility of the individual Jew to show concern for the image of the Jewish people that she/he created in public. The career of the Jewish People has been closely associated with their belief in and worship of God. The individual Jew who takes her/his religion seriously continues to regard her/himself as a "light unto the nations," not by missionizing among them, but by creating an example worthy of the name that she/he upholds.

The Language of Judaism, Simon Glustrom, Ktav Publishing House, Inc. (1973)

APPLYING OUR MITZVAH

Glueckel of Hamelin (1646-1724) is one of the most interesting characters in German Jewish history. Despite the fact that she was a businesswoman of enterprise and real ability, she found time to rear and to marry off twelve of her thirteen children, allying them with the most notable Jewish families of Europe.

During the years 1691-1719 Glueckel, who had moved from Hamelin to Hamburg, wrote her memoirs in Judaeo-German. This work of hers is a most unusual one, for autobiography is rare in Jewish literature in this age, and as a medium of self-expression by a woman of this period it is altogether unique.

For an insight into the social, economic, and cultural life of the Jews of Central Europe in the period 1650-1725 these memoirs are invaluable. They give us an intimate picture of the family life of the average well-to-do Jew, his relation to the state, his business problems, his religious background, and his spiritual life.

The Thief Who Died a Martyr, about 1670

At that time an East Indian ship with many uncut diamonds fell into the hands of the King of Denmark and lay at Gluckstadt. Since every sailor on it had diamonds, the Jews went to Gluckstadt and did business and made good profits. There were two Jews there who knew that a citizen in Norway had a large batch of these diamonds. They took evil counsel together, regrettably, and formed a partnership to get the diamonds out of that house where they were kept. It seems to me that the owner was a baker who had gotten them very cheaply.

So these two—this bad lot—came to Norway. At once they made a careful search for the man who had the diamonds and managed to get into his home. Gradually they became so friendly with this burgher that they found out where he kept his treasures, got the best of him, and took everything away from him. The man had sheltered them in his home. The next morning they left the house and rented a skiff and thought they had made a good job of it all. But the Almighty did not want this to succeed. When the burgher arose the next morning and asked about his two guests, the servant told him that they had left the house quite early. The burgher was rather disturbed for whoever has such a treasure is always worried. Therefore he went to the chest where he kept his treasures but found nothing. He immediately took it for granted that his two guests had done this to him. He ran straight for the sea and asked some boatmen if they had not seen two Jews pulling out. "Yes," said one of them to him, "Such-and-such a boatman took them away about an hour ago." He hired a boat immediately, put in four oarsmen, and started after them. It was not very long before they sighted the boat with the thieves, but when the thieves saw that they were being followed they threw the whole treasure into the sea.

In short, the burgher overhauled them and they had to go back with him although they argued a great deal with him, saying: "Consider what you're about to do. We are honest folk. It will not be discovered that we have any of the stuff. You are doing us an injustice. We'll hold you responsible for this." They had thrown the stuff into the water in order the better to deny the charges, but it is written in our Ten Commandments: "Thou shalt not steal!" Therefore, God, blessed be He, did not help them and they were again brought back to the place from which they had fled. They denied everything the while they were being stripped naked and everything was being carefully searched. But all this did not help them. They were put to such severe torture that finally they had to confess that they had done it, and that when they had seen that they were being pursued, they had thrown the diamonds into the sea, thinking that when they would be searched and nothing found on them, they would be able, by their denial, to get away with it. But, as has been said, God did not want this to happen and both were condemned to the gallows.

The one thief immediately accepted the Christian faith (and saved his life). The other had been a pious man all his life and also had a pious father and mother. He came from Wandsbeck (on the outskirts of Hamburg). He did not want to change his religion and chose to sacrifice his life. I knew him and his parents well, and all his life he had behaved himself as a pious, honest man. He must have been led astray by the other fellow, who was never any good, and so it was inevitable, unfortunately, that he should come to a bad end. Surely his soul is in Paradise for he must have actually attained future life through his conduct in his last hour. Out of respect for his family I don't want to give his name, but the whole story is well known in Hamburg. The Holy-One-Who-is-to-Be-Blessed will surely have accepted his martyrdom favorably, for he surrendered his life for God. He could have escaped just as easily as his companion but he fulfilled the commandment (Deuteronomy 6:5): "Thou shalt love the Lord thy God with all thy soul (even though you die a martyr to prove your love of God)." Hence his death must have been an expiation of all his sins. Therefore every one should learn from this example and not allow the evil inclination to seduce him with filthy lucre.

Did this second man perform *Kiddush ha-Shem*, and as Glueckel suggests, die a martyr? Explain your opinion:

_____
_____
_____
_____
_____
_____
_____

BE-HAR בְּהַר

וידבר יהוה אל משה
בהר סיני
לאמר

LEVITICUS 25:1–26:2

- And the rules go on:
- Rules for the **Sabbatical years**.
- Rules for the **Jubilee years**.
- Rules for **owning property** in the **Land of Israel**.
- A rule about **not lending money at interest**.

OUR TEXT—LEVITICUS 25:14

While we have seen little bits of this idea before, our verse of the week shows us that business is not separate from religion, but rather that the mitzvot specifically cover business practice.

וְכִי־תִמְכְּרוּ מִמְכָּר לַעֲמִיתֶךָ אוֹ קָנֹה מִיַּד עֲמִיתֶךָ אַל־תּוֹנוּ אִישׁ אֶת־אָחִיו.

כ	כִּי = _____	or .... = אוֹ	א
מ	sell .... = [מכר]	_____ = אָחִיו	
	תִמְכְּרוּ = _____	_____ = אִישׁ	
	מִמְכָּר = posession you are selling	do not .... = אַל	
ע	עִם = _____	_____ = יַד	י
ק	buy .... = [קנה]	cheat/trick .... = [ינה]	
		תּוֹנוּ = _____	

15. _____וְכִי־תִמְכְּרוּ מִמְכָּר לַעֲמִיתֶךָ

_____אוֹ קָנֹה מִיַּד עֲמִיתֶךָ

_____אַל־תּוֹנוּ אִישׁ אֶת־אָחִיו.

Now try reading this verse without vowels:

וכי תמכרו ממכר לעמיתך או קנה מיד עמיתך אל תונו איש את אחיו

150

EXPLORING OUR TEXT

AT WHOSE EXPENSE?

In the Torah there are a lot of business mitzvot. Which of them is best expressed by this story?

Leviticus 19:13   You shall not keep the wages of a worker overnight until the next morning.

Leviticus 19:35   You shall never be dishonest in the measurement of the weight, length, or volume of anything you are selling.

Leviticus 25:14   You shall not be dishonest in either buying or selling anything.

Leviticus 25:37   It is forbidden to lend a fellow Jew money at interest.

Consider this Hasidic story:

> Reb Zusia was a very poor man all his life. When his wife's dress became worn out and she was in need of a new one, he borrowed some money from a few friends, bought the needed material, and handed it to his wife to give to the tailor. A few weeks later, Reb Zusia asked his wife whether the tailor had finished the garment. With a sigh, she replied, "He finished the dress, but I don't have it." "What happened?" Reb Zusia asked in surprise. She began to explain, "When the tailor's future son-in-law had seen him sewing a dress, he had assumed that it was surely for his bride (the tailor's daughter).
>
> "But when he learned that it was not, the young man became angry, and the tailor began to worry lest the engagement be jeopardized. So, I immediately gave the dress to the girl as a present."

At this point in the story, Reb Zusia became concerned that a business mitzvah was being violated. Can you guess which one? What advice do you think he gave his wife?

_____

_____

_____

_____

> "And how much did you pay the tailor?" asked Rev Zusia. "For what?" asked his wife. "For making the dress," he replied. "Why on earth should I pay him for making the dress when it ended up being for his own daughter?" Reb Zusia stated firmly, "How could you even consider withholding the man's wages? The whole week long he has been working for you, and not for his daughter. He has been waiting anxiously to finish this job, so that he will be able to receive his payment in order to sustain his family. What is the poor man going to do now? Is it his fault that you decided to give the dress to his daughter?" Hearing these words, Reb Zusia's wife set out immediately to borrow some money, and paid the tailor his wages.

What is the "moral" of this story?

_____

_____

_____

_____

Write your own "Hasidic" story that teaches the importance of one of the other three business mitzvot.

_____

_____

_____

_____

MITZVAH OF THE WEEK
גְּנֵבַת דַּעַת Misrepresentation

The *Shulhan Arukh*, in dealing with the laws of theft, first legislates against blatant fraud, such as putting the good fruit on top. One is forbidden to beautify the article being sold in order to create a false impression. So one is forbidden to dye a slave's hair or beard in order to make him appear young. One is not allowed to give an animal bran to eat that makes her hair brown and upright, thus creating the impression that she is fat and sleek. Nor may one comb her artfully in order to create the same impression. One is not allowed to paint old baskets to make them look new nor is one allowed to soak meat in water to make it white and look fat.

In a book on business ethics, Rabbi S. Wagschal explains this mitzvah this way:

> We are forbidden from doing anything "misleading in business." What is considered misleading? A person is able to gauge what is counted as misleading by asking himself the following questions before offering goods for sale:
>
> 1) Do I want to hide anything from the buyer, e.g., any hidden faults?
>
> 2) Is the price correct?
>
> 3) Does the quality of the goods match their description?

Do I want to hide anything from the buyer, e.g., any hidden faults?

> **Example I:** Mixing good and bad quality: A vendor, who has a mixture of good and not-so-good quality of merchandise, must not place the good quality on top so as to create the impression that the whole lot is of good quality.
>
> **Example II:** Second-class goods sold as first-class: Second-class goods with minor faults, or of inferior quality (not noticeable to the customer), must not be sold as first-class goods.
>
> **Example III:** Faults in new or second-hand goods: A mechanical object that was returned as it was not working to perfection must not be sold to another person without pointing out the fault, e.g., electrical goods or clocks with even only a minor fault.
>
> **Example IV:** False claims: One must not say to a customer, "You will be getting an exceptional bargain," if in reality one is charging the normal price.
>
> **Example V:** Overcharging: A buyer who offers a high price for an object that is not so valuable, e.g., an antique, a piece of jewelry or a rare postage stamp, must be told by the vendor what the current price is.
>
> **Example VI:** Under-paying: If a vendor is not aware of the high value of the goods he is offering for sale, e.g., a rare antique, a painting or old seforim, and he is asking for a low figure, the buyer must offer the true market price of the goods.

A Torah Guide to the Businessman. Rabbi S. Wagschal, Feldheim Publishers, 5757-1990

BE-HUKOTAI בְּחֻקֹּתַי

אִם בְּחֻקֹּתַי תֵּלֵכוּ וְאֶת מִצְוֺתַי תִּשְׁמְרוּ וַעֲשִׂיתֶם אֹתָם

LEVITICUS 26:3–27:34

- God promises **five blessings** to the Children of Israel if they follow the law.
- Then God warns about **thirty-two curses if the promises are not kept**.
- Laws about **vows, tithes, things promised to God** and **things that need to be redeemed**.

OUR TEXT— LEVITICUS 27:2

In this *sidrah* is this verse where we learn about a very important Jewish legal category, the Oath. For Jews, the words "I swear to God" have very important and powerful ramifications.

דַּבֵּר אֶל־בְּנֵי יִשְׂרָאֵל וְאָמַרְתָּ אֲלֵהֶם אִישׁ כִּי יַפְלִא נֶדֶר בְּעֶרְכְּךָ נְפָשֹׁת לַיהוה.

כ	כִּי = _____	א	אִישׁ = _____
נ	נֶדֶר = vow		אֶל = _____
	נֶפֶשׁ = soul/human being		אֲלֵהֶם = _____
ע	עֵרֶךְ = value		[אמר] = _____
	בְּעֶרְכְּךָ = _____	ב	בְּנֵי יִשְׂרָאֵל = _____
פ	[פלא] = make a vow	ד	[דבר] = _____
	יַפְלִא נֶדֶר = explicitly makes a vow	י	יהוה = _____

2. דַּבֵּר אֶל־בְּנֵי יִשְׂרָאֵל _____

וְאָמַרְתָּ אֲלֵהֶם _____

אִישׁ כִּי יַפְלִא נֶדֶר _____

בְּעֶרְכְּךָ נְפָשֹׁת לַיהוה. _____

Now try reading this verse without vowels:

דבר אל בני ישראל ואמרת אלהם איש כי יפלא נדר בערכך נפשת ליהוה

EXPLORING OUR TEXT

Our teacher, Dr. Stephen Passamaneck, translated this Responsa case into English.

> A man, Feibush of Munich, swore a false oath before Jewish tax assessors in Regensburg, lying about his taxable income. Having been caught, he now stands repentently before us, the local *Bet Din*. What should be done with him?
>
> *Jacob Bazak, Jewish Law and Jewish Life, UAHC 1979*
> *Translated and Edited by Stephen M. Passamaneck*

What would you recommend that the *Bet Din* do?

_____
_____
_____
_____

MITZVAH OF THE WEEK
נֶדֶר TAKING AN OATH

In the Bible, and in the Talmud, taking an oath was a very serious action. It was something that Jews didn't want to do unless it was absolutely necessary. Even if people thought they were telling the truth in an oath, a mistake could cause them to swear falsely by God's name. These texts will help you understand that an oath was a very serious matter.

Hillel Gamoran, The Jewish Law Review Vol. 2

> You shall not tell a lie; *Adonai* will not clear anyone who swears falsely by God's name.
>
> *Exodus 20:7, The Ten Commandments*

> If a person intentionally gives false evidence about a neighbor, you should do to that person exactly what was planned for the neighbor. Thus you will sweep out evil from your community—others will hear and be afraid, and such evil things will not come again in your community.
>
> *Deuteronomy 19:18-20*

> If the court of law imposes an oath upon one of the parties, the court is permitted to bring about a settlement between them, even after the conclusion of the trial, to make sure that the one who was bound to take the oath will be exempt for the possible penalty of having taken a false oath.
>
> *Shulḥan Arukh, Ḥoshen Mishpat, Laws of Judges, 12.2*

A person taking an oath must be worthy, and there must be no suspicion of falsehood, either intentional or unintentional, in an oath. For that reason the Sages almost completely abolished oaths from court procedure and substituted other regulations. The punishment for taking a false oath is very severe since it involves the desecrating of God's name.

Adin Steinsaltz, The Talmud: A Reference Guide

How does the mitzvah of honesty in oaths fit into your life?

_____
_____
_____
_____

THE EPILOGUE

Here is the actual *T'shuvah* that Rabbi Jacob ben Judah Weil wrote.

Answer: We read in Talmud (*Shevu'oth* 39a): The entire world trembled when God on Sinai uttered the prohibition, "Thou shalt not take the Name of *Adonai* thy God in vain" (Exod. 20:7). The Sages designated a false oath as one of the most serious transgressions. R. Elazar of Worms wrote in his collection, the *Roke'ah*, no. 25, that a false oath is tantamount to denying the existence of God! Therefore I say this Feibush of Munich shall be flogged three (ceremonial) lashes just prior to the *v'Hu Rahum* portion of the evening worship service. This is to take place in the synagogue on three occasions:

A Monday, a Thursday, and the next following Monday (weekdays that are distinguished by a public reading of Torah, and more worshippers). After the lashes, he is to declaim in a voice clearly audible to all, in the German language, "I have sworn falsely on my tax declaration! 'I have sinned; I have done iniquity; I have acted illegally.'" Moreover, once Feibush's sin became public knowledge, it constituted a public desecration of God, which is not to be treated lightly.

The *Roke'ah* further provides that the malefactor "shall be flogged several times and shall fast for forty consecutive days, except upon Sabbaths and other religious holidays. When the forty-day period is over, he shall continue to fast for a number of days equal to the number of Sabbaths, etc., which fell during the original forty-day period. Thereafter he shall fast on Mondays and Thursdays for one full year. If he is physically incapable of sustaining the fast after the forty-day period, he shall give money to public charity and undertake another personal privation prescribed by the religious authorities of his city. He shall forever refrain from making any sort of oath—even on a matter which is manifestly true... etc."

Jacob Bazak, Jewish Law and Jewish Life, UAHC 1979
Translated and Edited by Stephen M. Passamaneck

Notice that Rabbi Weil was much more concerned about the "false oath" than the money not collected. Why is this an interesting priority?

_____

_____

_____

_____

What lesson can we learn from this case?

_____

_____

BE-MIDBAR

בְּמִדְבַּר

וידבר יהוה אל משה

במדבר

באהל מועד
באחד לחדש השני
בשנה השנית לצאתם
מארץ מצרים לאמר

NUMBERS 1:1–4:20

- A census is taken of men over twenty.
- Instructions are given for where each tribe should camp.
- Aaron's family is listed and other clans are identified.

OUR TEXT—NUMBERS 3:1-2

In this *sidrah*, a very innocent line listing the names of the sons of Aaron teaches us a very powerful lesson about the act of teaching.

וְאֵלֶּה תּוֹלְדֹת אַהֲרֹן וּמֹשֶׁה בְּיוֹם דִּבֶּר יהוה אֶת-מֹשֶׁה בְּהַר סִינָי.
וְאֵלֶּה שְׁמוֹת בְּנֵי אַהֲרֹן...

י	יהוה = _____	אַהֲרֹן = _____	א
	יוֹם = _____	אֵלֶּה = these are	
מ	מֹשֶׁה = _____	בָּנִים = _____	ב
שׁ	שֵׁם = _____	[דבר] = _____	ד
ת	תּוֹלְדוֹת = descendants	הַר סִינַי = _____	ה

1. וְאֵלֶּה תּוֹלְדֹת אַהֲרֹן וּמֹשֶׁה _____
   בְּיוֹם דִּבֶּר יהוה _____
   אֶת-מֹשֶׁה בְּהַר סִינָי. _____
2. וְאֵלֶּה שְׁמוֹת בְּנֵי אַהֲרֹן... _____

Now try reading this verse without vowels:

ואלה תולדת אהרן ומשה ביום דבר יהוה את משה בהר סיני
ואלה שמות בני אהרן...

EXPLORING OUR TEXT

To understand the power of this verse, we need to also read Rashi:

> **Why does the Torah state that Aaron's sons, Nadav, Avihu, Elazar and Itamar, were the sons of both Aaron and Moses, when in fact only Aaron was their biological father?**
> The Torah also credited Moses in order to teach us that one who teaches a child Torah is credited as if s/he had brought the child into the world (Sanhedrin 19b).

Explain this commentary's lesson in your own words:

_____
_____
_____

Here is a passage from the Mishnah. What does it teach about the relationship of parents and teachers?

> If a person goes looking for property lost by a parent and property lost by a teacher, the teacher's takes precedence over that of the parent's because even though the parent brought that person into the world, his teacher, who taught wisdom, brings that person into the World to Come...
>
> *Bava Mezia, 2.11*

_____
_____
_____

Write a few sentences about the best Jewish teacher you've ever had. (And because it would embarrass him or her, your present teacher doesn't count.)

_____
_____
_____
_____
_____

MITZVAH OF THE WEEK
וְשִׁנַּנְתָּם לְבָנֶיךָ AND YOU SHALL TEACH THEM DILIGENTLY

This mitzvah (Deuteronomy 6:7) applies to every person, old and young, rich and poor alike. Every person must set aside a specific time to study Torah each day. Included in this mitzvah is the obligation of every parent to teach his or her children Torah. A parent should begin to educate a child in Torah as soon a the child begins to speak, by teaching him the verse (Deuteronomy 33:4) "Moshe commanded us the Torah; it is a heritage of the congregation of Ya'akov." And when the child reaches the age of 5, the parent should begin teaching the child Torah.

In a book called *How to Be a Jewish Teacher*, our friend and teacher Rabbi Sam Joseph takes the mitzvah of being a Jewish teacher very seriously. He writes:

CHOOSING AND DECIDING TO TEACH

A roving commission of the foremost Rabbis was once sent to encourage education and to establish schools. They came to a town where there was no trace of instruction nor any teacher. They addressed the inhabitants and asked them to produce the guardians of the town. The heads of the municipality appeared. "These are not the guardians of the city," the Rabbis exclaimed. "Who are the guardians then?" asked the citizens with astonishment. "The guardians of the town are the teachers."

T. Jerus. Hag. I. 76

You have considered all the reasons why you cannot teach. You also know full well the reasons you should teach. Even more, you know that you are compelled—called—to teach in a Jewish school. It is something that you cannot resist. It is what you are going to be, one of the guardians of your town…

I welcome you to a long tradition of Jewish teaching. A great adventure and a great reward lie ahead. Teaching is a redemptive act. It is a concrete commitment to peace and justice, to transforming the world to express its Divine-given maximum potential.

As you teach, you can literally feed the hungry, shelter the homeless, free those who are imprisoned, and train a generation of peacemakers. As a teacher, you have the reward of learning from your students. Ben Zoma, a rabbinic figure, taught us, "Who is wise? An individual who learns from every person." The Bible teaches, "From all my students I have gained wisdom." Welcome to your calling. Welcome to your task. Welcome to your reward.

How do you plan on fulfilling the mitzvah of being a Jewish teacher?

_____

_____

_____

NASO נָשֹׂא

וידבר יהוה אל משה לאמר

נשא

את ראש

בני גרשון גם

לבית אבתם

למשפחתם

NUMBERS 4:21–7:89

- There are still more rules for the Kohanim.
- The clans of Levi are assigned to moving the Mishkan.
- Next come the rules of **Sota** and the **Nazir**.
- The Kohanim are taught the words of **Birkat Kohanim**.
- The chieftains bring gifts.
- Moses talks to God in the Tent of Meeting.

OUR TEXT—NUMBERS 7:9

In this *parashah* we learn something of the *Kohanim's* special relationship with the Mishkan and the Ark of the Covenant.

וְלִבְנֵי קְהָת לֹא נָתָן כִּי־עֲבֹדַת הַקֹּדֶשׁ עֲלֵהֶם בַּכָּתֵף יִשָּׂאוּ.

נ	[נתן] = _____	בָּנִים = _____	ב
	עֲבוֹדָה = work/service	כִּי = _____	כ
ע	עַל = _____	כָּתֵף = shoulder	
	עֲלֵיהֶם = _____	לֹא = _____	ל
ק	[קדש] = _____	[נשא] = carry/lift	נ
	קְהָת = Kehat	יִשָּׂאוּ = _____	

9. _____ וְלִבְנֵי קְהָת לֹא נָתָן

_____ כִּי־עֲבֹדַת הַקֹּדֶשׁ עֲלֵהֶם

_____ בַּכָּתֵף יִשָּׂאוּ.

Now try reading this verse without vowels:

ולבני קהת לא נתן כי עבדת הקדש עלהם בכתף ישאו

EXPLORING OUR TEXT

Jacob Milgrom is one of today's leading Bible scholars and teachers. Here is a short segment of his commentary on Numbers published by the Jewish Publication Society. This is an adult, scholarly piece of writing. Do your best with it. See what lessons you can find in it.

To leave the sanctuary or its sancta without protection was unthinkable. Indeed, no sooner did Israel recover the Ark from the Philistine than someone was consecrated to guard it (1 Sam. 7:1). Of the two major Levitical roles, guarding and removal, there can be no doubt which was more important: The labor force was to be activated only when the camp was on the move, but guard duty was perpetual responsibility. It is significant that when the Levites subsequently were apportioned their share of the Midianite spoils the text twice identifies them as the Tabernacle guards (Num. 31:30,47).

Ancient Israel's neighbors employed not only human but divine guards for the protection of the sanctuary. Thus the *lamassu* and *sedu* in Mesopotamia and the gargoyles in Egypt were placed in front of the temples. Israel, however, knew not of the world of demons. Its monotheism allowed for only one power in the universe. Therefore it had but to protect the sanctuary against the only remaining adversary—man.

Guard duty was performed around the clock. The nomadic *sadin* in the Arabian desert slept in the sanctuary of which he was the solitary guardian. So, at Shiloh, did young Samuel (1 Sam. 3:2-3), to whom this task was delegated because the priest Eli was nearly blind. According to one tradition, young Joshua was the full-time guard of the wilderness Tent-shrine since he "would not stir out of the Tent" (Exod. 33:11). Priests performed nocturnal guard duty in Mari (ARM 10.50.16-17) and in the Hittite temples ("Instructions for Temple Officials" iii. 9,12,30; ANET, p. 209). Akkadian *nasaru massarta* (the root [נצר] also means "guard" in Hebrew, e.g., Isa. 27:3).

In the Second (Herodian) Temple, the Levitical watch was stationed at twenty-four points: the five Temple gates, the four inner corners, the five gates of the Temple court, the latter's four corners, behind the Temple building, and in five chambers (Mish. Mid. I; Mish. Tam. I:I). According to Josephus, more than two hundred gatekeepers closed the Temple gates and these men probably remained at their posts (Apion 2,119). Philo records that Levite guards made the rounds day and night to ensure the purity of the Temple and its visitors (I Laws 156). These guards were supervised by an officer of the Temple Mount who at night "would make the rounds of every watch preceded by kindled torches" (Mish. Mid. I:2; cf. Papyrus Oxyrhinchus 5.840).

The guard duty was not just ceremonial. During the administration of the Roman governor Coponius (6-9 C. E.), the Temple was defiled apparently by Samaritans who painted bones there at night (Josephus, Ant. 18.29-30). When the object of *mishmeret* is not the Tabernacle but the Lord, the context always involves proscriptions and taboos, so that the basic meaning of "guarding" is extended to that of being wary of violations, for example, regarding priestly consecration (Lev. 8:35); sexual prohibitions (Lev. 18:30); the defiled priest and his food (Lev. 22:9); God's direction for the march (Num. 9:19,23); priestly taboos concerning the altar and the shrine (Num. 18:7a); and the priestly gifts (Numbers 18:18).

Mishmeret in the general sense of "duties" is not found until later biblical sources. *Mishmeret* as a service unit, the sense it assumes in rabbinic literature on the Second Temple, does not occur in the Bible at all. Thus the use of *mishmeret* exclusively for guard duty in the perspectives of Numbers attests to their antiquity.

ad loc, page 341-2

What important insights about the *Kohanim* and the *Mishkan* can you find in Milgrom's comments?

_____

_____

_____

MITZVAH OF THE WEEK
נְשִׂאַת אֲרוֹן הַקֹּדֶשׁ   CARRYING THE ARK

It was mitzvah for the *Kohanim* to carry *Aron ha-Kodesh* (the Holy Ark) on their shoulders whenever the need arose for it to be transported from one place to another. Most authorities agree that the entire tribe of *Levi* was permitted to carry the Holy Ark; in other words, both *Kohanim* and *Levi'im*. It was forbidden to transport the Holy Ark in a wagon (coach) or on the back of an animal.

Sefer ha-Hinukh

IT AIN'T HEAVY, IT'S MY TORAH!

> The first ark for the Ten Commandments was built while the Children of Israel were wandering in the desert. It was made of acacia wood covered with gold. A midrash says it was so heavy that it took the strength of many men even to budge it. But, then the midrash explained, once they lifted it, it carried its carriers.
>
> David Moshe of Tchortkov was a hasidic rabbi. Once, during the dedication of a new Sefer Torah, he had to lift a large heavy scroll for a long time. One of his students offered to help him, but he said: "Once you've picked it up, it is no longer heavy."

We no longer have an ark of the covenant. We cannot in our day and age literally perform this mitzvah. Make a metaphor out of it. How would you explain today's meaning of carrying the ark on your shoulders, not in a wagon!

_____

_____

_____

BE-HA'ALOTEKHA

בהעלתך

וידבר יהוה אל משה לאמר
דבר אל אהרן ואמרת אליו
בהעלתך
את הנרת
אל מול
פני המנורה
יאירו שבעת הנרות

NUMBERS 8:1–12:16

- The menorah is described.
- The members of the tribe of Levi become assistants to the Priests.
- We are taught the laws of the firstborn and of Passover.
- The Children of Israel again complain about food and a fire breaks out.
- The council of seventy elders is established.
- Moses marries a Cushite woman, Miriam complains and she gets leprosy.

OUR TEXT—NUMBERS 9:11

This is the *parashah* that introduces many of the mitzvot of Passover. Read our verse and figure out the Seder practices it describes.

בַּחֹדֶשׁ הַשֵּׁנִי בְּאַרְבָּעָה עָשָׂר יוֹם בֵּין הָעַרְבַּיִם יַעֲשׂוּ אֹתוֹ עַל-מַצּוֹת וּמְרֹרִים יֹאכְלֻהוּ.

מ	מַצָּה = _____	[אכל] = eat	א
	מָרוֹר = _____	יֹאכְלֻהוּ = they will eat it	
ע	עַל = _____	אַרְבָּעָה עָשָׂר = fourteen	
	[עשה] = _____	אֹתוֹ = _____	
	יַעֲשׂוּ = _____	בֵּין הָעַרְבַּיִם = twilight	ב
שׁ	שֵׁנִי = second	חֹדֶשׁ = _____	ח
		יוֹם = _____	י

11. _____ בַּחֹדֶשׁ הַשֵּׁנִי

_____ בְּאַרְבָּעָה עָשָׂר יוֹם

_____ בֵּין הָעַרְבַּיִם יַעֲשׂוּ אֹתוֹ

_____ עַל-מַצּוֹת וּמְרֹרִים יֹאכְלֻהוּ.

What specific parts of the Seder come from this verse? _____

_____

_____

Now try reading this verse without vowels:

בחדש השני בארבעה עשר יום בין הערבים יעשו אתו על מצות ומררים יאכלהו

EXPLORING OUR TEXT

This lesson will be much easier to do if you use a Haggadah.

Pesah has many mitzvot. Maimonides says there are 8 all together. Six of these involve removing the *Hametz*, one involves eating *Matzah* (together with *Maror*). One of them involves telling the Pesah story (through the Seder). We are going to look at the meaning of three terms: *Hametz*, *Matzah* and *Maror*.

HAMETZ

1. Define *Hametz*:

   _____
   _____
   _____

2. Describe what Jews traditionally do with *Hametz* before Passover. (Look in the section of the Haggadah that describes what to do before the Seder.)

   _____
   _____
   _____
   _____

3. What do you think is the "meaning" of removing *Hametz* from our homes and not eating it?

   _____
   _____
   _____

These two meditations are found in the Haggadah. One of them is read before searching for the *Hametz*. The other is read before burning the *Hametz*.

SEARCHING FOR HAMETZ

May it be Your will, God, that we merit to search our souls for the blemishes that we foolishly placed in it by following the evil inclination's advice, and that we merit true repentance. Please, God, in Your mercy and for Your honor, help us to be protected from the prohibition of *hametz,* even from a crumb; this year and every year, for as long as we live. Amen, may it be Your will.

BURNING THE HAMETZ

May it be Your will, God, that just as I have removed the *hametz* from my house and properties, so too, should You remove all the forces of evil, and the spirit of evil shall be removed from the earth. May our evil inclination be removed from us and may you grant us a pure heart. May all the forces of the "Other Side" and wickedness vanish like smoke and the kingdom of the wicked be eradicated. May You destroy all those that challenge the Divine Presence with vengeance and judgment, just as You destroyed the Egyptians and their idols in those days at this season, Amen.

4. Based on these meditations, what lesson can be learned from the searching, removing, and burning of *Hametz*?

_____

_____

MATZAH

1. Define *Matzah*:

_____

_____

2. In the Seder, we give Matzah two different origins. What are they? How can both opposite origins be true? (Hint: Look in *Ha Lahma Anya* right at the beginning of the *Maggid* section, the telling of the story part of the Seder and in the *What is Pesah, Matzah, and Maror?* piece at the end of *Maggid*.)

_____

_____

3. What do you think is the "meaning" of eating *Matzah*?

_____

_____

MAROR

1. What is *Maror*?

   _____

   _____

2. What is the "meaning" of *maror*?

   _____

   _____

Rabbi Nahman was a Hasid, a mystic, and a storyteller. Here are a couple of his comments about the deep meaning of *Maror*.

> ....Let us partake of the *Maror*—let us accept the painful experience of our past. We must realize that our personal *Maror* was necessary to implement our "redemption." We need to recognize that the depth of feeling we have for God, the depth of understanding we have of life, of ourselves, is only because of our past adversity (*Nahat HaShulhan*).
>
> The knowledge that God is always with us, the awareness that God will never forsake us—this is true peace and harmony. It is the tranquility and harmony we experience when we know that our life has meaning and purpose. It is the sweet serenity and at-one-ness with God that we feel when we realize that we are fulfilling God's Will.
>
> But we would never know it, we could never become aware of it, unless we first experience bitterness, the absence of serenity and peace; just as we cannot appreciate light without prior knowledge of darkness (*Lekkutei Maharan* I, 27:7; *Lekkutei Halakhot, Netilat Yadayim* 6:16).

3. What does Rabbi Nahman add to your understanding of *Maror*?

   _____

   _____

   _____

MITZVAH OF THE WEEK
חָמֵץ וּמַצָּה Hametz and Matzah

REMOVAL OF HAMETZ

It is a positive commandment of the Torah to remove the _hametz_ before the time when it is forbidden to eat, as it is said: "The first day ye shall put away _hametz_ out of your house" (Exodus 12:15), and, on the basis of a tradition, it has been learned that this "the first" is the fourteenth day _of Nisan_. Proof for this commandment is written in the Torah: "Thou shalt not offer the blood of My sacrifice with leavened bread" (ibid., 34:25); that is to say: Do not slaughter the Passover sacrifice when the _hametz_ is still in existence. The slaughtering of the Passover sacrifice is the afternoon of the fourteenth day.

What is this removal of which the Torah speaks? It is that one should annul the _hametz_ in his heart and consider it as dust; and he should take to heart that there is no _hametz_ at all in his possession; it is as dust, and as something of which there is no need whatsoever. According to the interpretations of the scholars, one is required to search for the _hametz_ in hiding-places and holes and to remove it entirely from his property. Thus, according to the interpretations of the scholars, _hametz_ is sought out and removed at night—at the beginning of the night of the fourteenth by the light of a candle—because at night all the people are at home and the light of a candle is helpful in searching.

EATING MATZAH

It is a positive commandment of the Torah to eat _matzah_ on the night of the fifteenth (of Nisan), as it is said: at evening ye shall eat _matzah_ (Exodus 12:18), in every place and at all times. This eating (of _matzah_) is not dependent on the Passover sacrifice. If one desires, one eats _matzah_ or rice or millet or parched grain or fruit. However, only on the night of the fifteenth is it obligatory; and if one eats (a piece of _matzah_) the size of an olive one has performed the duty (ibid.,6:1).

All are obliged to eat _matzah_, even women and servants. A child who is able to eat a piece of bread should be educated in the commandments and be fed _matzah_ the size of an olive (ibid., 6:10). According to the interpolations of the scholars one must not conclude by eating anything after the _matzah_... The sages have forbidden the eating of _matzah_ on the the eve of Passover so that there be a recognition of its eating in the evening... The early sages would hunger on the eve of Passover in order to eat the _matzah_ with good appetite (ibid., 6:11-12).

Mishneh Torah

The Great Matzah Debate

HAND-BAKED MATZOT

Until the middle of the nineteenth century all *matzot* were baked by hand according to detailed specifications that provided that: the kneading of the dough be continuous to prevent leavening from setting in; the dough be guarded from sudden heat until it is placed in the oven; no particles of the dough be left on the kneading table as they might become leaven and thus make the rest of the dough unfit for use; during the kneading all kernels of wheat not crushed during the milling must be sifted out. To assure that all these precautions were taken, the work was entrusted to adults only.

In many Jewish communities each householder had *matzot* baked in the local bakery on a day set aside for him and he supervised the entire operation so that he might share in the *mitzvah.* He and members of his family appeared before dawn at the bakery so that they might participate from the start to the finish. Extra help was still needed to handle the seasonal demand and employment was thus provided for many unskilled persons—the aged, women and children—who were engaged by the bakers as helpers.

Many a poor Jew earned the wherewithal to observe Passover by working in the *matzah* bakery. Special tasks were assigned to each employee, many of whom became expert in their particular functions. In the Mishnaic period, evidently three women sufficed for the process: one to knead, another to roll the dough, and a third to bake. In the course of later generations, a bureaucracy of functionaries developed. The *Mehl-Meister* measured the amount of flour required by the kneader. The *Vasser-Gisser* poured the cold water into the dough as the kneader required. The expert kneader may have had a number of assistants who continued the kneading of the batter, rolling the water out of the dough and thinning it into cakes. Then the *Redler* took over and with his cog wheel he made the perforation. He, in turn, passed the batter to the *Derlanger*, who bore it on a rolling pin to the *Shieber*. The latter, usually an expert at his task, was responsible for placing the dough in the oven. When the *matzah* was baked, he removed it from the oven and handed it over to the *Treger*, who proudly carried the finished product to the place where it was stored or packed.

It was the custom to start the fire for the baking of the *matzot* with the willows and the lulav used on *Sukkot* for, having been used for one mitzvah, they should be used for another.

THE DEBATE ON MACHINE-MADE MATZOT

In about 1857 the first *matzah*-baking machine was invented in Austria, beginning a heated controversy that raged for half a century. The newly invented machine kneaded the dough and rolled it through two metal rollers from which it came out thin, perforated and round. It was then placed in an oven. As the corners of the dough, cut to make the *matzot* round, were re-used, it was feared that the time elapsing until these pieces of dough were used again might allow them to become leavened. A later machine was developed that produced square matzot so that there would be no leftovers.

Other subsequent improvements in the machinery speeded up the entire process of production, leading to a general acceptance for the modern method. Meanwhile, many distinguished rabbis raised their voices in protest against the new machine, while others, equally respected, permitted its use.

1. What is your opinion? Should machine made *matzah* be Kosher for Passover. Should it be Kosher for Seder?

   _____

   _____

2. Even though the answer is almost obvious from our practice today, what do you think were the big issues in the debate?

   _____

   _____

   One of...most telling arguments was that the opportunity given to the poor to earn money for their Passover needs by working in *matzah* bakeries would be denied to them, as the use of machinery required fewer manual workers.
   He and his adherents also argued that *matzah shemurah*, particularly, must be made with the intention of fulfilling the precept which requires the understanding of a mature adult. They also claimed that there was a suspicion that the pieces of dough left in the wheels of the machine, which were difficult to clean, would become leavened. In the forefront of the rabbis who permitted the use of machinery was Joseph Saul Nathanson of Lemberg. They refuted the arguments of the opposition. If concern need be expressed about the displacement of the hand-bakers, the same solicitude should be shown to scribes whose replacement by the printing press had been universally accepted.
   They also held that these *matzot* are baked with the intent to comply with the law, as it is necessary for an adult to start the machine. They had no fear that dough would be left in the machines as they are cleaned well and often. Furthermore, they contended that the machine speeds the process and is more efficient than the men and women who worked in the bakery day and night. The views of Nathanson and those who sided with him have been accepted by most Jews.

   Philip Goodman, The Passover Anthology, JPS 1973

What can this debate teach us about the meaning of *matzah*?

_____

_____

_____

SHELAH LEKHA

שְׁלַח-לְךָ

וידבר יהוה אל משה לאמר

שלח לך אנשים ויתרו את ארץ כנען אשר אני נתן לבני ישראל איש אחד איש אחד למטה אבתיו תשלחו כל נשיא בהם

NUMBERS 13:1–15:41

- **Twelve spies** are sent to the Land of Israel and they make a report.
- The Children of Israel become afraid and **rebel**.
- God threatens to wipe out the Children of Israel but relents when Moses intercedes.
- God then decides that **all who knew Egypt would not enter the Land of Israel**.
- And, we are taught the laws of **Tzitzit**.

OUR TEXT—NUMBERS 15:38

In this *sidrah* we meet the third paragraph of the Shema. It has a new mitzvah to teach us.

דַּבֵּר אֶל־בְּנֵי יִשְׂרָאֵל וְאָמַרְתָּ אֲלֵהֶם וְעָשׂוּ לָהֶם צִיצִת עַל־כַּנְפֵי בִגְדֵיהֶם לְדֹרֹתָם וְנָתְנוּ עַל־צִיצִת הַכָּנָף פְּתִיל תְּכֵלֶת.

ל	לָהֶם = לְ + הֵם = ____	א	אֶל = ____
נ	[נתן] = ____		אֲלֵהֶם = ____
ע	עַל = ____		[אמר] = ____
	[עשה] = ____	ב	בְּנֵי יִשְׂרָאֵל = ____
פ	פְּתִיל = thread	ד	[דבר] = ____
צ	צִיצִת = ____		דּוֹר = ____
ת	תְּכֵלֶת = light blue	כ	כָּנָף = corner

.38 דַּבֵּר אֶל־בְּנֵי יִשְׂרָאֵל _____

וְאָמַרְתָּ אֲלֵהֶם _____

וְעָשׂוּ לָהֶם צִיצִת _____

עַל־כַּנְפֵי בִגְדֵיהֶם לְדֹרֹתָם _____

וְנָתְנוּ עַל־צִיצִת הַכָּנָף _____

פְּתִיל תְּכֵלֶת. _____

Now try reading this verse without vowels:

דבר אל בני ישראל ואמרת אלהם ועשו להם ציצת על כנפי בגדיהם לדרתם ונתנו על ציצת הכנף פתיל תכלת

EXPLORING OUR TEXT

The *Tallit* is a four-cornered garment with fringes on each of the four corners. Each of the fringes is called a tzitzit and must consist of an exact formula of 5 knots and 39 wrappings.

The mitzvah of *tzitzit* is mentioned twice in the Torah. Look at these two statements of the commandment. What do they actually command?

> Make tassels for yourself on the four corners of your garment which you use for protection (Deuteronomy 22:12).

> Make *tzitzit* for yourself on the corners of your garments... The *tzitzit* will be for you, that when you see them, you will **remember** all the LORD's mitzvot and perform them. So you will not search after your own heart and let your eyes lead you into lust.

> That you will **remember** and perform all My miztvot and be holy to your God. I am *Adonai*, Your God... (Numbers 15:38-40)

_____

_____

_____

_____

1. How do *tzitziyyot* help a Jew remember not to sin? Can you see the direct connection between this *aggadah* and the text from Numbers 15:39?

   > There once was a man who paid great attention to following the laws of the mitzvah of the *tzitzit*. Once he heard of a working-woman in a port city who charged 400 pieces of gold for her services. He sent her the 400 gold pieces and arranged a rendezvous. At the appointed time, he arrived at her city and waited outside her door until he was let in. She had arranged seven couches, one on top of the other. Six were of silver and the seventh was of gold. Next to the beds were seven ladders. Six were of silver and the seventh was of gold.

   > The woman was sitting naked on the seventh bed. The man was about to sin with the woman when his *tzitziyyot* hit him in the face. He slid down and sat on the floor. The woman joined him on the floor and said, "By Jupiter! I will not let you go until you tell me what you found wrong with me." The man said, "I swear that I have never seen a woman as beautiful as you! But our God has given us a commandment known as *tzitzit*." He then explained the mitzvah.

   > The woman said to him, "I will not let you go until you tell me your name, your city, and the school where you studied Torah." ...She sold all of her possessions except for her bed. One-third of the money she gave to the government (to allow her to leave), and one-

third of the money she gave to the poor. All she kept was a third of the money and her seven beds. She went to Rabbi Hiyya's academy and studied to become a Jew. Eventually she and the man who had visited her were married. Rabbi Hiyya told her, "The same beds you used for sin, you may now enjoy in a permissible manner" (*Menahot* 44a).

_____

_____

_____

2. How do the *tzitziyyot* help to remind Jews of the responsibility of the mitzvot? How does looking at them help to urge us to do mitzvot?

FACT:

 248 = number of bones in the human body
 248 = number of positive ("Thou Shalt") mitzvot
 365 = number of days in a year
 365 = number of negative ("Thou Shalt Not") mitzvot
 (613) = total number of mitzvot

FACT:

א	Alef	1	ל	Lamed	30
ב	Bet	2	מ	Mem	40
ג	Gimel	3	נ	Nun	50
ד	Dalet	4	ס	Sameh	60
ה	Heh	5	ע	Ayin	70
ו	Vav	6	פ	Peh	80
ז	Zayin	7	צ	Tzade	90
ח	Het	8	ק	Kuf	100
ט	Tet	9	ר	Resh	200
י	Yud	10	ש	Shin	300
כ	Kaf	20	ת	Tav	400

צ Tzade = _____
י Yud ≈ _____
צ Tzade = _____
י Yud ≈ _____
ת Tav ≈ _____

_____ value of the word *tzitzit*
+ 8 = number of strings in a *tzitzit*
+ 5 = number of double knots in a *tzitzit*

_____

= _____

The 8 threads remind us of the 8 days that elapsed between the Families-of-Israel leaving Egypt and their arriving at the Reed Sea.

The five knots correspond to the five books of Moses.

Tur, O.H. 24

The 39 wrappings correspond to the numeric value of the words יהוה אֶחָד, God is one.

The four corners remind us that no matter in what direction one looks, God is there.

O.H. 8:4

MITZVAH OF THE WEEK
צִיצִית Tzitzit

1. The actual mitzvah taught in the Torah was to put fringes on every four-cornered piece of clothing you wore. Originally, if you didn't wear four-cornered clothes, you didn't have to do this mitzvah.

2. Because Jews want to perform as many mitzvot as possible, the rabbis suggest that one intentionally wear a four-cornered garment in order to do this mitzvah and say the brakhah. The *tallit katan* (a.k.a. *tzis-tzis*) is a small *tallit*, worn like an undershirt, which fulfills this mitzvah.

3. The custom of wearing a big *tallit* during morning services (and a few other ocassions) grew from the *tallit katan*. It was a way of adding "honor" and "beauty" to the mitzvah. Jews like to embellish their mitzvot. It is the same reason we don't use an ordinary cup for Kiddush, even though any cup is "kosher" for Kiddush.

4. Today, in many settings, women are also wearing *Tallitot*.

A GIRL'S 'TALLIT'

I'm a bit exhausted. I've just been all over the city shopping for a *tallit*. For my daughter. During the last 10 years, I've prayed with women wearing *tallitot, kippot* and even wrapping themselves in *tefillin*. It's always been a bit of a conflict for me, at times an amusement, and at other moments a fascination, watching these objects evolve into appropriate feminine designs. On the one hand, I believe in women's complete equality within Jewish observance. On the other, I'm not certain that wrapping parts of the body in what has traditionally been a man's holy object is a necessity of women's liberation.

A year ago, when I realized that my daughter might actually participate in the donning of these garments and objects, my rather distant reaction became immediate, the subject of several discussions. Wearing the *tallit* for a bat mitzvah is not mandatory, I was told. It's optional. Inwardly, I found myself hoping that my daughter would choose not to. But, particularly after Camp Ramah, "where everyone wears a *tallit,*" she has chosen to wear one. First we went to a bookstore on one side of the street. The man who greeted us as we walked in was from Iran. I immediately thought to myself, "In their community women don't wear *tallitot*. This guy is going to think I'm crazy."

He didn't. He pulled out a drawer with the women's *tallitot*. One pink *tallit* after another. "So this," I said to myself, "is what the *tallit* makers think of as women's liberation." "I don't wear pink," my daughter said. "Good for her," I thought. Then she found some others, nice ones, silk, multicolored, batik, scenes of Jerusalem. She held each one in her hands. Folding them one way. Folding them another. I remembered taking my nephew a month earlier. We were in and out in a split second.

My daughter was going to be different. She was determined to make this as experiential as the Gap or the Limited. As she stood back showing me the *tallitot*, and I was confronted with the reality of her draped in this traditional men's garment, I had to hold myself back from saying, "Take it off. You look ridiculous." But before I had a chance, she removed it. I was about to breathe a sign of relief when she said, "Let's go across the street now, and see what they have." She was enjoying this.

Across the street stood an Orthodox women in a *sheitel*. "Do you have *tallitot* for women?" I asked. She took a deep breath, "I guess." "Does that means 'yes' or 'no?'" I asked. She ignored me and moments later brought out the pink stuff. "Do you have anything else?" She motioned to a rack of hanging *tallitot*. There my daughter tried about 10 more, shaking her head after each one. The woman had disappeared. "O.K.," my daughter said, "now , let's go somewhere else…"

…I wonder if I'm ever going to get used to seeing her wearing her *tallit* in synagogue. I know that when I put on my *tallit* I feel a sense of holiness; I feel that wrapped in my oversized *tallit* I look biblical. I feel that I blend in with the other men; that we look like one. Will she feel the same? Or will she feel that this only a symbol of achievement from the women's movement? Or does the fact that she sees her fellow campers at Ramah wearing one give her a connection to that experience that has so deeply touched her soul?

Will it connect her to Sarah, Leah and Rebecca or more to Betty Friedan, Letty Cottin Pogrebin and Rabbi Laura Geller? And what's wrong with that? As with all Jewish rituals, traditions, holidays and celebrations, I tend to look at many sides, exploring them, questioning them, searching for meanings and origins. With the woman's *tallit* I do the same, particularly as my daughter becomes a bat mitzvah. I have to ask myself:

Was wearing one born as a symbol of creation, where the feminist movement created a new equal ritual? Or was it born as a symbol of defiance, where the women said, "Look, men, we can do just as you do"? I'm not sure that any of this is my issue. It's hers. She's the one who is being bat mitzvahed. She's the one who is becoming responsible for the commandments. She is the one who is entering into Judaism as a woman. She'll resolve these questions for herself. Daddy's going to have to let go. That's part of what bat mitzvah is all about.

Gary Wexler

KORAH

קֹרַח

ויקח קרח בן קהת בן יצהר בן לוי ודתן ואבירם בני אליאב ואון בן פלת בני ראובן

NUMBERS 16:1–18:32

- **Korah and his followers rebel** against Moses and Aaron.
- God ends the rebellion.
- Then we are taught more laws:
- Duties of the Kohanim and the Levites.
- Laws of the firstborn that should go to the priests.
- Laws of tithing.

OUR TEXT—NUMBERS 18:24

A tithe is ten percent. In this *parashah* we have a mitzvah that has to do with tithing.

כִּי אֶת־מַעְשַׂר בְּנֵי־יִשְׂרָאֵל אֲשֶׁר יָרִימוּ לַיהוה תְּרוּמָה נָתַתִּי לַלְוִיִּם...

נ _____	[נתן] = _____	א אֲשֶׁר = _____
	נָתַתִּי = _____	ב בְּנֵי־יִשְׂרָאֵל = _____
ר lift _____	[רום] = _____	כ כִּי = _____
	יָרִימוּ = _____	ל לֵוִי = Levite ....
	תְּרוּמָה = _____	מ מַעְשַׂר = tithe ....

24. כִּי אֶת־מַעְשַׂר בְּנֵי־יִשְׂרָאֵל _____
אֲשֶׁר יָרִימוּ לַיהוה תְּרוּמָה _____
נָתַתִּי לַלְוִיִּם... _____

Now try reading this verse without vowels:

כי את מעשר בני ישראל אשר ירימו ליהוה תרומה נתתי ללוים

EXPLORING OUR TEXT

The word *Ma'aser* means a tenth. To understand how it impacts on the idea of tzedakah we need to look at the rules for Jewish farmers. While there are all kinds of rules—rules about vineyards, rules about orchards, rules about herds, and so on—we are only going to look at the rules on fields. Use a piece of paper with a grid of squares 10 across by 10 down as your field. As you read each of these rules, mark off the portions of the field that must be taken as tithes.

MA'ASER

1/10th of everything that grows in the land, whether it is grain that has grown in the ground, or fruit that has grown on a tree, must be set apart and given to Adonai (Leviticus 27:30). This means giving it to the tribe of Levi for the work which they do in running the worship in the tent of meeting (Numbers 18:21). Mark the *Ma'aser* on your field by coloring in 1/10th of your crop (10 squares).

MA'ASER SHENI

Take 1/10th of the crop that remains after the Ma'aser and eat it before Adonai your God in the place that is chosen for the Divine Dwelling place (the Tabernacle and later the Temple) (Deuteronomy 14:23).

Ma'aser Sheni means the "second tithe" (1/10th). There are 90 squares left in your field after *Ma'aser*. We need to mark 1/10th of the 90. Mark the *Ma'aser Sheni* on your field by marking 9 more squares.

Ma'aser Oni means "the poor tithe" (1/10th). Every third year, the Torah tells us to take the second 1/10th (after the *Ma'aser* has already been taken) and use it as a gift to the poor instead of a personal pilgrimage food. Because we've already marked these squares, don't mark anything.

PE'AH

And when you reap the harvest of your fields, you shall not totally harvest the field. You must leave the corners of the field...for the poor and the stranger (Leviticus 23:22).

Pe'ah (means corner). This mitzvah orders farmers to leave the corners of their fields (at least 1/60th) for people in need. This allows poor people to come and do the work to harvest their own food, without having to ask for tzedakah. To indicate *Pe'ah* mark and color two squares of your field.

SHIKHEHAH

When you reap the harvest of your field and you forget a sheaf in the field, do not go back to get it. Leave it for the stranger, the fatherless and the widow (Deuteronomy 24:19).

Shikhehah means "forgotten." This a mitzvah for which you can't plan. You can't plan to forget something. You also can't ever know how much you'll forget. For the sake of this exercise, mark two more squares for *shikhehah*.

LEKET

And when you reap the harvest of your fields...you shall not gather the gleanings of your harvest (Leviticus 19:9).

Leket means "gleanings." Gleanings are things that the people harvesting dropped or didn't bother to pick. Like *shikhehah*, you can't plan the amount of gleanings that will be left. For this exercise, mark two squares of *Leket*.

Pe'ah, Shikhehah and **Leket** are all gifts to the poor, which allow the poor to work for their own food without having to beg or ask for help. How much should be given to tzedakah? If the person can afford it, as much as is needed by the poor. But if the person cannot afford that much, the person should give up to 20% of what s/he has. That is the highest degree of tzedakah. 10% is considered average, and less than that is considered "cheap" (*Yoreh De'ah* 249.1).

1. Based on the texts you've studied on farming, where do you think the rabbis came up with these figures?

   _____
   _____
   _____

2. Why do you think the rabbis set two limits on giving, one for how much one could give and another for how little one should give?

   _____
   _____
   _____

MITZVAH OF THE WEEK
מַעֲשׂר MA'ASER

Allocations is a big word, one that has to do with money. Collecting tzedakah is only part of the job. It is a big responsibility, but the other responsibility is in deciding how the money will be allocated. The big problem with tzedakah is that the need is bigger than the resources, so someone is forced to make the choice of which good work to fund. Working on allocations is not an easy or fun responsibility, but it is an important one.

Use this exercise to help in your allocation process:

PART I—THE AMOUNT OF MONEY

A) The amount of tzedakah money we have to distribute is _____

B) With one dollar I could buy myself _____

   With five dollars I could buy myself _____

   With twenty dollars I could buy myself _____

   If I had all of our tzedakah money to spend on me, I would buy myself _____

C) A mitzvah that could be accomplished with one dollar is _____

A mitzvah that could be accomplished with five dollars is _____

A mitzvah that could be accomplished with twenty dollars is _____

A mitzvah that could be accomplished with a hundred dollars is _____

PART II—OUR PAST HISTORY OF GIVING

What do we know about where our tzedakah money went last year?

Place	Kind of Work	Amount

PART III—PLANNING FOR THIS YEAR

What sort of rules or standards should we set for the people or places that receive tzedakah from us?

1) _____

2) _____

3) _____

Based on these standards, what questions do we want to ask about each recipient?

1) _____

2) _____

3) _____

4) _____

5) _____

Use a blank sheet of paper to decide where you want your tzedakah money to go to this year.

HUKKAT חֻקַּת

וידבר יהוה אל משה
ואל אהרן לאמר
זאת **חקת** התורה
אשר צוה יהוה לאמר
דבר אל בני ישראל ויקחו אליך
פרה אדמה תמימה אשר אין
בה מום אשר לא עלה עליה על

NUMBERS 19:1–22:1

- There are still more laws to teach: Laws of the **red heifer**; rituals and laws of **purification**.
- Miriam and Aaron die.
- The people complain again and **Moses strikes the rock** for water.
- The King of Edom refuses to let the Children of Israel pass through his land.
- They fight battles with the Canaanites, Amorites and Og, king of Bashan.

OUR TEXT—NUMBERS 20:11

In this week's *sidrah*, Moses commits the "sin" that keeps him from ever entering the land of Israel.

וַיָּ֨רֶם מֹשֶׁ֜ה אֶת־יָד֗וֹ וַיַּ֧ךְ אֶת־הַסֶּ֛לַע בְּמַטֵּ֖הוּ פַּעֲמָ֑יִם וַיֵּצְא֙וּ מַ֣יִם רַבִּ֔ים וַתֵּ֥שְׁתְּ הָעֵדָ֖ה וּבְעִירָֽם׃

11. _____ וַיָּרֶם מֹשֶׁה אֶת־יָדוֹ

ע	community = עֵדָה		cattle = בְּעִיר	ב
פ	time = פַּעַם		יָד = _____	י
	_____ = פַּעֲמַיִם		[יצא] = _____	
ר	much/a lot = רַבָּה		staff/stick = מַטֶּה	מ
	_____ = רַבִּים		מַטֵּהוּ = _____	
	lift up = [רום]		מַיִם = _____	
	_____ = יָרֶם		hit = [נכה]	נ
שׁ	drink = [שתה]		וַיַּךְ = _____	
	_____ = וַתֵּשְׁתְּ		rock = סֶלַע	ס

_____ וַיַּךְ אֶת־הַסֶּלַע בְּמַטֵּהוּ פַּעֲמָיִם

_____ וַיֵּצְאוּ מַיִם רַבִּים

_____ וַתֵּשְׁתְּ הָעֵדָה וּבְעִירָם.

Now try reading this verse without vowels:

וירם משה את ידו ויך את הסלע במטהו פעמים ויצאו מים רבים ותשת העדה ובעירם

EXPLORING OUR TEXT

When the commentators read this story carefully, they wound up disagreeing on Moses' "crime." They came up with a number of different possibilities.

Maimonides: His sin was that he got angry and insulted the people rather than being patient and working with them.

Nahmanides: His sin was comparing himself to God, by saying, "Shall *we* bring forth water for you..." rather than giving God all the credit.

Albo: His sin was lack of faith. He did not believe that God's command to talk to the rock would be enough to effect the miracle.

Rashi: He failed to reinforce the people's faith, because the miracle would have been greater if he had followed God's command and only spoken to the rock.

Read the entire story in Numbers 20 and decide which of these four interpretations you like, or if you can find a better one. Explain your thinking.

_____
_____
_____
_____
_____
_____

MITZVAH OF THE WEEK
לֹא תְּבַיֵּשׁ Do Not Embarrass

Though it is a little hard to find in the Torah, *Sefer ha-Hinnukh* tells us, "There is no greater anguish for a person than that of embarrassment, therefore, God commanded us not cause anyone else embarrassment, especially public embarrassment." (This is based on a midrashic reading of Leviticus 19:19, "Do not bear sin because of another...") In the Talmud we are told, "One who embarrasses another has no place in the world to come."

To understand this more deeply, look at this story from the Talmud:

A certain man had a friend named Kamtza and an enemy named Bar Kamtza. He once gave a party and ordered his servant to invite Kamtza. The man went and brought Bar Kamtza instead.

"What are you doing here?" the man said. Said Bar Kamtza, "Since I'm here, let me stay, and I'll pay for what I eat and drink."

"No," replied the man.

"Then let me pay half the cost of the party."

"No."

"Then let me pay for the entire party!"

"No, again."

And the man took Bar Kamtza by the hand and threw him out.

Said Bar Kamtza, "Since the rabbis were all at the party and did not stop him, they must have agreed with him. I will go and inform against them to government." He went to the emperor and said, "The Jews are planning a revolt against you."

"How can I tell?" asked the emperor.

"Send them an offering for sacrifice at their Temple," said Bar Kamtza, "and see whether they will use it on their altar." So the emperor gave him a fine calf to deliver to the Jews. While on the way, he made a blemish on its mouth—or some say on its eye—in a place that would make it unfit for Jews to use on their altar.

The rabbis were inclined to sacrifice it anyway so as not to offend the government. But Rabbi Zechariah ben Avkilus said to them, "People will say that we offer blemished animals on our altar." Then it was proposed to kill Bar Kamtza so he would not inform the emperor that his offering had been refused. But again Rabbi Zechariah ben Avkilus interfered. "Are we to condemn a man to death for making a blemish on an animal meant for sacrifice?" he argued. As a result of this incident, Rabbi Johanan said, "Through the scrupulousness of Rabbi Zechariah ben Avkilus our house has been destroyed, our Temple burned, and our people exiled from their land."

Babylonian Talmud, tractate Gittin, 55b-56a

Give your explanation of the meaning of this *aggadah*.

_____

_____

_____

BALAK

בָּלָק

ויראבלק בן צפור את כל אשר עשה ישראל לאמרי

NUMBERS 22:2-25:9

- **Balak**, king of Moab, **sends for Bil'am** to curse the Children of Israel.
- Bil'am gets in a fight with **his ass**.
- Bil'am **blesses** the Children of Israel rather than **cursing** them.
- Bil'am prophesies that the foes of the Children of Israel will be conquered.
- The Children of Israel take part in the sacrifices to Ba'al-Peor.

OUR TEXT—NUMBERS 22:6

In this *sidrah* we have the story of Bil'am and his famous talking animal. Here is a foreign prophet who ultimately gives Israel a famous blessing.

...כִּי יָדַעְתִּי אֵת אֲשֶׁר־תְּבָרֵךְ מְבֹרָךְ וַאֲשֶׁר תָּאֹר יוּאָר.

ב	[ברך] = _____	curse = _____	**א** [ארר] =
	מְבֹרָךְ = _____	יוּאָר = _____	
	תְּבָרֵךְ = _____	תָּאֹר = _____	
י	[ידע] = know	אֲשֶׁר = _____	
	יָדַעְתִּי = _____	אֵת = _____	
כ	כִּי = _____		

6. ...כִּי יָדַעְתִּי _____

אֵת אֲשֶׁר־תְּבָרֵךְ מְבֹרָךְ _____

וַאֲשֶׁר תָּאֹר יוּאָר. _____

Now try reading this verse without vowels:

כי ידעתי אשר תברח מברך ואשר תאר יואר

EXPLORING OUR TEXT

In the Talmud, the rabbis claim that Bil'am is a false prophet, a soothsayer. It is a commandment not to listen to a false prophet. There is also a mitzvah to kill false prophets. The rabbis therefore wonder why God allows a false prophet to give an important blessing. To understand this question, we need to learn about false prophets. Here is a lesson from Joel's childhood Rabbi, Beryl D. Cohan:

> These prophets roamed the country the way gypsies do. There were many of them. The Bible speaks of "a company of prophets." This is true of all the false prophets: they moved about in large groups. The true prophets were lonely men, who lived and thought very much alone. They were alone even when they were in crowded cities. Notice, further, that these prophets played musical instruments: the psaltery, tabret, pipe, harp. By playing these instruments, at a fast tempo, no doubt, they "prophesied."
>
> The true prophets never engaged in much emotionalism; they did not rave and chant and carry on. They were highly thoughtful, serious men, given to meditation and prayer, pretty much in solitude. Heavy burdens rested on their hearts, and worries upon their minds. These raving, chanting, dancing prophets were foretelling the future—foretelling the future the way gypsy fortune-tellers do—and were paid for their services.
>
> The true prophets never received pay for their speaking. Perhaps you have heard your parents, or some other adults, talk about fortune-tellers. Their business is to predict what will happen. For that they are paid. Many people consult fortune-tellers; it is a foolish practice, but, nevertheless, many do. Some people do it for the fun of it; others are more serious about it. How does a fortune-teller know what will happen? She (usually it is a woman) will gaze into a crystal ball, or read the palms of the questioner's hands.
>
> The fortune tellers are supposed to have some mystic powers ordinary people do not have. The truth is that they do not know, and have no facts to enable them to predict what will happen the next day or the next week, or month or year. There are legitimate and honest ways of reading the future. A weather man, for example, will forecast the weather a day or several days ahead. He has certain facts to help him.
>
> He makes his prediction on the basis of what is known as "cause and effect." A physician will foretell how a certain disease will run its course, or how a certain medicine will produce certain results. Businessmen, by studying business situations, will predict what will happen in the business world. These, and others—engineers, social workers, political scientists and many others—think and speak in terms of "cause and effect."
>
> But, legitimate as their predictions may be, they will not be too sure of themselves. The false prophets were only fortune-tellers who had no basis whatever for their predictions except their supposed mystic powers. They told people mostly what the people wanted to hear, for a price. The true prophets, as we shall read later, did predict certain events; but they did it on the basis of social and moral causes.

If a city was corrupt, if a government neglected the poor and the needy, if treaties were made with bad countries, if judges were dishonest, they predicted that misery and revolution would come upon the land. In this sense they did predict the future. We shall hear them say, over and over again: "It shall come to pass," and, "thus saith the Lord."_____ predicting that this or that would happen if the people and their kings and priests persisted in their bad ways.

What we learn of these false prophets from the story of Saul, and from many other stories in the Bible, is, first, that they moved in gangs; second, that they would whip themselves into violent excitement by playing musical instruments; third, they foretold the future the way gypsy fortune-tellers do—-for a fee, without any factual basis or good logic for their predictions. The true prophets, we shall see, differed from them on all these points.

MITZVAH OF THE WEEK
NOT LISTENING TO A FALSE PROPHET

In his book of Jewish law, the *Mishneh Torah*, Maimonides expands this section into 50 inter-related mitzvot about false prophets and idolatry.

Read this list. Put an E in front of all the mitzvot that are easy for you to accept. Put an H in front of all the mitzvot that are hard for you to accept. Put a ? in front of all those you have a hard time understanding. Discuss the list with your class.

_____ 24   Not to inquire into idolatry (Lev. 19:4)

_____ 25   Not to follow the whims of your heart or what your eyes see (Num. 15:39)

_____ 26   Not to blaspheme (Ex. 22:27)

_____ 27   Not to worship idols in the manner they are worshipped (Ex. 20:5)

_____ 28   Not to worship idols (in the four ways we worship God) (Ex. 20:5)

_____ 29   Not to make an idol for yourself (Ex. 20:4)

_____ 30   Not to make an idol for others (Lev. 19:4)

_____ 31   Not to make (human) forms even for decorative purposes (Ex. 20:20)

_____ 32   Not to turn a city to idolatry (Ex. 23:13)

_____ 33   To burn a city that has turned to idol worship (Deut. 13:17)

_____ 34   Not to re-build it (as a city) (Deut. 13:17)

_____ 35   Not to derive benefit from it (Deut. 13:18)

_____ 36   Not to missionize an individual to idol worship (Deut. 13:12)

_____ 37   Not to love the missionary (Deut. 13:9)

_____ 38   Not to cease hating him (Deut. 13:9)

_____ 39 Not save him (Deut. 13:9)

_____ 40 Not to say anything in his defense (Deut. 13:9)

_____ 41 Not to refrain from incriminating him (Deut. 13:9)

_____ 42 Not to prophesize in the name of idolatry (Deut. 18:20)

_____ 43 Not to listen to a false prophet (Deut. 13:4)

_____ 44 Not to prophesize falsely (in the name of God) (Deut. 18:20)

_____ 45 Not to be afraid of killing the false prophet (Deut. 18:22)

_____ 46 Not to swear in the name of an idol (Ex. 23:13)

_____ 47 Not to perform "ov" (medium) (Lev. 19:31)

_____ 48 Not to perform "yid'oni" (magical seer) (Lev. 19:31)

_____ 49 Not to pass (your children through the fire) to Molech (Lev. 18:21)

_____ 50 Not to erect a column (as a public place of worship) (Deut. 16:22)

_____ 51 Not to bow down on smooth stone (Lev. 26:1)

_____ 52 Not to plant a tree (in the Temple courtyard) (Deut. 16:21)

_____ 53 To destroy idols and their accessories (Deut. 12:2)

_____ 54 Not to derive benefit from idols and their accessories (Deut. 7:26)

_____ 55 Not to derive benefit from ornaments of idols (Deut. 7:25)

_____ 56 Not to make a covenant with idolaters (Deut. 7:2)

_____ 57 Not to show favor to them (Deut. 7:2)

_____ 58 Not to let them dwell in our land (Ex. 23:33)

_____ 59 Not to imitate them in customs and clothing (Lev. 20:23)

_____ 60 Not to be superstitious (Lev. 19:26)

_____ 61 Not to go into a trance (to foresee events, etc.) (Deut. 18:10)

_____ 62 Not to engage in astrology (Lev. 19:26)

_____ 63 Not to mutter incantations (Deut. 18:11)

_____ 64 Not to attempt contacting the dead (Deut. 18:11)

_____ 65 Not to consult the "ov" (Deut. 18:11)

_____ 66 Not to consult the "yid'oni" (Deut. 18:11)

_____ 67 Not to perform acts of magic (Deut. 18:10)

_____ 68 Men must not shave the hair off the sides of their head (Lev. 19:27)

_____ 69 Men must not shave their beards (with a razor) (Lev. 19:27)

_____ 70 Men must not wear women's clothing (Deut. 22:5)

_____ 71 Women must not wear men's clothing (Deut. 22:5)

_____ 72 Not to tattoo the skin (Lev. 19:28)

_____ 73 Not to tear the skin (in mourning) (Deut. 14:1)

_____ 74 Not to make a bald spot (in mourning) (Deut. 14:1)

APPLICATION: CULTS

In our day and age, "religious cults" probably represent the most dangerous "false prophets." Read this material and then create your own guide on how to avoid cults.

JEWS IN CULTS: WHY WE'RE VULNERABLE AND HOW THEY SNARE OUR CHILDREN
Arnold Markowitz

Pablo Cohen, a musician who joined the Branch Davidians after meeting David Koresh in Israel, died in the inferno in Waco, Texas. Although Jews constitute less than three percent of the U.S. population, 10 to 20 percent of cult members are Jewish. Jews comprise at least 40 percent of members of Eastern meditation or mass therapy cult-like groups in major urban centers. Even though Jews are disproportionately attracted to cults, the Jewish community is doing little to combat this threat to its children.

WHAT IS A CULT?

A cult is not easy to define. The word is used with respect to a range of religious groups. Some groups commonly referred to as cults object to the term's being applied to them. Cults do have some aspect of other religious groups. And not every religious group that tries to attract adherents is a cult. It is not the religious group behind every caller at the door wanting to give you a Bible or every Hebrew Christian organization trying to convince Jews that the messiah has already come. In a country devoted to free speech and freedom of religion, it is crucial that we distinguish alternative religions from objectionable cults.

According to the Interfaith Coalition of Concern about Cults (ICCC), a coalition of Catholic, Protestant and Jewish groups, destructive cults often: Have a self-appointed messianic-type leader who focuses followers' veneration upon him- or herself, claims special or divine selection and exercises considerable autocratic control over members' lives. Use deception and misrepresentation to recruit and retain members and to raise funds. Use techniques aimed at controlling individual thought and personal privacy that frequently lead to an effectively coerced reconstitution of personality.

HOW DO CULTS RECRUIT?

"It is important to remember that for the most part, people join cults. Cults recruit people," writes Steven Hassan, former member of the Unification Church (the Moonies) (*Combating Cult Mind Control*). Recruiters lie, flirt, imply a romantic or sexual interest or promise great benefits to their target if he or she will attend a meeting. At the meeting, new recruits are often isolated and showered with interest, attention, flattery and approbation—what the Moonies call "love bombing." At subsequent meetings, the Bible or some other philosophical or political work is distorted to promote the group's beliefs.

The cult is usually deceptive; initially, many recruits don't know the real name, leader or true purpose of the group. After a short time, the cult invites the recruit to attend a retreat—perhaps a weekend or longer—in an isolated location away from outside influences. During the retreat, questions and doubts are discouraged, delayed or avoided. In time, the recruit is told that the group's truths have been revealed to their leader. As the recruit attends meetings and retreats he or she becomes dependent on the group for approval and indoctrinated with the group's beliefs.

Lengthy study sessions and limited sleep lead to disorientation; frequently recruits are moved at night to unfamiliar places and have no time for reflection and questioning. The result of these techniques may be to induce delusions about the leader's powers and about the effectiveness of a group's doctrine. The psychological surrender to the leader, as well as to the group and its doctrine, leaves followers dependent, suggestible and diminished in their ability to think critically.

Who Joins Cults?

There is a common belief that only weird, disturbed, dysfunctional kids or other malcontents join cults. There is no evidence to support such stereotypes. While a quarter of the Jews who join cults are depressed, according to my experience, three-quarters are relatively balanced, successful people. Social and economic factors examined in various studies (Drs. Mark Sirkin and Bruce Grellong, 1988) found cult members come from upper-middle income, intact and educated families.

When comparing Jews who had belonged to a cult with a control group of Jews not involved in cults, there is no difference in academic performance, number of friendships, after-school activity or employment. From early childhood until mid-adolescence, Jewish cult members develop as well as their peers. They do, however, have more experiences in psychotherapy, tend to be more dissatisfied with life, change colleges more frequently and often experience a major loss prior to joining the cult.

Cult members are idealistic and altruistic young people who have difficulty tolerating the ambiguity of adult life. They seek the perfect answer and see compromises as weak and polluted. They have trouble deciding on a political view. It is difficult for them to find and accept a suitable mate for fear that a more perfect person may come along later. They often have difficulty establishing religious-personal values.

Signs and Symptoms of Cult Involvement:
- Sudden changes in life plan (dropping out of school or changing careers).
- Unusual state of euphoria, excitement or other rapid change in personality.
- New friends, new and different activities that offer a life transformation.
- Dramatic decrease in social activities with former friends.
- Dogmatism about social, religious or philosophical issues.
- Weekends or evenings away or involvement in vaguely described meetings or attempts at secrecy.
- Open discussion of new interests or ideas about religion, spiritual matters or philosophy.
- Major change in diet such as becoming a vegetarian for spiritual reasons. However, many teenage and college students become vegetarians for other reasons.

Moment Magazine

Create your own guide on how to avoid cults:

_____

_____

_____

_____

PINHAS פִּינְחָס

וידבר יהוה אל משה לאמר

פינחס בן אלעזר

בן אהרן הכהן

השיב את חמתי מעל בני ישראל

בקנאו את קנאתי בתוכם

ולא כליתי את בני ישראל בקנאתי

NUMBERS 25:10–30:1

- Pinhas is rewarded for killing the people who cursed God.
- Israel fights a war against the Midianites.
- A census is taken.
- The **daughters of Zelophehad force a change in the laws of property inheritance**.
- **Joshua** is chosen to be Moses' successor.
- Another list of sacrifices is presented.

OUR TEXT—NUMBERS 29:1

In this *sidrah* we get a whole cluster of holiday celebration practices. Among them is this favorite High Holy Day mitzvah:

וּבַחֹדֶשׁ הַשְּׁבִיעִי בְּאֶחָד לַחֹדֶשׁ מִקְרָא-קֹדֶשׁ יִהְיֶה לָכֶם כָּל-מְלֶאכֶת עֲבֹדָה לֹא תַעֲשׂוּ יוֹם תְּרוּעָה יִהְיֶה לָכֶם.

מ	מְלָאכָה = labor	א	אֶחָד = _____
	מִקְרָא = assembly	ה	[היה] = _____
ע	עֲבוֹדָה = work/service		יִהְיֶה = _____
	[עשה] = _____	ח	חֹדֶשׁ = month
	תַעֲשׂוּ = _____	י	יוֹם = _____
ק	[קדש] = _____	כ	כָּל = _____
שׁ	שֶׁבַע = seven	ל	לֹא = _____
	שְׁבִיעִי = _____		לָכֶם = _____
ת	תְּרוּעָה = shofar blast		

1. וּבַחֹדֶשׁ הַשְּׁבִיעִי _____
   בְּאֶחָד לַחֹדֶשׁ _____
   מִקְרָא-קֹדֶשׁ יִהְיֶה לָכֶם _____
   כָּל-מְלֶאכֶת עֲבֹדָה לֹא תַעֲשׂוּ _____
   יוֹם תְּרוּעָה יִהְיֶה לָכֶם. _____

Now try reading this verse without vowels:

ובחדש השביעי באחד לחדש מקרא קדש יהיה לכם כל מלאכת עבדה לא תעשו יום תרועה יהיה לכם

EXPLORING OUR TEXT

The sound of the shofar is like a bugle call, awakening us from our sleep. We are so busy with day-to-day interests, school, work, play, that we tend to become unaware of our true purpose in life, as though in a deep sleep. At Rosh ha-Shanah, when we start a new year, we are awakened to plan to do mitzvot and learn Torah during the coming year. Sa'adya Gaon pointed out ten different ways the shofar inspires us to live a better life in the New Year.

1. When a new king begins to rule, a proclamation is issued, accompanied by trumpet blasts. Every year on that day, his rule is again proclaimed, also with the sound of a trumpet. The creation of the world was completed on Rosh ha-Shanah, and God's rule of the world began. Every year on that day, we reproclaim God's rule with the shofar's blast.

2. When a king issues a decree, the horns blow and a warning is announced. The Ten Days of T'shuvah (Penitence) begin on Rosh ha-Shanah. "Improve your ways!" we are warned, and as this warning is issued, the shofar blows.

3. When Moses and the Children of Israel received the Torah on slopes of Mt. Sinai, the sound of the shofar filled the air. On this day of Rosh ha-Shanah, we dedicate ourselves to Torah again, as the sound of the shofar fills the air.

4. The words of our prophets of old rang out like a shofar blast. We remind ourselves of their corrective words of ethical instruction when we hear the shofar blast.

5. Our enemies blew on their trumpets when they destroyed our Holy Temple. When we blow the shofar on Rosh ha-Shanah we pray the New Year will bring the rebuilding of the Temple to forgive us our sins.

6. Isaac willingly offered himself as a sacrifice, as God commanded, but at the last minute he was replaced by a ram. On Rosh ha-Shanah we blow on a ram's horn to remind ourselves and God of our ancestors' devotion.

7. "Could the shofar sound in the city, and the people not tremble with fright?" (Amos 3). The shofar makes us tremble in fear of God's judgment.

8. "Near is the great day of (judgment of) God; near, very quick, the day of the shofar" (Zefaniah 2). The Rosh ha-Shanah shofar reminds us of the final day of judgment.

9. "And it will be on that day, the Great Shofar will be sounded, and the lost will come from the Land of Ashur, and the rejected from Egyptland" (Isaiah XXIII). The sound of the shofar reminds us of the Messiah's great horn—we hope and pray it be sounded this year to gather all the Jews scattered about the globe.

10. "The inhabitants of the dust…when the shofar will be heard" (Isaiah XVIII). The shofar reminds us of the day of when the dead will arise from their sleep.

Which of these metaphors for the sounding of the shofar do you find most powerful? Why?

_____
_____

Which do you find least satisfying? Why?

_____
_____
_____

Write you own "meaning" for hearing the shofar.

_____
_____
_____
_____
_____

MITZVAH OF THE WEEK
שׁוֹפָר Shofar

It is a mitzvah to listen to the sound of a shofar (ram's horn) on Rosh ha-Shanah, the first day of Tishri. Laws: The horn of a non-kosher animal, a cow's horn or the horn of wild animal may not be used as a shofar. It is preferable to use a ram's horn, and it is necessary that the horn be bent and not straight. If one reverses the shofar and blows in it from the wrong end regardless of how he reverses it he cannot fulfill his obligation. The sounds of the shofar are the *teki'ah*, a single, long note; the *sh'varim*, three shorter notes, and the *teru'ah*, a staccato sound, at least nine very short consecutive sounds.

It is the custom to sound one hundred notes on the shofar. These consist of thirty at the "sitting sounds" right after the initial brakhah; another thirty during the silent *Mussaf Amidah*; another thirty during the hazzan's repetition of the *Mussaf Amidah*, following and finally, ten sounds during the *Kaddish* the *Mussaf Amidah*. Hence, 30, 30, 30, 10 = 100.

MATTOT

מַטּוֹת

NUMBERS 30:2–32:42

- The laws of vows are given.
- Israel fights against the Midianites. This provides the opportunity to teach some new laws:
- Rules for dividing the spoils of war.
- Rules for purifying warriors.
- Two tribes ask to stay on the east bank of the Jordan River. Their rights and responsibilities are clarified.

OUR TEXT—NUMBERS 31:17

Genocide is a big word. It means murdering a whole people and trying to drive them out of existence. In this *parashah* we seem to find that in some cases, genocide is a mitzvah.

וְעַתָּה הִרְגוּ כָל-זָכָר בַּטָּף וְכָל-אִשָּׁה יֹדַעַת אִישׁ לְמִשְׁכַּב זָכָר הֲרֹגוּ.

י	[ידע] = _____	אִישׁ = man	א
כ	כָּל = _____	אִשָּׁה = woman	
ע	עַתָּה = now	[הרג] = kill	ה
ש	[שכב] = to lie down	זָכָר = _____	ז
	מִשְׁכַּב = lying with/cohabitation	טָף = children	ט

17. _____ וְעַתָּה הִרְגוּ כָל-זָכָר בַּטָּף
_____ וְכָל-אִשָּׁה יֹדַעַת אִישׁ
_____ לְמִשְׁכַּב זָכָר הֲרֹגוּ.

Now try reading this verse without vowels:

ועתה הרגו כל זכר בטף וכל אשה ידעת איש למשכב זכר הרגו

EXPLORING OUR TEXT

1. By God's command, what were the Israelites supposed to do to the Midianites? (You may need to open your Bible and read more of the text to figure this out.)

   _____

   _____

2. If this commandment had been fulfilled, what would have been the results?

   _____

   _____

3. Why was this commanded? What did Midian do to deserve this treatment? (You may want to look at chapter 25 of Numbers to get a deeper understanding)

   _____

   _____

4. What is your moral evaluation of this command? Is it morally justified in your eyes?

   _____

   _____

To understand the "ethics" of this commandment, it is helpful to look at another mitzvah found Deuteronomy 7:2, "You shall utterly destroy them." Interpreting this commandment, *Sefer ha-Hinukh* says:

> It is a mitzvah to wipe out the seven nations who resided in *Eretz Yisrael* before the Families-of-Israel settled there. It is a mitzvah not to let any of them live.

While there is an obvious military strategy involved in this "mitzvah," the commentators ask the question, "Why is this the right thing to do?" (They feel like we do, that just because it is practical, doesn't mean it should be a mitzvah.) *Sefer ha-Hinukh* summarizes their answer:

> The seven nations were the Hittites, Girgashites, Amorites, Canaanites, Perrizzites, Hivites, and Jebusites. Those people of the seven nations who sincerely agreed to give up their idolatry were allowed to remain unharmed.

> The seven nations not only failed to observe the seven mitzvot given to Noah and all humanity (see *parashat Noah*) but in fact were even more immoral and corrupt, going out of their way to do things which God found disgusting. God made this mitzvah more severe than usual acts of war to keep them from corrupting our people and others.

Summarize this argument:

_____
_____
_____

Avraham Cronbach (ז״ל) was a leading American Reform rabbi during World War II. He was a founder of the Jewish Peace Fellowship. When asked about this commandment, he said:

> I think this is a place where Moses misunderstood what God really wanted.

Explain his idea in your own words:

_____
_____
_____

What is your own "final take" on this command to exterminate a non-Jewish people?

_____
_____
_____
_____

MITZVAH OF THE WEEK
מִלְחֶמֶת מִצְוָה Milhemet Mitzvah

In the Torah we are given a series of rules for war. We learn that some wars are commanded, some permitted, and some forbidden. And we also learn that all wars have rules.

1. At first, the king may wage only a mitzvah-war. Which wars are considered wars for mitzvah purposes? The war against the seven nations (of Canaan), the battle against Amalek, and a defense of Israel from attacking enemies. Thereafter, the king may wage an optional war, a war against other peoples, to extend Jewish territory and to augment his military prestige.

2. In the case of a mitzvah-war, the king does not have to obtain the sanction of the Supreme Court. He may at any time set out independently and compel the people to come out with him. But in case of an optional war, he can bring out the people only by a decision of the court of seventy-one.

3. The king may break through anyone's property to make a road for himself, and no one may protest against him. No limit is prescribed for the king's road. He makes use of as much as he needs. He is not required to proceed by a detour because of somebody's vineyard or field. He takes the straight line and pursues his battles.

No war is to be waged with anyone in the world before offering him terms of peace, whether it is an optional or a *mitzvah*-war, as it is written: "When you approach a town to attack it, you shall first offer it terms of peace" (Deuteronomy 20:10). If the inhabitants have responded peaceably and accepted the seven precepts imposed upon the descendants of Noah, none of them should be slain, but only taxed, as it is written: "They shall do forced labor for you and serve you." The tax imposed upon them consists in being prepared to serve the king physically and financially, as in the case of building walls and fortifying strongholds, or constructing a palace for the king, and the like.

It is forbidden to be false to the peace made with them, to deceive them when they have accepted the terms of peace and the seven precepts.

When a city is besieged in order to capture it, it must not be surrounded on all four sides but only on three sides, so as to leave room for a refugee and anyone who wishes to escape.

What would wars be like if armies really fought by these kinds of rules?

_____

_____

_____

The following two excerpts were taken from a book called *The Seventh Day*, which is made up of conversations with Israeli soldiers after the 1967 War (known as The Six Day War). It says some remarkable things about an army rooted in the Torah. (This is not to say the Israeli Army always manifests the best Jewish values—and never has done anything that might be considered unethical—but they often do!)

> Peter: The CO got the whole battalion together and gave us a talk. He really did a good job. He spoke about a relative of his who'd been in the Etzion bloc during the war in 1948 and had been taken prisoner, along with some of the others. He kept emphasizing the point that these boys had been taken into the home of one of the Arab Mukhtars so that they could later be turned over to the Arab Legion. Then along came some of the irregulars who wanted to finish them off. They told the Mukhtar to bring them out and hand them over—and he went outside with his gun and stood up to them and said:
>
> "They're my guests, under my roof, and I shall deliver them over to the Legion.

Anyone who wants to do anything about it will have to finish me off first." He really saved their lives. The CO kept repeating this story, at every possible opportunity, and when the boys started cursing the Arabs, he used to say, "Okay, you're right up to a point, but there are good Arabs, too. There are Arabs who do know what honor and honesty mean, who do know how to behave." He used to explain to them, "We're going to have to live with the Arabs — if not now, then in another ten years' time. It's inevitable. Any cruelty we show now will simply arouse more hatred. Some people claim that if we behave properly to them, see to their wounded, give them water, cigarettes and treat them fairly it doesn't have results. But I think it can have results." And he convinced them. The boys believed in him. Once he'd talked to them, the problem was over. There wasn't any cruelty. A couple of them had some extreme views on the subject, and he felt it. He got hold of them and discussed it with them personally, very quietly and convincingly. And they accepted his point of view.

Hagi: I'll tell you an odd story about looting. In my company we had a religious CO from Kibbutz Tirat Zvi. On the first day, after we'd gone through Jenin, we moved on to the objective and found all the Jordanians had gone. We dug ourselves in there because there were reports that they might mount a mortar barrage, and we stayed there until later that night. Then we went down into the village. While we were up there the administrative personnel had gone into the village. When we got to the base we found the storemen and the cooks—all that lot—absolutely rolling in things that they'd looted from the village. Wrapped up in carpets, women's jewelery — it was a horrible scene. At that moment, everybody thought: "For God's sake, what do they need all that stuff for? Then, I remember, the CO got the whole company together, formed them all up in a semi-circle and stuck all the storemen and cooks in the middle along with their loot.

Then he started quoting them chapter and verse of the Bible: "Thou shalt not plunder! Thou shalt not....! Thou shalt not....!" It was really impressive. After he'd finished, one of the storemen got up and asked him, "What about that bit in the Bible: 'And when Jehosophat and his men came to take away the spoil,' what do you make of that, then?" So the CO began to explain that Rashi, commenting on the verse, says that it should be taken to mean that a conquering army takes only what it really needs during the fighting. That's to say, if they have no food, and since they have to live somehow, then they take what they need, but nothing more than that— no property. I stood in a corner and I thought to myself, "What a peculiar army this is, standing there and listening to all this stuff." But there really was something in it. After that parade, there was no more looting in our company. No one touched any booty. The example set up by the CO and the officers influenced them all.

MAS'EI

מַסְעֵי

NUMBERS 33:1–36:13

- We are on the eve of entering the Promised Land.
- Israel's **journey** from Egypt to the Jordan is **reviewed**.
- We are taught **laws** concerning the **settlement** of Canaan.
- The **boundaries** of the Land of Israel are defined along with **Priestly Cities,** and the **Cities of Refuge** are described.
- A careful distinction betweeen **murder** and **manslaughter** is taught.
- Also, we are introduced to laws of inheritance for women who marry men of other tribes.

OUR TEXT—NUMBERS 35:12

The Masai are an African tribe. They have nothing to do with our *sidrah*. Mas'ei is the last Torah portion in Numbers. It tells of the last few moments of Jewish life in the wilderness. Included in it are a few laws about murder cases and a concept called Cities of Refuge.

וְהָיוּ לָכֶם הֶעָרִים לְמִקְלָט מִגֹּאֵל וְלֹא יָמוּת הָרֹצֵחַ עַד-עָמְדוֹ לִפְנֵי הָעֵדָה לַמִּשְׁפָּט.

	מִשְׁפָּט = judgment	גֹּאֵל] = redeemer/avenger	ג
ע	עַד = until	מִגֹּאֵל = _____	
	עֵדָה = community	[הָיָה] = _____	ה
	עִיר = city	לִפְנֵי = before	ל
	[עָמַד] = stand	[מוּת] = _____	מ
ר	[רָצַח] = murder	יָמוּת = _____	
	רֹצֵחַ = _____	מִקְלָט = shelter/refuge	

12. וְהָיוּ לָכֶם הֶעָרִים _____

לְמִקְלָט מִגֹּאֵל _____

וְלֹא יָמוּת הָרֹצֵחַ _____

עַד-עָמְדוֹ _____

לִפְנֵי הָעֵדָה לַמִּשְׁפָּט. _____

Now try reading this verse without vowels:

והיו לכם הערים למקלט מגאל ולא ימות הרצח עד עמדו לפני העדה למשפט

EXPLORING OUR TEXT

When a man killed someone unintentionally he could find security by fleeing to one of the six levitical cities. The blood avenger, who as next to kin to slain the person had the traditional task of hunting down the killer, could not violate the sanctuary of these cities. A trial would be held in the locale where the slaying occurred, and, if lack of malice aforethought was established the manslayer would be sent back to the city of refuge to stay there securely until the death of reigning High Priest (Num. 35:25).

The distinguishing features of the biblical provisions are the restriction of asylum to the unintentional slayer and the connection of the institution with the death of the High Priest. The link between these two characteristics was the fundamental postulate that homicide—even if accidental—could not be expiated by ransom like other transgressions. Only death could compensate for the loss of a life, and thus the death of the High Priest became the symbol of communal expiation.

It is clear that these rules arose from social traditions that knew of family feuds as normal consequences of manslaughter. The *go-el* was charged by his family to be not only avenger but redeemer, which is the strict meaning of the word. In the event of the depletion of family life by the loss of blood, the *go-el* had a responsibility to secure for the family an equivalent of that loss by other blood. "His mission was not vengeance, but equity. He was not an avenger, but a redeemer, a restorer, a balancer."

The biblical law reckoned with this tradition and therefore insisted here and elsewhere that only the person involved in the killing was to be held responsible. "He who sins shall die; the son shall not be responsible for the sins of his father, neither the father for those of his son" (Ezek. 18:20). With the Torah's establishment of judicial rules and processes, the law was generally taken out of the hands of private persons. But the privileges of the avenger were so firmly rooted among the people that the provisions for the cities of refuge must be looked upon as a gradual and intermediate shift from private to public law enforcement. In fact, the Torah still granted the avenger the right to kill when his victim left the city of refuge (Num. 35:27).

Since ultimately only death could expiate the sin, it was not until the High Priest had died that the process was completed and full expiation extended to the manslayer himself. The killing of a human being, though it occurred without evil intent, was a moral injury to the total community. The holy people had a special God-relationship that was founded on zealous regard for the sanctity of every life.

The Torah–A Modern Commentary, Gunther Plaut

1. Explain the concept of a City of Refuge.

   _____

   _____

2. Explain the need for Cities of Refuge.

   _____

   _____

3. What kinds of "Cities of Refuge" do we both have and need in our society?

   _____

MITZVAH OF THE WEEK
שְׁנֵי עֵדִים Two Witnesses

Compare these two laws from the Codes to the two verdicts below:

From the Mishneh Torah: Sanhedrin 16.6

The Torah teaches us (Ex. 23:1/Deut. 19:15) that a court shall not find a man guilty through his own admission of guilt. This is done only on the evidence of two witnesses.

From the Mishneh Torah: Sanhedrin 20.1

The court cannot find someone guilty on just circumstantial evidence, but only on the conclusive testimony of witnesses. Even if the witness saw the assailant chasing the victim, gave him a warning, and then lost sight of him, or followed him into a ruin and found the victim in death agony, while the sword dripping with blood was in the hands of the slayer, the court does not condemn the accused to death, since the witnesses did not see him at the time of the slaying.

CASE 1

From the Responsa of Rabbi Simon ben Zemah Duran:

FACTS: A blind man went on a trip with a companion who was a known criminal. They shared sleeping quarters. At the end of the trip a collection of gems was missing from the hem of the blind man's robe.

DECISION: Rabbi Simon suggests that the court throw the accused in jail until he confesses or until the gems are found. He explains, "It is well known that a thief does not practice his craft before witnesses! If we needed to limit prosecution of theft to those cases with valid witnesses, justice would be impaired." He based his argument on a story told in the Talmud, *Bava Metzia* 24a. A valuable object was stolen from Mar Zutra. Later he saw a rabbinical student wash his hands and dry them on someone else's clothes.

He said, "This one has no respect for personal property; he is the thief." The student was bound and later confessed. Rabbi Simon concludes his responsum, "I have already imprisoned a Jew of this place, whom a traveler accused being a thief. The stolen article was later found in his possession and I was praised by the community...."

CASE 2

From the Responsa of Rabbi Israel ben Petahiah Isserlein:

FACT: Two men are known to be enemies. One threatens the other. During the dancing of the Hoshana celebrations on Sukkot, the party who was threatened was pushed and his shoulder broken. Leaving the synagogue, his enemy bragged about the revenge he has taken.

DECISION: Rabbi Israel begins, "We cannot impose liability... on the basis of supposition and circumstance." He goes on to explain selections of talmudic laws that prevent this. Still he concludes, "I am both intellectually and morally certain that this sort of incident requires significant preventative measures...it does appear and matters do demonstrate that R. Gershom did intend to injure and harm R. Eliezer..." Rabbi Israel's verdict came in three parts. The guilty party was required to:

(1) Pay for the medical expenses of the victim,

(2) pay a fine to tzedakah, and

(3) publicly make atonement (accepting responsibility and asking forgiveness) before the whole community.

4. What seems wrong with these verdicts?

_____

_____

_____

5. Both of these Responsa came from rabbis who were among the leading scholars of their era, who were authors of major *halakhic* works. They knew and followed Jewish law. How can you explain these verdicts?

_____

_____

_____

These two texts are the key to solving this riddle.

From the Mishneh Torah, Kings 3:10

If one person kills another and there is no clear evidence, or if no warning has been given him, or there is only one witness, or if one accidentally kills a person whom he hated, the king may, if the situation calls for it, put him to death in order to ensure the stability of the social order.

From the Mishneh Torah, Sanhedrin 23:1, 3

In monetary matters, the judge should act in accordance with what he is inclined to believe is the truth when he feels strongly that his belief is justified, even though he has no actual proof... If this is true, then why does the Torah require the testimony of two witnesses? The answer: When two (acceptable) witnesses give testimony, the judge is bound to decide on their evidence, even if he does not know whether the evidence submitted by them is true or not.

When a judge has reason to suspect the testimony given by a witness...he should relentlessly interrogate the witness as carefully as if it was a murder trial...If after this interrogation he still has doubts, although he has no valid grounds on which to disqualify him, he should withdraw the case and let another judge...handle it. For matters of this nature are matters of the heart, and the Torah teaches us: "Judgment is God's" (Deut. 1:17).

6. Based on these texts, how do you explain the Responsa decisions on the previous page?

_____

_____

_____

DEVARIM דברים

אלה הדברים

אשר דבר משה אל כל ישראל

בעבר הירדן במדבר בערבה

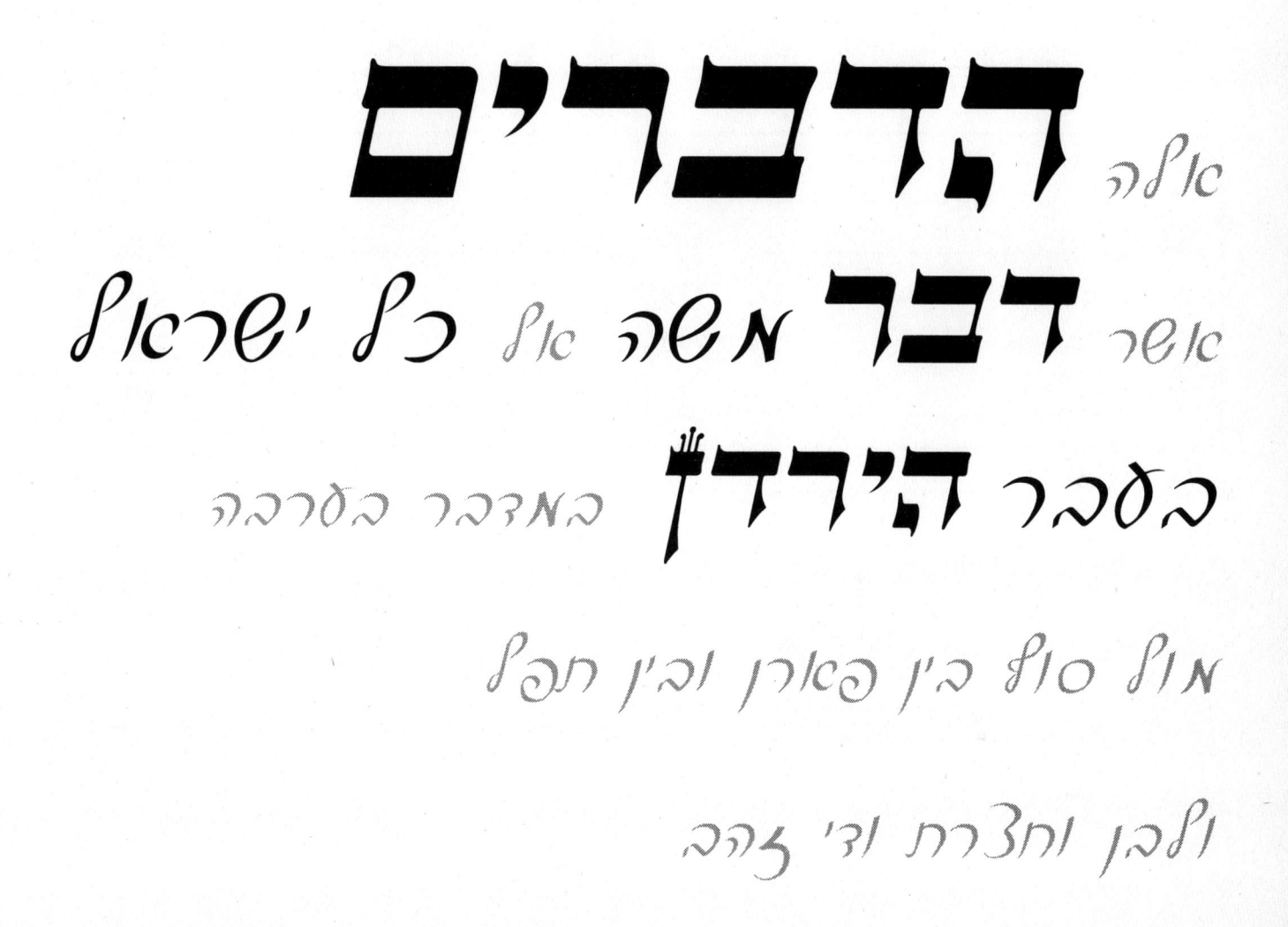

מול סוף בין פארן ובין תפל

ולבן וחצרת ודי זהב

DEUTERONOMY 1:1–3:22

- Moses begins his review:
- The review of the **journey from Sinai to Kadesh**.
- The **appointment of assistants** for Moses.
- The **journey to Horeb**, and then to **Kadesh-Barne'a**.
- The people's **refusal to enter** the Land of Canaan.
- The allotment of conquered land.

OUR TEXT—DEUTERONOMY 1:1

Our *sidrah* begins with Moses getting ready to die. He begins to reteach the whole Torah to the Jewish People.

אֵלֶּה הַדְּבָרִים אֲשֶׁר דִּבֶּר מֹשֶׁה אֶל־כָּל־יִשְׂרָאֵל בְּעֵבֶר הַיַּרְדֵּן...

כ	כָּל = _____	these are = אֵלֶּה	א
מ	מֹשֶׁה = _____	_____ = אֲשֶׁר	
ע	עֵבֶר = side	_____ = [דבר]	ד
	בְּעֵבֶר = on the other side	Jordan = יַרְדֵּן	י
		יִשְׂרָאֵל = _____	

1. אֵלֶּה הַדְּבָרִים_____

   אֲשֶׁר דִּבֶּר מֹשֶׁה_____

   אֶל־כָּל־יִשְׂרָאֵל_____

   בְּעֵבֶר הַיַּרְדֵּן..._____

Now try reading this verse without vowels:

אלה הדברים אשר דבר משה אל כל ישראל בעבר הירדן

EXPLORING OUR TEXT

Moses Assembles the People before his Death

When God informed Moses that he would die after battling Midyan, Moses requested, "Please, God, permit me to review the entire Torah with the people before my passing! I wish to clarify any difficulties which they may have and to acquaint them thoroughly with the details of the Torah laws."

The Almighty honored Moses' request. On 1 Shevat 2488, thirty-seven days before Moses' death He told him, "Assemble the people to review the mitzvot with them, and to instruct them in those mitzvot which they have not yet heard from you."

Moses himself had learned all the mitzvot from God either at Mt. Sinai or in the first year after that in the Tent of Meeting.

Deuteronomy Rabbah 1.6

1. What Jewish practice is suggest by this piece of midrash?
   _____
   _____

2. How do Jews usually perform this mitzvah?
   _____
   _____

MITZVAH OF THE WEEK
STUDYING TORAH OVER AND OVER AGAIN

In a mitzvah found formally in the next *sidrah* (Deuteronomy 6:7), "And you shall teach them diligently...." we learn, "This mitzvah to study Torah regularly applies to every Jew, young, old, rich and poor. Every Jew should set aside time to study Torah every day" (*Sefer ha-Hinukh*).

Usually Jews organize their Torah study around the weekly Torah portions. This is the story of their development.

The practice of reading the Pentateuch (Torah) in public is undoubtedly ancient. The sources, however, do not permit the definite tracing of the historical development of the custom. The command to assemble the people at the end of every seven years to read the law "in their hearing" (Deut. 31:10-13) is the earliest reference to a public Torah reading. A second mention is made in the time of Ezra when he read the Torah to all the people, both men and women, from early morning until midday, on the first day of the seventh month (Neh. 8:1-8). These two occasions are isolated instances and do not help to establish when the custom of regular Torah readings arose.

The Mishnah shows that by the end of the second century C.E. there were regular Torah readings on Mondays, on Thursdays, and on Sabbaths; special readings for the Sabbaths during the period from before the month of *Adar* to before Passover; and special readings for festivals, including those of Hanukkah and Purim, and for fast days (Meg. 3,4-6). The length of the reading, however, seems not to have been fixed by that time.

R. Meir states, for instance, that the practice was to read a short portion on Sabbath mornings, that portion that followed on Sabbath afternoon, and further portions on Monday and Thursday, beginning on the following Sabbath morning from the end of the Thursday portion. According to R. Judah, the procedure was to begin the reading at each Sabbath morning service where it had ended on the morning of the previous Sabbath (Meg. 31b).

The passage in the Babylonian Talmud (Meg. 29b) is the earliest reference to a fixed cycle of consecutive readings. It states that "in the West" (Palestine), they completed the reading of the Torah in three years. The old division of the Pentateuch into 153, 155, or 167 *sedarim* ("divisions") is based on this triennial cycle.

In Babylon and other communities outside Palestine, an annual cycle was followed according to which the Pentateuch was divided into 54 *sedarim* (singular, *sidrah*, i.e., *parashah*). This became the universal Jewish practice, except for certain isolated instances. In Palestine, the triennial cycle was also superseded by the annual, possibly under the influence of Babylonian immigrants.

The Reading of the Torah Today.

The Pentateuch is divided into 54 portions; one is to be read each Sabbath. Two such portions are sometimes read on a single Sabbath; otherwise the cycle could not be completed in one year. On festivals, a special portion dealing with the theme of that festival is read from one scroll and the relevant portion of Numbers 28:16-29:39 from the second scroll. The regular portion is not read on a Sabbath coinciding with a festival.

Each weekly portion is divided into seven smaller ones; the actual point of division, however, varies in the different rites. The Ashkenazi and Sephardi Jews do not read the same haftarot on certain Sabbaths. There are also occasions when different portions are read in Israel and the Diaspora (as a consequence of the observance of second days of festivals outside Israel). The cycle of readings begins on the Sabbath after Sukkot and is completed on the last day of this festival (Simhat Torah).

How is Torah read in your synagogue?

_____

_____

How do Jews whom you know try to make Torah study a regular part of their lives?

_____

_____

VA-ETHANNAN ואתחנן

ואתחנן אל יהוה
בעת ההוא לאמר

DEUTERONOMY 3:23–7:11

- Moses prays to be allowed to enter the Land of Israel and is again refused by God.
- Moses warns against **idolatry**.
- Moses assigns three **Cities of Refuge**.
- We review the Sinai experience and the commandments.
- We are taught the **Shema** and v'**Ahavta**.

OUR TEXT—DEUTERONOMY 6:8

This *parashah* contains the first paragraph of the *Shema*. It has a lot of *mitzvot* hidden in it.

וּקְשַׁרְתָּם לְאוֹת עַל־יָדֶךָ וְהָיוּ לְטֹטָפֹת בֵּין עֵינֶיךָ.

ע	עֵינַיִם = _____	אוֹת = sign	א
	עֵינֶיךָ = _____	בֵּין = _____	ב
ט	עַל = _____	טוֹטָפֶת = frontlet	ט
ק	[קשר] = tie/bind	יָד = _____	י
	קְשַׁרְתָּם = _____	יָדֶךָ = _____	

8. וּקְשַׁרְתָּם לְאוֹת עַל־יָדֶךָ _____

וְהָיוּ לְטֹטָפֹת בֵּין עֵינֶיךָ. _____

Now try reading this verse without vowels:

וקשרתם לאות על ידך והיו לטטפת בין עיניך

EXPLORING OUR TEXT

Open a copy of the first paragraph of the Shema. (A Siddur or a Torah will both have it.) See how many mitzvot you can find hidden in the words.

_____

_____

_____

_____

_____

MITZVAH OF THE WEEK
תְּפִלִּין Tefillin

SOVEREIGNTY

1. We have quoted the statement of Rabbi Yoḥanan to the effect that one who wants to accept the sovereignty of God should perform his hygienic needs, then put on his tefillin and recite the SHEMA. The purpose of the tefillin is best expressed in the prayer that is said before putting them on. God has commanded us to wear the tefillin on the arm in memory of God's outstretched arm; opposite the heart to intimate that we ought to subject our hearts' desires and designs to the service of God, blessed be God; and on the head, opposite the brain, to intimate that the mind, and all senses and faculties, ought to be subjected to God's service, blessed be God (O.H. 25:5).

2. The tefillin consist of two black leather boxes. Each of these contains four passages of the Torah that mention the mitzvah of tefillin: i.e., the first two sections of Deut. 6:4-9 and 11:13-21, and Exodus 13:1-10 and 11-16, each paragraph of which is interpreted as containing a reference to the tefillin (vv 9 and 16).

3. The *Shel Rosh*, or headpiece, has the four passages in four separate compartments, whereas in the *Shel Yad*, or handpiece, they are all written on one parchment in one compartment (O.H.. 32:2). This has been interpreted as meaning that while we should encourage honest differences of opinion, we should nevertheless strive to achieve a uniformity of practice.

4. The tefillin are put on before beginning the daily morning prayers (O.H. 25:4). On the ninth of *Av*, however, they are worn at *Minḥah*. The tefillin are not worn on the Sabbath or on the major festivals (the High Holy Days, Sukkot, Shemini Atseret, Pesaḥ, and Shavu'ot). This is because tefillin are a "sign upon thy hand." Since Sabbaths and festivals themselves serve as such signs, tefillin are not necessary on these occasions (B. Erub. 96a; O.H. 31:1).

5. The practices of the Sephardim and the Ashkenazim differ during the intermediate days of Pesah and Sukkot. The Sefardim do not put on tefillin during intermediate days but the Ashkenazim do. The Hasidim follow the practice of the Sephardim. In Israel, too, the general custom is not to put on tefillin

6. The accepted practice today is that one starts to put on tefillin at the age of thirteen, when he becomes a Bar Mitzvah. According to the Talmud, when a child becomes mature enough to observe the rules concerning the tefillin his father should buy him a pair and teach him to use and care for them properly. While the precise time of attaining such maturity may vary with the mental capacity of each child, the practice has become uniform, on the assumption that maturity has always been achieved by the age of thirteen

Klein, *Jewish Practice*

It is impossible to learn how to put on tefillin from a book. It is a "hands-on thing." If you don't know how to do it, get someone to show you.

What did you learn from actually putting tefillin on?

_____
_____
_____
_____
_____
_____

EKEV עֵקֶב

עֵקֶב תִּשְׁמְעוּן וְהָיָה
אֵת הַמִּשְׁפָּטִים הָאֵלֶּה וַשְׁמַרְתֶּם
וַעֲשִׂיתֶם אֹתָם וְשָׁמַר
יהוה אֱלֹהֶיךָ לְךָ
אֶת הַבְּרִית וְאֶת הַחֶסֶד
אֲשֶׁר נִשְׁבַּע לַאֲבֹתֶיךָ

DEUTERONOMY 7:12–11:25

Moses reviews some important ideas:
- **Following God's laws will bring blessings** of prosperity and health.
- We should not be **self-righteous**.
- We must learn the lessons of our **history**.

OUR TEXT—DEUTERONOMY 8:10

This text talks about rules for what you have to do when you enter the land of Israel and start to live there. But, hidden in these words is a daily mitzvah we know well.

וְאָכַלְתָּ וְשָׂבָעְתָּ וּבֵרַכְתָּ אֶת־יהוה אֱלֹהֶיךָ עַל־הָאָרֶץ הַטֹּבָה אֲשֶׁר נָתַן־לָךְ.

ט	_____ = [טוב]	eat .... = [אכל]	א
י	_____ = יהוה	_____ = אֱלֹהֶיךָ	
ל	_____ = לָךְ	_____ = אֲשֶׁר	
נ	_____ = [נתן]	_____ = אֶרֶץ	
שׂ	satisfy .... = [שׂבע]	_____ = [ברך]	ב

וְאָכַלְתָּ וְשָׂבָעְתָּ _____ .10

וּבֵרַכְתָּ אֶת־יהוה אֱלֹהֶיךָ _____

עַל־הָאָרֶץ הַטֹּבָה _____

אֲשֶׁר נָתַן־לָךְ. _____

Now try reading this verse without vowels:

ואכלת ושבעת וברכת את יהוה אלהיך על הארץ הטבה אשר נתן לך

EXPLORING OUR TEXT

1. How does the mitzvah of Birkat ha-Mazon come out of our verse?
   _____

2. We already know that according to the Torah, God wants us to say a brakhah after we eat. In this exercise we will try to figure out why.

    In Psalm 24:1 we find this sentence:
    > The earth and everything on it belongs to Adonai.
    > The world and everyone who lives on it, too.

3. Explain this verse in your own words. _____

4. Based on this biblical verse, why should we say a brakhah after eating? _____

5. Maimonides was a famous Jewish teacher and thinker who wrote an important book on Jewish law called the *Mishneh Torah*. In it he says:
    > Anyone who eats any food or enjoys anything without saying a brakhah is a thief.

6. If God created the world, and lets us use part of it for our own needs, then a brakhah is a way of saying thank you.

    The brakhah we say after eating can also teach us a second lesson. See if you can figure it out. If God lets us use part of the earth for our own needs, what can a brakhah after eating teach us about people who are hungry?

    _____
    _____
    _____

MITZVAH OF THE WEEK
בִּרְכַּת הַמָּזוֹן Birkat ha-Mazon

Birkat ha-Mazon is the flag-ship Brakhah for the entire Brakhah-system. It is the one and only Brakhah with a clean and precise biblical origin. All other Brakhot evolve from Birkat ha-Mazon.

The Torah says (Deuteronomy 8:10) "**after you have eaten, and you are satisfied, then you should bless** Adonai, your God." Reading rabbinically, the message is obvious. Step 1: eat. Step 2: be nourished. Step 3: Say Birkat ha-Mazon.

RULES

1. Birkat ha-Mazon must be said after every act of eating that involves a piece of bread that is the size of an olive or bigger.

2. When three or more adults have eaten together Birkat ha-Mazon should be said together. The zimmun is added when three or more eat and bless together (*Brakhot* 7.1). When ten or more join in zimmun, the word ELOHEINU is added to the text.

3. Birkat ha-Mazon must be said where a meal is eaten—part of making the table into an altar (*Brakhot* 8.7).

4. The table cloth should be left on the table during Birkat ha-Mazon. Knives should be removed or covered.

5. There are additions to Birkat ha-Mazon for Shabbat, for Rosh Hodesh (New Moon), for each of the festivals, for Purim and Hanukkah, and Birkat ha-Mazon is expanded to include the Shevah Brakhot during "wedding week."

BIRKAT ha-MAZON: The Four Blessings
The First Three Brakhot.

Originally, Birkat ha-Mazon was called the 3 blessings; the fourth brakhah was added later. (*Brakhot* 38b). The first brakhah speaks **universally** of God as CREATOR and the ONE-Who-FEEDS. The second brakhah speaks of ERETZ YISRAEL, TORAH, and COVENANT—all **particular** GIFTS God gave Israel. The third paragraph speaks of future hopes for Jewish people via JERUSALEM.

The progression is essentially: CREATION, REVELATION, and REDEMPTION (the same as the Shema and Her Brakhot).

Like a superhero, almost every Jewish prayer has a midrashic origins story. BIRKAT ha-MAZON is no exception. Each brakhah has it own origin.

Moses wrote the **first** brakhah: "**The ONE-Who-FEEDS-All**" when God first fed Israel with manna. Joshua wrote the **second** brakhah: "**for the land and for the food**" when the people of Israel first entered the Promised Land. David and Solomon co-wrote the **third** brakhah: "**The ONE-Who-in-KINDNESS rebuilds JERUSALEM**." David wrote: "**On Israel your people and on JERUSALEM Your city**." Solomon wrote: "**and on Your great and Holy House**" (*Brakhot* 48a).

These origin stories tell us that BIRKAT ha-MAZON is also a progression of Jewish experiences. We move from the WILDERNESS to conquering the LAND to building the TEMPLE.

Rav Kook looked at this progression in a second way. He suggested that it is a hierarchy of human need, first for FOOD, then for SECURITY and finally for a bright and promising FUTURE—a spiritual connection.

Moshe Tuttenaur suggests that BIRKAT ha-MAZON should really be called "BIRKAT ha-ARETZ," the blessing for the LAND (of Israel). If you go back to the Torah (Deuteronomy 8) you find out that (a) the word Eretz is used 7 times, (b) that the 7-Minim (kinds of fruit grown in the LAND of ISRAEL is introduced, and the verse which "commands" BITKAT ha-MAZON actually reads: (Deuteronomy 8:10) "**AFTER YOU HAVE EATEN, AND YOU ARE SATISFIED, THEN YOU SHOULD BLESS ADONAI, YOUR GOD For the Good Land Which Has Been Given to You**." The core idea here was supposed to be, God gave you the LAND and the LAND gave you food. Calling it BIRKAT ha-MAZON is a "diaspora" kind of thing. (This comes from the tape of a Shiur my friend and teacher Stuart Kelman shared with me.)

The Fourth Brakhah

The fourth brakhah is different; it seems to be a breech born brakhah. Its form is all wrong—something is amiss. Whereas this last brakhah needs no P'TIHAH, one is present: it begins BARUKH. Whereas every brakhah should have a HATIMAH, it should be sealed with the ACTIVE element and therefore made into an official prayer. Instead, it drifts off into a series of hopes and never quite finishes. This last brakhah, in fact stands in need of explanation—and that is just what the commentators and midrash-makers do:

At first, they only said "**The ONE-Who-is-GOOD to all—Who is GOOD every day**." Later other insertions were added. (The *Rosh*) Why doesn't it end with a barukh-formula? Because it was really a short (one line blessing). The rest was added later. (*Tosefta*) This brakhah does not really connect to the other brakhot in BIRKAT ha-MAZON since it is really not part of BIRKAT ha-MAZON. It was added to remember the memory of the defenders slain at Betar (*Rashi*).

The last brakhah "**The ONE-Who-is-GOOD to all—Who is GOOD every day**" was written in reference to those who were slain in Betar, during the Bar Kokhba revolution against the Romans. This blessing was created by the rabbinic court in Yavneh. The "**The ONE-Who-is-GOOD**" refers to God preserving the bodies even though they had not been taken care of at the time of death. The "**Who is GOOD every day**" is thanks for finally being able to bury them (*Brakhot* 48a).

"It was the fourth brakhah which really grew to giant size. People took more liberties with it, because it was the last of the brakhot to be officially added" (Abraham Milgram, *Jewish Worship*, p. 294) When you go to a rock and roll concert, often there is an encore. After the band has played their planned set of songs, they often come back and play some more material. Sometimes, this is brand new material, sometimes it is "oldies." (In those days, Psalms were "oldies-but-goodies." Ideas like the Messiah were brand new material.) I like to think of the ending of the fourth brakhah of BIRKAT ha-MAZON as the encore.

Joel Lurie Grishaver, *Making Sense of the Siddur*

Retell the story of the four brakhot of Birkat ha-Mazon:

1. When we say the first brakhah we are like _____
   _____

2. When we say the second brakhah we are like _____
   _____

3. When we say the third brakhah we are like _____
   _____

4. When we say the last brakhah we are like _____
   _____

RE'EH

רְאֵה

ראה
אנכי
נתן לפניכם היום
ברכה וקללה

DEUTERONOMY 11:26–16:17

- God sets before the Children of Israel the choice of doing right rather than wrong, of choosing **the blessing** rather than **the curse**.
- We also receive warnings against eating and pouring **blood** and against **false prophets**.
- Laws are also reviewed: **shemitah** and **yovel**, and the **pilgrimage festivals**.

OUR TEXT—DEUTERONOMY 15:8

This verse is the place that everyone's favorite mitzvah, giving Tzedakah, is anchored in the Torah.

כִּי־פָתֹחַ תִּפְתַּח אֶת־יָדְךָ לוֹ וְהַעֲבֵט תַּעֲבִיטֶנּוּ דֵּי מַחְסֹרוֹ אֲשֶׁר יֶחְסַר לוֹ.

ל	_____ = לוֹ	enough/sufficient .... = דַּי	ד
ע	lend .... = [עבט]	lacking/deficient .... = [חסר]	ח
	(you will surely) lend = הַעֲבֵט תַּעֲבִיטֶנּוּ	_____ = יֶחְסַר	
פ	open .... = [פתח]	_____ = מַחְסֹרוֹ	
	(you will surely) open ...... = פָתֹחַ תִּפְתַּח	_____ = יָד	י
		_____ = כִּי	כ

8. _____ כִּי־פָתֹחַ תִּפְתַּח אֶת־יָדְךָ לוֹ

_____ וְהַעֲבֵט תַּעֲבִיטֶנּוּ

_____ דֵּי מַחְסֹרוֹ

_____ אֲשֶׁר יֶחְסַר לוֹ.

Now try reading this verse without vowels:

כי פתח תפתח את ידך לו והעבט תעביטנו די מחסרו
אשר יחסר לו

EXPLORING OUR TEXT

The Case: Young v. New York City Transit Authority, CA 2, No. 90-7115, 5/10/90; rev'g 58 LW 2456

The New York City Transit Authority issued a regulation which banned begging and panhandling in New York City subways. It did, however, allow organized charities to solicit funds. A beggar named Young challenged the legality of this regulation and the case was heard before the New York State Supreme Court.

What do you think the Jewish result of this case would be?

_____

_____

_____

_____

Jewish Sources

If a poor stranger comes to you and says: "I am hungry, give me something to eat," you should not suspect the stranger. Rather feed him or her immediately. If, however, the stranger has no clothing and says, "Clothe me," the stranger's claim should be checked (Mishneh Torah, Laws of Gifts to the Poor, 6.6).

Levi Yitzhak was the rabbi of the town of Berditchev. Once, he was invited to a meeting to discuss the following new procedure: In order to keep the poor from begging door to door, a box was placed in the synagogue. Each person would then put in according to her or his abilities. And the poor would take out according to their needs.

Rabbi Levi Yitzhak was angry. He said, "There is nothing new in this procedure. It is very, very old. It started in the city of Sodom. There they had a community charity box where the well-to-do could leave their donations—and no one had to look his or her poor brothers or sisters in the eye" (Tiferet Bet Levi).

The New York State Supreme Court upheld the ruling that panhandling is legal. The United States Supreme Court later overturned it.

MITZVAH OF THE WEEK
צְדָקָה Tzedakah

Rabbi Moses Maimonides was one of the greatest Jewish scholars of all times. He spent much of his time writing books that help Jews apply the laws and teaching of the Torah to the way they live and treat other people. This text, from one of his books of law, the Mishneh Torah, is the way he solved the problem of the tzedakah contest.

There are 8 different ways of giving tzedakah—each way is better than the one that comes after it.

1. The best way of giving is to help a person help him/herself by entering into a partnership of helping that person find a job.

2. The next best way of giving tzedakah is where the person who gives doesn't know who will receive the money, and the person who receives the money doesn't know who has given it.

3. The next best way of giving tzedakah is where the person who gives knows who will get the money, but the person who receives the tzedakah doesn't know who gave it.

4. The next case is one where the person who receives the tzedakah knows who has given it, but the person who is giving the tzedakah has no knowledge of the person in need.

5. The next best case is the person who gives money directly to the person in need before the person has to ask.

6. The next best case is the person who gives money directly to the person in need after being asked.
   Up to now, all these cases include people who have given the right amount of tzedakah in a cheerful way.

7. Below this is a person who gives directly to the poor person, but gives less than s/he should, even though the tzedakah is given cheerfully.

8. Below this is the person who gives tzedakah with a scowl.
   No matter how it is given, giving tzedakah is a mitzvah.

SHOFTIM שֹׁפְטִים

שֹׁפְטִים

שֹׁפְטִים וְשֹׁטְרִים

תִּתֶּן לְךָ בְּכָל שְׁעָרֶיךָ

אֲשֶׁר יְהוָה אֱלֹהֶיךָ נֹתֵן לְךָ

לִשְׁבָטֶיךָ וְשָׁפְטוּ

אֶת הָעָם

מִשְׁפַּט צֶדֶק

DEUTERONOMY 16:18–21:9

More laws are reviewed:
- The appointment of **judges**.
- Laws against worshipping **idols**.
- Laws concerning the **High Court**, a **King**, and the **Priests** and **Levites**.
- **Criminal laws** and the **laws of warfare**.

OUR TEXT—DEUTERONOMY 20:19

In this *sidrah* we get some Jewish rules of war. In our verse, a war rule has big ecological ramifications.

כִּי־תָצוּר אֶל־עִיר יָמִים רַבִּים לְהִלָּחֵם עָלֶיהָ לְתָפְשָׂהּ לֹא־תַשְׁחִית אֶת־עֵצָהּ...

ע	עֵץ = _____		ה■ = her		
	עֵצָה = _____		יוֹם = _____		י
צ	[צור] = lay siege _____		יָמִים = _____		
	תָצוּר = _____		כִּי = _____		כ
ר	רַבִּים = _____		לֹא = _____		ל
ש	[שחת] = destroy/waste _____		[לחם] = wage war		
	תַשְׁחִית = cause destruction _____		לְהִלָּחֵם = _____		
ת	[תפש] = capture _____		עִיר = city		ע
	לְתָפְשָׂהּ = to capture it/her _____		עַל = _____		
			עָלֶיהָ = _____		

19. כִּי־תָצוּר אֶל־עִיר _____

יָמִים רַבִּים לְהִלָּחֵם _____

עָלֶיהָ לְתָפְשָׂהּ _____

לֹא־תַשְׁחִית אֶת־עֵצָהּ... _____

Now try reading this verse without vowels:

כי תצור אל עיר ימים רבים להכלחם עליה לתפשה לא תשחית את עצה...

EXPLORING OUR TEXT

Here are five Jewish sources—our verse and those that have grown out of it.
Number them in the order in which you think they were written.

_____ **Text A** Kiddushin 32a

Whoever breaks vessels, or tears garments, or destroys a building, or clogs up a well, or does away with food in a destructive manner violates the negative mitzvah of *bal tash-hit* (do not waste).

_____ **Text B** Mishneh Torah, Mourning 14.24

One should be trained not to be destructive. When you bury a person do not waste garments by burying them in the grave. It is better to give them to the poor than to cast them to worms and moths. Anyone who buries the dead in an expensive garment violates the negative mitzvah of *bal tash-hit*.

_____ **Text C** Sheviith 4.10

How much fruit should an olive tree produce so that it may be considered a fruit-bearing tree and should not be cut down (*lo tash-hit*)? Rabbi Simeon ben Gamaliel taught a rova (1 rova + 33.6 cubic inches).

_____ **Text D** Deuteronomy 20:19-20

When you besiege a city for a long time, making war against it in order to capture it, you shall not destroy (*lo tash-hit*) the trees by wielding an axe against them, for you may eat of them. You should not cut them down. Are the trees in the field people that they should be besieged by you?

_____ **Text E** Shulhan Aruch, Laws of Body and Soul, Section 14

It is forbidden to destroy anything that can be useful to people.

The Bible
All of Jewish law is based on the Bible. The Bible is made up of three parts: the Torah, the Prophets, and the Writings. The Torah especially is filled with laws and rules about the ways people should live together. The Bible, however, was written for a period when most Jews were farmers. It was a time when life was simple, when there was little business and almost no cities.

The Mishnah
The Mishnah is the first part of the Talmud. It was written by a group of scholars called the Rabbis who lived between 200 B.C.E. and 200 C.E. The Mishnah is divided into 6 orders, and there are many books in each of these orders. The Mishnah groups laws found in the Bible and adds and adapts laws for later societies. In the Mishnah, almost every word is part of a simple statement of the rule and its application.

The Gemara
The Gemara is the second part of the Talmud. Between 200 and 500 C.E. additional "rabbis" added their own comments to the Mishnah. This updating and expansion of the Mishnah again helped to adapt the laws to the latest changes and problems in society. Unlike the Mishnah, which is basically a direct law code, the Gemara is filled with dialogue, stories and other interesting tangents. The Talmud (Mishnah and Gemara together) forms the heart of the Jewish legal process.

The Codes
As the times changed people had questions about how the laws of the Talmud should be applied in their day and in their situation. They ran into two problems. First, as society continued to change and evolve, new problems arose that called for new interpretations. Second, it was often difficult to find a particular law in the Talmud. The solution came with the creation of the "Codes." The Codes were books that organized the law by subject and included all the rules that had been added to deal with new situations. While there are many Codes of Jewish law, the two most famous are the Mishneh Torah, which was written by Maimonides (Moses ben Maimon) in the 12th century, and the Shulhan Aruch, which was written in the 16th century by Joseph Caro.

The Responsa
Meanwhile, the Jewish legal process didn't stop with the Codes. People still faced situations that demanded interpretations of the law. When a local rabbi felt unable to work out a correct answer he would draft a letter to a leading scholar of his age (in those days, no women were rabbis). These letters and their answers were collected as volumes of Responsa. These, too, became part of the literature Jews consult to find the right application of the Torah to their situation.

The following letter was sent by the board of a synagogue to a famous scholar—one of the leading rabbis of this generation. The congregation whose board composed the letter was faced with a Jewish legal question they didn't know how to answer. To find a solution they followed an ancient Jewish practice of consulting an outstanding **halakhic** figure of their generation.

There is a whole body of Jewish literature made up of letters requesting legal advice and answers received. These are called **responsa.** Each **responsum** is made up of two parts: the **sh'elah** (the request) and the **t'shuvah** (the answer).

THE MITZVAH OF THE WEEK
בַּל תַּשְׁחִית Bal Tash-<u>h</u>it

Write your own description of this mitzvah:

___
___
___
___
___
___

APPLYING OUR MITZVAH

Our Sh'elah

Dear Rabbi:

We seek your counsel in helping this congregation resolve a question of great moral and practical significance.

Like many congregations, our synagogue has a contract with a caterer who has the exclusive right to provide food for functions in our social hall. For this privilege Mr. Reuben pays an annual fee and donates a fixed percentage of his income to the congregation. He is also expected to provide certain free food services to the congregation. He is a good man, and the relationship is indeed beneficial to the community.

In our community, there is a shelter which houses and feeds those without homes. Our congregation makes regular donations to this shelter, and some of the members volunteer time there. Recently the shelter requested that we turn over food which is left over after weddings and B'nai Mitzvah celebrations. Normally this food is thrown out, since state health codes forbid it being served again.

Based on this request, our board enacted a congregational policy that all left-over foods would indeed be donated to the shelter. When this policy was presented to our caterer, he refused to follow it. He explained that it would cost him substantial time and money to make this food available. Most of our board is also in business, and understanding the caterer's position, reversed the policy.

When our rabbi learned of the change, he instructed the board that there is a principle of Jewish law called *bal tash-<u>h</u>it* which forbids Jews from wasting any valuable resource. He said that it was our obligation to see to it that this food was not destroyed. While his position seems correct morally, it seems unfair to ask either the congregation or the caterer to bear the expense of making this food available. Our rabbi suggested that we write to you, and seek your insight. Thank you.

The board of Anshei <u>H</u>esed

When a rabbi writes a *t'shuva* (response) to a legal problem, s/he doesn't just give her/his own opinions. Writing a halakhic response is a research project. A rabbi checks all previous sources and finds the cases and laws that apply.

Write your own *t'shuva* (response) to this letter.

KI TEITZEI

כִּי תֵצֵא

כִּי תֵצֵא
לַמִּלְחָמָה עַל אֹיְבֶיךָ וּנְתָנוֹ יְהֹוָה אֱלֹהֶיךָ בְּיָדֶךָ וְשָׁבִיתָ שִׁבְיוֹ

DEUTERONOMY 21:10–25:19

Still more laws are reviewed:
- **Family laws** including marriage, rights of a firstborn, and the disobedient child.
- **Laws of kindness**.
- **Laws** of restoring **lost property**.
- **Miscellaneous laws:** distinction of sex in apparel; sparing a mother bird; parapets on roof-tops; against mixing seeds; unlike animals working together; sh'atnez; and the laws of tzitzit.

OUR TEXT—DEUTERONOMY 22:1

This *parashah* is once again Moses reviewing basic Jewish laws. All Jewish laws of lost and found come from this verse.

לֹא-תִרְאֶה אֶת-שׁוֹר אָחִיךָ אוֹ אֶת-שֵׂיוֹ נִדָּחִים וְהִתְעַלַּמְתָּ מֵהֶם הָשֵׁב תְּשִׁיבֵם לְאָחִיךָ.

ר	[רָאָה] = _____	או = or..............	א
	תִרְאֶה = _____	אָח = brother/fellow/neighbor..........	
שׂ	שֶׂה = sheep _____	לֹא = ...	ל
	שֵׂיוֹ = _____	מֵהֶם = _____	מ
שׁ	[שׁוּב] = return _____	[נדח] = abandon _____	נ
	הָשֵׁב תְּשִׁיבֵם = you must return _____	נִדָּחִים = _____	
	שׁוֹר = ox _____	[עלם] = turn away _____	ע
		הִתְעַלַּמְתָּ = _____	

1. _____ לֹא-תִרְאֶה אֶת-שׁוֹר אָחִיךָ
   _____ אוֹ אֶת-שֵׂיוֹ נִדָּחִים
   _____ וְהִתְעַלַּמְתָּ מֵהֶם
   _____ הָשֵׁב תְּשִׁיבֵם לְאָחִיךָ.

Now try reading this verse without vowels:

לא תראה את שור אחיך או את שיו נדחים והתעלמת מהם השב תשיבם לאחיך

EXPLORING OUR TEXT

The Mishnah expands this verse by stating when a finder must try to return a lost object and when the lost object may be kept.

BAVA METZIA 2.1

If a person finds a lost object when may the finder keep the object and when must the found object be publicly advertised?

The following objects belong to the finder:
- scattered fruit,
- scattered money,
- small sheaves of grain (on a public street),
- cakes of figs,
- loaves of bakers' bread,
- strings of fish,
- pieces of meat,
- bundles of combed flax,
- strips of purple wool.

These belong to the finder according to Rabbi Meir.

Rabbi Judah says: "Everything which has personal markings or 'changes' must be publicly advertised."

"Explain!"

"For example, if one finds a bundle of figs with a potsherd in it or a loaf with a coin in it."

Rabbi Shimon ben Elazar says: "All brand-new items with no identification or sign of use need not be advertised."

BAVA METZIA 2.2

The following must be advertised as found by the finder:
- If one found fruit in a container
- or just an empty container,
- money in a bag
- or just an empty bag,
- a pile of fruit,
- a pile of money,
- three coins on top of each other,
- small sheaves of grain in a private area,
- homemade loaves of bread,

These must be advertised.

Restate the basic principles in your own words:

A find may be kept when _____

A finder must try to return a lost object when _____

MITZVAH OF THE WEEK
RETURNING LOST OBJECTS

It is a mitzvah to return lost property to its owner. One is obligated to return a fellow Jew's lost property even if it is worth as little as a *shekel* (the value of a piece of silver weighing a half a grain of barley). The finder is obligated to care for the found article until it is claimed by its rightful owner. If it is something that may deteriorate or die, such as fresh food or an ill animal, he may sell it and hold the money for the owner. In the interim, the finder is required to make the public aware of his finding. In earlier times, these announcements were made after davening or between Minhah and Ma'ariv. Nowadays, notices are posted on the bulletin board in the local shul.

The owner may claim the lost article only if he can properly identify it with a unique characteristic or a definitive description of the object, such as size, color or some kind of imperfection. This mitzvah applies even to real property. For example, if one sees that an onrushing river is about to demolish the home or field of a fellow Jew, he must work intensely to put up a dam in order to prevent a disaster.

Sefer ha-Hinukh

Use your understanding of these two mishnayot to explain what should be done with each of these found objects. Put a "K" in front of every item you can Keep. Put an "A" in front of every item you must Advertise. Circle every case where you think the Mishnah's categories should be reconsidered.

____A) A wallet with $5 and no identification found on the floor of a classroom with 18 students and one teacher.

____B) A wallet with $5 and no identification found on the floor of a cafeteria of a company with 250 employees.

____C) A wallet with $5 and no identification found in Madison Square Garden.

____D) A bag of groceries left on a bus stop bench.

____E) Two bleacher tickets to a World Series baseball game.

____F) A six-pack of diet cola left on a mailbox.

____G) A briefcase left in a taxi.

____H) A briefcase left in a synagogue board room.

____I) A bag with six of the latest CD's, all unopened.

____J) A homemade green sweater with the name "Buz" woven into the sleeve.

____K) A green polo sweater (size medium).

____L) A lottery ticket.

____M) Tickets 137 through 145 to the Beth El Congregation dinner with the name "Heller" written on the back of the first ticket.

____N) A blank videotape left in a VCR you rented.

____O) Three sheets of brand-new plywood sitting in a vacant lot.

____P) An empty gym bag left in the lobby of an apartment building.

____Q) An empty gym bag left by a basketball court in a public park.

____R) $25 in quarters spilled in the alley.

____S) A briefcase with $5,000 left behind in a public phone booth.

____T) A bundle of figs and a potsherd left in the middle of a shopping center.

____U) A pair of expensive skis (which probably fell off a car roof) sitting by the side of the road. On each is the mark H.I. Stu.

____V) A brand new Walkman radio, still in the box, left on the railing of a freeway overpass.

____W) A case of baseball bats left in an alley.

____X) a dog found at the back door without any identification tags.

____Y) A rough draft of an essay for the Optimists' competition with the initials D.M.

____Z) A golf ball with "Love, Joanne" imprinted in gold letters, found near a public golf course.

Rabbi Morley Feinstein, *The Jewish Law Review*

KI TAVO

כִּי תָבוֹא

וְהָיָה כִּי־תָבוֹא אֶל־הָאָרֶץ אֲשֶׁר יְהוָה אֱלֹהֶיךָ נֹתֵן לְךָ נַחֲלָה וִירִשְׁתָּהּ וְיָשַׁבְתָּ בָּהּ

DEUTERONOMY 26:1–29:8

Even more laws are reviewed:
- Rituals of presenting **first fruits** and **tithing**.
- Descriptions of the **three tithes**—to the Levites, to the owner of Jerusalem, and to the poor and dependent.
- Procedures for crossing the Jordan River.
- The command to build an altar immediately after the crossing.

OUR TEXT—DEUTERONOMY 28:9

Having retaught most of the laws, Moses launches into his big sermon.

יְקִימְךָ יהוה לוֹ לְעַם קָדוֹשׁ כַּאֲשֶׁר נִשְׁבַּע־לָךְ כִּי תִשְׁמֹר אֶת־מִצְוֹת יהוה אֱלֹהֶיךָ וְהָלַכְתָּ בִּדְרָכָיו.

ק	_____ = [קדש]	way/path .... = [דרך]	ד
	establish/get up .... = [קום]	his .... = יו■	
	_____ = יְקִימְךָ	_____ = דְּרָכָיו	
שׁ	take an oath/swear ... = [שבע]	walk/go .... = [הלך]	ה
	_____ = נִשְׁבַּע	_____ = הָלַכְתָּ	
	guard/keep .... = [שמר]	as/when .... = כַּאֲשֶׁר	כ
	_____ = תִשְׁמֹר	_____ = מִצְוֹת	מ
		_____ = עַם	ע

9. _____ יְקִימְךָ יהוה לוֹ לְעַם קָדוֹשׁ

_____ כַּאֲשֶׁר נִשְׁבַּע־לָךְ

_____ כִּי תִשְׁמֹר

_____ אֶת־מִצְוֹת יהוה אֱלֹהֶיךָ

_____ וְהָלַכְתָּ בִּדְרָכָיו.

Now try reading this verse without vowels:

יקימך יהוה לו לעם קדוש כאשר נשבע לך כי תשמר את
מצות יהוה אלהיך והלכת בדרכיו

EXPLORING OUR TEXT

R. Hama son of R. Hanina further said:

What is the meaning of the verse: "You shall walk after Adonai your God?

Is it possible for a human being to walk after the Shekhinah; for has it not been said, "Adonai your God is devouring fire? (Deut. 4:24)

Sotah 14b

The real meaning is to walk after the attributes of the Holy One.

As God clothes the naked so should you also clothe the naked, for it is written, "And Adonai the God made for Adam and for his wife coats of skin, and clothed them."

The Holy One visited the sick so should you also visit the sick, for it is written, "And Adonai appeared to Abraham after his circumcision by the oaks of Mamre."

The Holy One comforted mourners so should you also comfort mourners, for it is written, "And it came to pass after the death of Abraham that God blessed Isaac his son."

The Holy One buried the dead so should you also bury the dead, for it is written, "And God buried Moses in the valley."

Based on this interpretation in the Talmud, what mitzvah is found here?

_____

_____

_____

_____

MITZVAH OF THE WEEK
WALKING AFTER GOD

It is a mitzvah to emulate God's righteous ways. One should strive to perfect oneself in the following character traits: compassion, kindness and graciousness towards others; forgiveness for iniquity; honesty, humility and tolerance.

Sefer ha-Hinukh

Look up these two passages in the Torah:

Genesis 1:27

Exodus 34:6

How do they expand our understanding of this mitzvah?

_____

_____

_____

List ten things you can do to fulfill this mitzvah:

1. _____
2. _____
3. _____
4. _____
5. _____
6. _____
7. _____
8. _____
9. _____
10. _____

NITZAVIM נִצָּבִים

נצבים אתם היום כלכם לפני יהוה אלהיכם ראשיכם שבטיכם זקניכם ושטריכם כל איש ישראל

DEUTERONOMY 29:9–30:20

- Moses speaks to all who have and will enter into the **covenant.**
- Moses explains that God does not want to punish the Children of Israel—**if they seek God**, God will show mercy.
- Moses explains that God's commandments are not hard and distant, but practical to follow.

OUR TEXT—DEUTERONOMY 30:19

Moses' life is almost over. He is finishing up his "State of the Wilderness." Our verse is one of the great soundbites from that address.

הַעִדֹתִי בָכֶם הַיּוֹם אֶת־הַשָּׁמַיִם וְאֶת־הָאָרֶץ הַחַיִּים וְהַמָּוֶת נָתַתִּי לְפָנֶיךָ הַבְּרָכָה וְהַקְּלָלָה וּבָחַרְתָּ בַּחַיִּים.

מ	death = [מות]		א ארץ = _____
נ	give = [נתן]		את = _____
ע	witness = עד	in/in the = בְּ/בַּ	ב
	הַעִדֹתִי = _____	בָכֶם = _____	
פ	face = פָּנִים	choose = [בחר]	
	לְפָנֶיךָ = _____	[ברך] = _____	
ק	curse = קְלָלָה	[חי] = _____	ח
שׁ	heavens = שָׁמַיִם	יוֹם = _____	י

19. _____הַעִדֹתִי בָכֶם הַיּוֹם

_____אֶת־הַשָּׁמַיִם וְאֶת־הָאָרֶץ

_____הַחַיִּים וְהַמָּוֶת נָתַתִּי לְפָנֶיךָ

_____הַבְּרָכָה וְהַקְּלָלָה

_____וּבָחַרְתָּ בַּחַיִּים.

Now try reading this verse without vowels:

העדתי בכם היום את־השמים ואת־הארץ
החיים והמות נתתי לפניך הברכה והקללה ובחרת בחיים

248

EXPLORING OUR TEXT

WHETHER OR NOT TO FIGHT ON SHABBAT (I Maccabees, chapter 2, verses 31-41)

This story took place during the beginning of the Jews' rebellion against the Greeks (during the Hanukkah Story). The Maccabees were just being formed. Before they were organized, some Jews had already begun to fight back.

> Word soon reached the king's officers and the forces in Jerusalem, the city of David, that Jews who had defied the king's order had gone down into hiding-places in the wilds. A large group of soldiers went quickly after and found them, and occupied a position opposite. The soldiers prepared to attack them on the Sabbath.
>
> "There is still time," the soldiers shouted. "Come out, obey the king's command, and your lives will be spared."
>
> "We will not come out," the Jews replied. "We will not obey the king's command or profane the Sabbath."

These Jews had fought back against the Greeks in order to follow Jewish law and observe Jewish customs. They had a hard choice to make. In order to win their fight for religious freedom, they would have to break the very Jewish laws they were fighting to defend.

If you were one of these Jewish rebels in the forest—would you break Shabbat and fight back against the Greeks? Why? _____

_____

_____

This is what actually happened (at least this is the way the story is told in the first book of Maccabees):

> Without more ado the attack was launched; but the Jews did nothing in reply; they neither hurled stones, nor barricaded their caves. "Let us meet death with a clear conscience," they said…
>
> So they were attacked and massacred on the Sabbath, men, women, and children, up to a thousand in all, and their cattle with them.
>
> Great was the grief of Mattathias and his friends when they heard the news. They said to one another, "If we all do as our brothers have done, if we refuse to fight the king's soldiers for our lives as well as for our laws and customs, then they will soon wipe us off the face of the earth."
>
> That day they decided that, if anyone came to fight against them on the Sabbath, they would fight back, rather than all die as their brothers in the caves had done.

MITZVAH OF THE WEEK
פִּקוּחַ נֶפֶשׁ Pikuah Nefesh

The obligation to save another person is based on a principle in Halakhah (Jewish law) called *Pikuah Nefesh*, saving a soul. Protecting a human life is a major Jewish obligation.

Our rabbis learned this lesson from the Torah:

> Do not stand idly by the blood of your neighbor (Leviticus 19:16).

Leviticus 19:16 teaches us that as Jews we are not allowed to stand by and watch someone else be injured or killed. That would be "Standing Idly by the Blood of Your Neighbor." If someone is going to be hurt or killed, a Jew is must try to prevent this injury or death. This is the same idea as "choosing life."

> The Mishnah says: "Whenever a human life is endangered, the laws of the Sabbath are suspended."
>
> The more eagerly someone goes about saving a life, the more worthy s/he is of praise.
>
> If a person sees a child fall into the sea on the Sabbath, s/he may spread a net and rescue the child—the sooner the better—and s/he need not get permission from a court of law, even though in spreading the net s/he may also catch fish (which is forbidden on the Sabbath).
>
> If a person sees a child fall into a pit, s/he may break through the earth on one side and step down to pull the child up—the sooner the better—and s/he need not get permission from a court of law, even though in the process of rescuing the child s/he may be building stairs.
>
> And if a person sees a door shut on a room in which an infant is alone, s/he may break down the door to get the baby out—the sooner the better—and s/he need not get permission from a court of law, even though by breaking down the door s/he may knock off chips that can be used for firewood.
>
> Babylonian Talmud, Yoma, page 84b

PIKUAH NEFESH OR NOT?

YES____ NO____ 1. It is Yom Kippur, about 2:00 in the afternoon. Jon has been fasting. Jon is really hungry. He tells his friend, "I'm so hungry I could die," but he doesn't feel faint or anything. Can Jon eat?

YES____ NO____ 2. It is Yom Kippur. Your little sister is a diabetic. You are concerned that her insulin level is out of balance and that her blood sugar level is dangerously low. She wants to continue the fast. You think she should eat. Should you insist that she eat?

YES____ NO____ 3. It is the seventh night of Hanukkah. Cynthia's whole family is due at the JCC to see a Hanukkah play. The family lights the candles and then prepares to leave. Cynthia's mom wants to blow out the candles because she is worried that there might be an accident if they burned with no one around. Cynthia's brother says that it is against Jewish law to blow out Hanukkah candles. Should the family blow the Hanukkah candles out?

YES____ NO____ 4. Shabbat candles are supposed to be lit before sundown. In the winter, no one in Amy's family is home before sundown. Amy asks the rabbi if the family may light candles after Shabbat has started. Rabbi Shana answers, "Shabbat candles are supposed to be kindled one hour before sundown." She doesn't tell Amy not to light them after sundown. She just told Amy what one is supposed to do. Is it better to follow the rules and not have candlelighting as part of one's family ritual?

YES____ NO____ 5. Larry does not keep kosher but one day a bully in his school threatens to beat him up unless Larry eats a ham sandwich. The bully knows that Larry is Jewish and that Jews don't eat ham. Normally eating the sandwich wouldn't bother Larry. Should he eat it?

VA-YELEKH

וַיֵּלֶךְ

וילך משה וידבר את הדברים האלה אל כל ישראל

DEUTERONOMY 31:1–31:30

- Moses announces that **Joshua** will soon take over as the leader, but makes the Children of Israel realize that God will still be with them.
- Moses gives Joshua public recognition that he has confidence in him as a leader.
- Moses hands the law to the Levites to be deposited in the *Aron*.

OUR TEXT—DEUTERONOMY 31:19

Even though it is not obvious upon first reading, in this *sidrah* the Torah gives us one of the Torah mitzvot.

וְעַתָּה כִּתְבוּ לָכֶם אֶת־הַשִּׁירָה הַזֹּאת וְלַמְּדָהּ אֶת־בְּנֵי־יִשְׂרָאֵל שִׂימָהּ בְּפִיהֶם לְמַעַן תִּהְיֶה־לִּי הַשִּׁירָה הַזֹּאת לְעֵד בִּבְנֵי יִשְׂרָאֵל.

ל	learn/teach = [למד]		_____ = אֶת	א
	so that = לְמַעַן		_____ = בְּנֵי יִשְׂרָאֵל	ב
ע	witness = עֵד		_____ = [היה]	ה
	now = עַתָּה		_____ = זֹאת	ז
פ	mouth = פֶּה		_____ = [כתב]	כ
	_____ = בְּפִיהֶם	to _____ = לְ	ל
שׁ	put = [שִׂים]		_____ = לִי	
שׁ	song = שִׁירָה		_____ = לָכֶם	

19. וְעַתָּה כִּתְבוּ לָכֶם _____

אֶת־הַשִּׁירָה הַזֹּאת _____

וְלַמְּדָהּ אֶת־בְּנֵי־יִשְׂרָאֵל _____

שִׂימָהּ בְּפִיהֶם _____

לְמַעַן תִּהְיֶה־לִּי הַשִּׁירָה הַזֹּאת _____

לְעֵד בִּבְנֵי יִשְׂרָאֵל _____

Now try reading this verse without vowels:

ועתה כתבו לכם את השירה הזאת ולמדה את בני ישראל שימה בפיהם למען תהיה־לי השירה הזאת לעד בבני ישראל

EXPLORING OUR TEXT

WRITING A TORAH

> Every Jew is commanded to write a *Sefer Torah* for his/her own use. Even if s/he has inherited a *Sefer Torah*, it is a *mitzvah* to write one at his/her own expense. If s/he writes it with his/her own hand, it is as if s/he has received it him/herself at Mt. Sinai. If s/he does not know how, s/he should have others write it for him/her. Anyone who corrects a single letter in a *Sefer Torah* is credited with writing all of it.
>
> <div style="text-align:right">Rambam, <i>Mishneh Torah</i>, Laws of the Sefer Torah, 7:1</div>

The rabbis based the mitzvah that obligates every Jew to write a *Sefer Torah* on this biblical verse:

וְעַתָּה כִּתְבוּ לָכֶם אֶת הַשִּׁירָה הַזֹּאת

Therefore, write down this song for yourself (Deuteronomy 31:19).

Even today, a *Sefer Torah* is handwritten by a *sofer* (scribe). Writing it is a long, hard process. It takes between nine months and a year of work to finish a Torah. It has to be written with the best permanent black ink, on parchment made from the skins of "clean" (kosher) animals. For a pen, the *sofer* must use a quill or a reed. Metal, which is used to make weapons, cannot be used for making a Torah. All of the separate parchments must be sewn together with sinews from kosher animals and the *sofer* must use a thorn for a needle.

The *sofer* cannot write a single letter from memory. The *sofer* must read from a correct text, pronounce every word out loud, and only then copy it. Every letter and every word must be perfectly spaced. Every letter must be clearly drawn so that a child can recognize it. In addition, the *sofer* has to add crowns to thirteen letters. The letters צ, ץ, ג, ז, ן, נ, ט, ע, שׁ have three-stroke crowns and the letters ה, י, ח, ק, ד, ב have one-stroke crowns.

Here is a passage handwritten by a *sofer*. Add the crowns on your own.

ועתה כתבו לכם את השירה הזאת

To understand how hard it is to write a *Sefer Torah*, look at this list of conditions that can make it unkosher (and therefore unusable):

> If it was written on the skin of an unclean animal.
>
> If a clean skin was not made into parchment.
>
> If the parchment was not made specifically for a *Sefer Torah*.
>
> If it was written on the wrong side of the parchment.
>
> If just one section was written on the wrong side of the parchment.
>
> If it was written without traced lines.
>
> If it was not written with indelible ink.
>
> If it was written in any language but Hebrew.
>
> If the *sofer* was a heretic or impure.
>
> If the *sofer* wrote the name of God without *kavanah* (devotion).
>
> If one letter was omitted.
>
> If one letter was added.
>
> If two letters touch.
>
> If one letter can be misread as another.
>
> If a letter can't be read.
>
> If one word looks like two.
>
> If two words look like one.
>
> If the *sofer* changed the form of any section.
>
> If it is not sewn together with the dry tendons of clean animals.
>
> Rambam, Mishneh Torah, Laws of the Sefer Torah, 10.1

One Hasidic rabbi took the laws for writing a *Sefer Torah* and explained them this way:

> The many letters in the Torah represent the many souls of the Jewish people. If one single letter is left out of the Torah, it is unfit for use. If one single soul is left out of the union of the Jewish people, the Divine Presence will not join them. Like the letters, the souls must join together in a union. Then why is it forbidden for one letter to touch another? Because every soul must have its own unique relationship with its Creator.
>
> Rabbi Uri of Strelisk, from *Tales of the Hasidim: Later Masters*, by Martin Buber, p. 147

MITZVAH OF THE WEEK
סֵפֶר תּוֹרָה WRITING A TORAH

It is a mitzvah for every Jew to write a Torah scroll for him/herself.

If one is unable to write a Torah scroll him/herself, s/he can fulfill this mitzvah by hiring a qualified *sofer* (scribe) who will write one for him/her. The *sofer* must be both skilled in this art and a religious Jew.

The writing of a *Sefer Torah* must be done in accordance with certain rules and specifications.

- It must be written by hand.

- It must be written on sheets of parchment made from the skin of a kosher animal.

- It must be written with special Hebrew lettering.

- Before beginning to write a *Sefer Torah*, the *sofer* must declare that the work is to be a *Sefer Torah*.

- The sheets of parchment that make up the Torah scroll must be sewn together with the tendons of a *kosher* animal.

- The *sofer* must have before him/her a Torah scroll from which the *sofer* reads, pronouncing every word before inscribing it.

It is forbidden to sell a *Sefer Torah* unless it is to raise money for a poor bride to marry, to study Torah, or to pay the ransom for Jewish captives.

A *Sefer Torah* that is beyond repair or is decayed must be buried in a Jewish cemetery.

Since a Torah Scroll is the holiest religious article, it must be given the highest respect. Therefore, when someone passes by with a *Sefer Torah* in hand, we must rise and remain standing and never turn our back to it.

HA-AZINU הַאֲזִינוּ

הַאֲזִינוּ

הַשָּׁמַיִם וַאֲדַבֵּרָה וְתִשְׁמַע הָאָרֶץ אִמְרֵי פִי

DEUTERONOMY 32:1–32:52

- Moses sings "**The Song of Moses**," a farewell to the people.
- Moses is ordered to ascend Mt. Nebo.

OUR TEXT—DEUTERONOMY 32:52

The speeches are over. Moses begins to say his good-byes. Our verse literally is pointing him towards his grave.

כִּי מִנֶּגֶד תִּרְאֶה אֶת־הָאָרֶץ וְשָׁמָּה לֹא תָבוֹא אֶל־הָאָרֶץ אֲשֶׁר־אֲנִי נֹתֵן לִבְנֵי יִשְׂרָאֵל.

כ	because .... = כִּי		_____ = אֶל	א
ל	_____ = לֹא		_____ = אֲנִי	
נ	opposite .... = נֶגֶד		_____ = אֶרֶץ	
	_____ = מִנֶּגֶד	that/which _____ = אֲשֶׁר		
	give .... = [נתן]		_____ = אֶת	
ר	see .... = [ראה]	come _____ = [בוא]		ב
ש	there .... = שָׁם	_____ = בְּנֵי יִשְׂרָאֵל		

52. _____ כִּי מִנֶּגֶד תִּרְאֶה אֶת־הָאָרֶץ
_____ וְשָׁמָּה לֹא תָבוֹא
_____ אֶל־הָאָרֶץ אֲשֶׁר־אֲנִי נֹתֵן
_____ לִבְנֵי יִשְׂרָאֵל.

Now try reading this verse without vowels:

כי מנגד תראה את־הארץ ושמה לא תבוא אל־הארץ
אשר־אני נתן לבני ישראל:

EXPLORING OUR TEXT

What is an ethical will? It is a letter a parent writes to his/her children. In it, a mother describes what she has learned during her life and the lessons she hopes to pass on to her children and future generations. The blessings Moses gives the Jewish people in this *parashah* are like an ethical will. Some ethical wills are very lengthy and contain many details, while others are only several sentences in length. An ethical will becomes part of a family's inheritance and heritage. It is considered by some to be much more important than the passing on of material possessions.

An ethical will can preserve a memory and, to some extent, shape the way that a person is remembered. That is one of the greatest challenges and the greatest dangers in writing an ethical will: We all wish we had done more in our lives. We have to fight the desire to be remembered for things that we wish we had done, but never got around to doing. Here are several excerpted examples of ethical wills. As you read them, ask yourself what they tell you about the authors.

The RAMBAN (Rabbi Moshe ben Nahman), a great scholar who lived in the 13th century in Spain, wrote the following to his children and students:

> "Listen, my child, to the instruction of your father, and do not forget the teaching of your mother" (Proverbs 1:8). Speak with kindness to all people always. This will save you from anger, the major cause of misdeed...Always be humble; regard every person as greater than yourself...Study Torah regularly so that you can fulfill its commandments. When you finish your studies, think carefully about what you have learned; try to translate your learning into action...When you pray, do not think about worldly matters, think only of God...Read this letter once a week, and be regular in carrying out its requirements. By doing so you will always walk in the path of God and you will be worthy of all of the good which is due to the righteous.

1. Underline the values that the Ramban wants to pass on to his children.

2. Why does he ask that the letter be read every week?

IMAGINE...You are going to be a parent. Not years from now, but in the next few days! To say the least, it will be quite an adjustment. Before the birth of your child, close your eyes, take a deep breath and think for a moment about having a child. What are your hopes and dreams for your child? What kind of person do you hope he or she will be? What kind of Jew?

Use the space below to write your thoughts down in the form of a letter to your unborn child that you will present when he or she is ready to start a family.

_____
_____
_____
_____
_____
_____
_____
_____
_____
_____
_____
_____
_____
_____
_____
_____
_____

Remember Me, an Instant Lesson by Rabbi Philip Warmflash. Published by Torah Aura Productions.

MITZVAH OF THE WEEK
OBEYING A LAST WILL AND TESTAMENT

It is a mitzvah to carry out the wishes of the person who has died. Thus it is a duty of the legal heirs to carry out the wishes of the person who wrote the will, and this is a duty the courts will enforce. However, the above rule is not always to be applied as a strict legal duty, and when the duty is merely a moral one, the court will not compel compliance with the wishes of the person who wrote the will's directions (Shevut Ya'akov, vol. 1, no. 168).

V'ZOT HA-BRAKHAH וְזֹאת הַבְּרָכָה

וְזֹאת הַבְּרָכָה אֲשֶׁר בֵּרַךְ מֹשֶׁה אִישׁ אֱלֹהִים אֶת בְּנֵי יִשְׂרָאֵל לִפְנֵי מוֹתוֹ

DEUTERONOMY 33:1–34:12

- Moses **blesses** the Children of Israel before his death—he blesses each tribe individually.
- Moses goes up to **Mt. Nebo** to the **top of Pisgah** to die. Before he closes his eyes, he gets a chance to see the **Land of Israel**.

OUR TEXT—DEUTERONOMY 34:5

This is the end of the Torah. Not quite the last verse, but close to it. This is the moment that Moses dies.

וַיָּמָת שָׁם מֹשֶׁה עֶבֶד־יהוה בְּאֶרֶץ מוֹאָב עַל־פִּי יהוה.

ע	servant = עֶבֶד		א	אֶרֶץ = _____
	_____ = עַל		י	יהוה = _____
פ	mouth = פֶּה	Moav = מוֹאָב	מ	
	_____ = פִּי	death = [מוֹת]		
שׁ	there = שָׁם			מֹשֶׁה = _____

5. וַיָּמָת שָׁם מֹשֶׁה _____
עֶבֶד־יהוה _____
בְּאֶרֶץ מוֹאָב _____
עַל־פִּי יהוה. _____

Now try reading this verse without vowels:

וימת שם משה עבד־יהוה בארץ מואב על־פי יהוה

EXPLORING OUR TEXT

This script comes from *Midrash P'tirat Moshe*, a collection of rabbinic fantasies about the way Moses died. It is not supposed to be a collection of true facts about his death; rather, it is a way of talking about deeper truths. Our version is drawn from the editing found in *Sefer ha-Aggadah*.

PROLOGUE:

Narrator:	AND ADONAI SAID TO MOSES:
God:	BEHOLD, IT IS GETTING CLOSE TO YOUR DAYS TO DIE (Deuteronomy 31.14).
Narrator:	Even Moses had to die. It says in the book of Job:
Bible:	EVEN IF HE GOES UP TO HEAVEN, AND HIS HEAD REACHES UP TO THE CLOUDS, STILL HE SHALL DIE (Job 20:6).
Narrator:	This is the story of Moses who went up to heaven, walked on clouds like an angel, spoke to God face-to-face, and received the Torah from God's hand. Yet as soon as he reached the time for the natural end to his life, God told him:
God:	BEHOLD, IT IS GETTING CLOSE TO YOUR DAYS TO DIE (Deuteronomy 31.14).

SCENE 1: "I'LL HUFF, AND I'LL PUFF AND I'LL PRAY YOUR GATES DOWN."

Narrator:	When Moses realized that God's decree about his death had been sealed, he drew a circle in the dirt, stood inside it, and shouted:
Moses:	Master-of-the-Universe, I will not move out of this circle until You change Your mind and take back the decree.
Narrator:	He put on sack cloth and ashes and stood praying and petitioning God. Soon, heaven, earth, and all of creation were shaking. Everyone was afraid that God was going to destroy the world and start again.
God:	Close the gates of heaven. Do not let Moses' prayers and requests enter. I do not want to hear them.
Narrator:	But Moses' cries began to cut through the heavenly gates like a blow torch. God ordered the ministering angels:
God:	Bolt every gate in heaven!
Moses:	Master-of-the-Universe! You know all the pain and suffering which I endured until the Families of Israel believed in You. You know how hard it was to teach them Torah and the Mitzvot. All I want is to see a little of their happiness after all those years of pain in the wilderness. Is that too much to ask? Yet, now You tell me, "You shall not pass over the Jordan." Oh God! In that case Your Torah is a lie—it is junk—because Your own law says: "AN EMPLOYER IS COMMANDED TO PAY HIS HIRED SERVANT ON THE DAY HE FINISHES WORK" (Leviticus 19:13). So how come I had to work for forty years to try to get Israel to be a holy and faithful nation—and I get nothing?
God:	This is still my decree!

SCENE 2 MOSES PLAYS "LET'S MAKE A DEAL."

Moses: If You won't let me enter the Promised Land alive, then how about letting me be brought in dead, like Joseph's bones?

God: Moses, when Joseph went down to Egypt he did not hide the fact that he was a Hebrew. He told everyone about his Jewish identity. However, when you arrived in Midian, you let people think you were an Egyptian.

Moses: Well, if You won't bring me into the Land, then at least let me be like one of the beasts of the field which eats grass, drinks the stream waters, and looks out at the world.

God: Stop! Enough! No!

Moses: Then let me fly like a bird which goes searching in all directions for its food and then comes back to its nest at day's end.

God: Enough already! Stop! No more!

SCENE 3: A FRIEND IN NEED...

Narrator: Next Moses turned to the heavens and the earth.

Moses: Intercede for me. Help me to change God's mind.

Heavens & Earth: We have ourselves to worry about. Our time is limited, too. We've been warned. Remember?

Bible: THE HEAVENS SHALL DISAPPEAR LIKE SMOKE AND THE EARTH SHALL WEAR OUT LIKE OLD CLOTHES. (Isaiah 51:6).

Narrator: Then Moses asked the sun, moon, and stars to help.

Moses: Pray for me!

Sun, Moon, Stars: We've got our own worries. We will die, too. We've been warned, too. Listen:

Bible: ALL OF THE OBJECTS OF HEAVEN SHALL BE DISSOLVED (Isaiah 34:4).

Narrator: Moses went to the mountains and hills.

Moses: Pray for me!

Mountains & Hills: We can't help you—we first have to beg for ourselves. We've got to save ourselves. We've been warned as well:

Bible: FOR THE MOUNTAINS WILL DEPART AND THE HILLS WILL BE REMOVED (Isaiah 54:10).

Narrator: Next on Moses' list was the sea.

Moses: Pray for mercy for me.

The Sea: Son of Amram, what makes today different than yesterday? Aren't you the same Son of Amram who beat me with his staff and divided me into 12 tiny streams? I had no way of defending myself against you—because you stood at God's right hand. I had nowhere I could go for help. Now the tables are turned, you come and ask me to help you. Why should I help you?

Moses:	Would that I were back in the old days. I used to stand by the Reed Sea like I was a king—but now I cry for help and no one listens to me.
Narrator:	Next Moses sneaked into heaven and cornered one of the ministering angels.
Moses:	I beg of you—please pray for mercy for me.
Angel:	Moses, my teacher, why are you going to all this bother? It can't do any good. I already know from the Inner Court that your prayers will not be heard on this matter.

SCENE 4: SOLO, THE FACE-TO-FACE.

Narrator:	Moses places his hands on his head and starts to cry.
Moses:	To whom can I go? Who will intercede with God to have mercy on me?
Narrator:	God was getting angrier and angrier at Moses. The more he begged, the more God got angry. That is until Moses prayed with the words:
Moses:	ADONAI, ADONAI THE GOD, THE MERCIFUL, THE GRACIOUS (Exodus 34:6).
Narrator:	Right away God's anger subsided. God again spoke to Moses:
God:	Moses, do you remember that I took two oaths? The first was to destroy Israel after they had worshiped the Golden Calf. The second was that you would die and not enter the Promised Land. I gave up and cancelled the first oath when you prayed. Now you want Me to forget My second prayer. You are holding onto both ends of the rope—it doesn't work that way. If you want Me to answer this prayer, then I will restore the first oath and destroy Israel. Otherwise, if you want that prayer to remain in effect, you must withdraw your present prayer.
Moses:	Master-of-the-Universe, better Moses and a thousand like him have to die—before a single fingernail on one Israelite be hurt.
	Master-of-the-Universe! Are You really going to let the feet which came up on high and the face which looked face-to-face with God and the hands which received the Torah directly from You to sleep in the dirt?
God:	That is My plan and that is the law of life. Each generation will have its own teachers and its own leaders. Until now, you've been the one to serve Me. From now on, that will be Joshua your servant's responsibility.
Moses:	Master-of-the-Universe I have to die because it's Joshua's turn to become the leader—why not just let me be his disciple?
God:	If that is what you want to do—go and do it.

SCENE 5: MOSES, THE SERVANT OF JOSHUA.

Narrator:	So Moses got up early in the morning and went to the door of Joshua's tent. Joshua was seated, busy teaching Torah. Moses quietly entered with his hand on his heart. Joshua was focused on his teaching and didn't notice Moses. Meanwhile, many Israelites had gone to Moses' tent door, wanting to study Torah with him. They asked:

Israelites:	Where is Moses our teacher?
Narrator:	They were told that he had gone to Joshua's tent. They followed and found him standing there while Joshua sat and taught Torah.
Israelites:	Joshua! What is the meaning of this? How can you sit and teach while Moses is standing?
Narrator:	Joshua raised his eyes and saw Moses standing. He cried:
Joshua:	Rabbi, Rabbi, Father, Father!
Israelites:	Moses, teach us Torah.
Moses:	I am not permitted.
Israelites:	We will not abandon you!
Moses:	From now on you must learn Torah from Joshua.
Narrator:	They accepted this command and sat down to hear the teachings of Joshua. Joshua sat at the head, Moses at his right hand and the sons of Aaron at his left. Joshua taught Torah in the presence of Moses, his teacher. This is the way the mantle of authority and wisdom passed from Moses to Joshua.
	Later, Moses and Joshua went to the *Mishkan*. There, the cloud of the *Shekhinah* came down and divided them. Then it was gone.
Moses:	What did God have to say?
Joshua:	I am not allowed to tell you, just as you were not permitted to tell me everything when God used to speak to you.
Moses:	Better one thousand deaths than a single jealousy! Oh Master-of-the-Universe—up to now I sought life, but now I am ready to return my soul to You!

SCENE 6: MEANWHILE, BACK IN HEAVEN...

God:	WHO WILL NOW RISE UP FOR ME AGAINST EVIL DOERS? (Psalm 94:16) Who will now defend Israel against My anger? Who will stand by to pray for them when they are at war? Who will seek My mercy when they sin against Me?
Narrator:	The first to speak was Metatron, God's personal ministering angel—and Israel's number 1 advocate. Metatron was the angel who kept the book of Israel's good deeds.
Metatron:	Master-of-the-Universe! Moses is now dying in accordance with Your law—why then do You mourn?
God:	Let me tell you a story:
	Once there was a king of flesh and blood who had a son who angered him by his wild and rebellious behavior. In fact, the king often got so angry that he wanted to kill the son, but was prevented from doing so by the queen, who saved her son. Then the queen died and the king deeply mourned her. When his ministers asked

        the reason for the depth of his sadness, he answered, "I am not only mourning for my wife but also for my son. Many times I have been so angry at him that I would have killed him—if not for his mother. His mother saved him every time."

        This is exactly how I feel. I am mourning not only for Moses but for Israel, because every time they angered Me, Moses stood by them, defended them, and took away My anger.

Narrator:	God then spoke to Gabriel, the angel who guards paradise and will eventually blow the great shofar:
God:	Go and bring home the soul of Moses.
Gabriel:	Master-of-the-Universe, how can I be witness to the death of one who is the equal of the six-hundred-thousand Israelites?
Narrator:	So then God turned to Michael, another one of the four angels in God's inner circle. He is the "commando" angel who always defends Israel. He was the angel who taught Moses Torah.
God:	Go and bring home the soul of Moses.
Michael:	I was his teacher and he was my pupil. How can I bring about his death?
Narrator:	Finally God turned to Sammael, the chief of the angels who worked for Satan—the prosecuting angel. He is the angel of death. Now Sammael had been waiting hourly for Moses' death and had been asking:
Sammael:	When will the moment come when I will be able to take away his soul? When will I get to see Michael weep as my mouth fills with joy?
God:	Go and bring home the soul of Moses.
Narrator:	When God finally gave him the command, he clothed himself in anger, put on his sword, wrapped himself in his cloak of terror and went out to Moses.

SCENE 7: MOSES VS. SAMMAEL

Narrator:	When Sammael came to Moses, Moses was busy writing God's name in a *Sefer Torah*. Moses glowed with light. He was as bright as the sun. He looked a lot like an angel. Sammael was afraid. He was terrified. He couldn't speak.
Moses:	Wicked-one, what are you doing here?
Sammael:	I have come to take away your soul.
Moses:	Who sent you?
Sammael:	The One-Who-Created-All-Things.
Moses:	Get away from here. I wish to praise the Holy-One-Who-is-to-Be-Praised: "I SHALL NOT DIE BUT LIVE IF I TELL OF GOD'S WORKS" (Psalm 118:17).
Sammael:	Don't be so high and mighty. God already has someone to sing praises: "THE HEAVENS DECLARE THE GLORY OF GOD" (Psalm 19:2).

Moses:	I can shut them up. "HEAVENS—LISTEN AND I WILL SPEAK—LET THE EARTH HEAR THE WORDS OF MY MOUTH" (Deuteronomy 32:1).
Sammael:	But all living things must return their souls to me!
Moses:	Yes, but I have more power than any other living thing.
Sammael:	What is your power?
Moses:	I am the son of Amram, who at the age of three prophesied that I would receive the Torah in the midst of flames. I went into a king's place and removed the crown from the king's head. When I was eighty, I performed signs and miracles in Egypt and brought out six-hundred-thousand Jews despite the might of Egypt. I divided the sea, I climbed up and made a way to heaven. I fought a battle with the angels who didn't want me to receive the Torah. I spoke to God face-to-face and received the Torah from His right hand and taught it to Israel. I also caused the sun and the moon to stand still in heaven. Who else in all the world has done such things? Go away, I will not give my soul to you.
Narrator:	Sammael went back to God and told him what had happened.
God:	Go back and bring the soul of Moses back here.
Narrator:	Sammael unsheathed his sword and stood at Moses' side. Moses became angry with him. He took his staff with God's name inscribed on it. He hit Sammael with all his might and the angel fled. Moses continued to chase him away. Then Moses took a beam of light from between his eyes and blinded the angel of death.

SCENE 8: GOD STEPS IN

God:	Moses, the hour has come. You must now depart from the world.
Moses:	Master-of-the-Universe. Remember when You appeared to me from the burning bush. Do you remember how I stood on Mt. Sinai for forty days and forty nights? I beg You, do not deliver me into the hands of the angel of death.
God:	Fear not, Moses. I, Myself, will attend to you and bury you.
Moses:	All right, but please give me a couple of moments. I want to bless Israel. All these years they have only gotten orders, warnings, and scoldings from me.
Narrator:	So Moses began to bless each tribe separately. When he saw that the hour was drawing to a close, he united the tribes together into a single blessing.
Moses:	I have troubled you much with the Torah and the mitzvot. Now forgive me.
Israelites:	Moses, our teacher and our leader, you are forgiven.
Narrator:	Then the people drew close to him.
Israelites:	We have frequently made you very angry and given you much distress. Forgive us!
Moses:	You are forgiven.
God:	The moment has arrived for you to depart from this world.

Moses:	Bless the Name of The-One-Who-Lives-and-Exists-Forever.
Narrator:	He then turned back to the Israelites and said:
Moses:	Please, when you enter the Land, remember me and my bones and say, "Alas for the son of Amram, who ran bravely before us but whose bones fell in the wilderness."
God:	Now you must depart from the world.
Moses:	Now you see the destiny of all living things.
Narrator:	Moses sanctified himself like the angels. Then God descended with his four closest ministering angels from the highest heaven to retrieve the soul of Moses. The angels stood around Moses.
God:	Moses, close your eyes. Now, place your hands on your breast. Bring your feet together. Precious soul, I set a time of one-hundred-and-twenty years for you to be in the body of Moses. Now the time has come for you to depart. Please leave the body—do not wait.
Moses' Soul:	Master-of-the-Universe. I know that You are the God of all spirits and the Master of all souls. You created me and placed me in the body of Moses for one-hundred-and-twenty years. Now I ask, is there a better body in the entire world than that of Moses? I love him and I don't want to leave him.
God:	Come with Me and I will raise you to the highest heaven and set you down beneath the throne of my glory—right alongside the cherubim and seraphim.
Narrator:	At that moment God kissed Moses and removed his soul with a kiss. Then God wept:
God:	THERE HAS NEVER ARISEN IN ISRAEL SINCE THEN ANOTHER PROPHET WHO CAN BE COMPARED TO MOSES (Deuteronomy 34:10).
Narrator:	And the heavens wept:
Heavens:	THE GODLY MAN IS PERISHED FROM THE EARTH (Micah 7:2).
Narrator:	The earth wept:
Earth:	AND THE MOST UPRIGHT AMONG MEN IS NO MORE (Micah 7:2).
Narrator:	The ministering angels wept:
Angels:	HE DID ADONAI'S JUSTICE (Deuteronomy 33:21).
Narrator:	Israel wept:
Israelites:	HE BROUGHT ADONAI'S JUDGMENT TO ISRAEL (Deuteronomy 33:21).
All:	HE ENTERS INTO PEACE. EVERY ONE THAT WALKS IN RIGHTEOUSNESS RESTS PEACEFULLY (Isaiah 57:2).

Copyright Acknowledgements

Every effort has been made to ascertain the owners of copyrights for the selections used in this volume, and to obtain permission to reprint copyrighted passages. Torah Aura Productions will be pleased, in subsequent editions, to correct any inadvertent errors or omissions that may be pointed out.

Jason Aronson Inc. Publishers: *Love, Marriage, And Family In Jewish Law And Tradition* by Michael Kaufman, copyright © 1992 by Jason Aronson Inc., Northvale, NJ.

The Jewish Publication Society: *Does God Belong in the Bedroom* by Michael Gold, copyright © 1992.

Silver Dawn Music: "Light One Candle" by Peter Yarrow, copyright © 1983. Used by Permission. All Rights Reserved.

"Jews in Cults: Why We're Vulnerable and How They Snare Our Children" by Arnold Markowitz reprinted from *Moment* magazine (August 1993). To order the "Jews in Cults" issue, please call 1-800-221-4644.

Charles Scribner's Sons, an imprint of Macmillan Publishing Company: *The Seventh Day* by Henry Near. Reprinted with the permission of the publisher. Copyright © 1970 Henry Near.

Union of American Hebrew Congregations: *The Torah: A Modern Commentary* by W. Gunther Plaut, copyright © 1981.

Union of American Hebrew Congregations: *Jewish Law and Jewish Life*, by Jacob Bazak, translated by Stephen Passamaneck, copyright © 1979.

Ktav Publishing: *In God's Mirror* by Harold M. Shulweiss, copyright © 1990.

Jason Aronson Inc. Publishers: *The Language of Judaism* by Simon Glustrom, copyright © 1988 by Jason Aronson Inc., Northvale, NJ.

Jewish Theological Seminary of America: *A Guide to Jewish Religious Practice*, by Isaac Klein, copyright © 1979 by Ktav Publishing.

Berit Mila Board of Reform Judaism: *Berit Mila in the Reform Context*, edited by Dr. Lewis M. Barth, copyright © 1990 by Berit Mila Board of Reform Judaism, New York.

Bloch Publishing Company: *Book of Kashruth*, by Seymour E. Freedman, copyright © 1970.

From *Tales of the Hasidim: The Later Masters* by Martin Buber. Copyright © 1947, 1948 and renewed 1975 by Schocken Books, Inc. Reprinted by permission of Schocken Books, Pantheon Books, a division of Random House, Inc.

From *Art of Jewish Living: The Passover Seder*, by Ron Wolfson, copyright © 1988 by Federation of Jewish Men's Clubs.